Mythical Past, Elusive Future

History and Society in an Anxious Age

Frank Füredi

PLUTO PRESS
LONDON • BOULDER, COLORADO

First published 1992 by Pluto Press
345 Archway Road, London N6 5AA
and 5500 Central Avenue,
Boulder, Colorado 80301, USA

Reprinted 1993

British Library Cataloguing in Publication Data
Füredi, Frank
  Mythical past, elusive future
  I. Title
  907

  ISBN 0-7453-0530-X hbk

Library of Congress Cataloguing in Publication Data
Füredi, Frank, 1948-
  Mythical past, elusive future: history and society
  in an anxious age / Frank Füredi
  320p. 22.1cm.
  Includes bibliographical references and index
  ISBN 0-7453-0530-X : £25.00
  1. Historiography--History--20th century. I. Title.
D13.F87 1992
907′ .2--dc20   91-33093
                                                 CIP

Typeset in 10 on 12pt Palatino by Peter Marsden using Ventura
Printed in Finland by WSOY

Contents

Preface

This book is about change. More specifically it is about perceptions of change in contemporary society. It attempts to explain the overwhelming preoccupation with the past that characterises end-of-twentieth-century societies. Society has adopted that well-known characteristic of the aged of always going on about the past, ignoring the present and steadfastly evading the future.

Our consciousness of the past and of the future is strongly shaped by contemporary experience. With this perspective, this book seeks to provide a sociological account of history and a historical analysis of our view of society. By reconstructing society's view of itself through its consciousness of the past, we can gain useful insights about its predisposition to change and develop.

The contemporary frenetic concern with history is the point of departure. The sense of the past seems to preside over vast areas of social life. In culture, intellectual life and private hobbies, past times are impregnated with nostalgia. The contemporary romantic sensibility does not merely pertain to aesthetic matters. The search for and assertion of roots and identities are now important issues in the public domain.

Finally there is the politicisation of history itself. An outburst of controversies about history during the past decade in the main industrial capitalist societies indicates that the meaning of the past is now a focus for political debate.

The veneration of the past reflects a mood of conservatism. The revival of tradition is preferred to experimenting with new ideas. Western leftist thought has also been overtaken by this outlook. The left-wing legacy of an enthusiastic attitude towards the future and towards change has given way to a cautious reorientation on the past. As a result the characteristic distinction between left and right-wing thought has little meaning today. The ascendancy of the past over the

vii

sense of change is strikingly shown by the decline of futuristic and radical thought. The creative tension between those who wanted to preserve and those who wanted change has given way to arguments about who can claim what past.

The book does not aim only to explain. It provides a critique of History (note the capital 'H'), a mode of thought that relies on the past to provide authority for human action. Instead of History, the book argues for historical thinking. It restates the case for the main insights of the Enlightenment, in particular the potential for progress. It is motivated by the belief that the more we seek the sanction of the past the more we evade our responsibility for making history.

A few words on the structure of the book. Chapters 1 and 2 provide an overview of the contemporary debates on history, providing a comparative account of these debates in Britain, Germany, Japan and the United States. By examining the relationship between society and the perception of history, Chapter 3 attempts to isolate precisely what kind of debate is in demand.

Chapters 4, 5 and 6 try to explain why History is in such demand today. They argue that the present debate about history is the culmination of a series of frustrated attempts to elaborate an intellectually acceptable positive vision of society. The revival of History represents an attempt to deploy the tradition of the past as a substitute for a positive vision of the future. It thus seeks to contain the negative effects of the crisis of ideas. Chapter 5 suggests that this revival of History has been achieved through a reaction against the 1960s – though Chapter 6 argues that the right-wing offensive against the 1960s in reality represents an attempt to come to terms with ideological problems that have their roots not in the 1960s but in the years between the two world wars.

Chapter 7 contends that the revival of History represents the closure of the historical mind. It re-states the main intellectual themes advanced against the idea of change. This chapter suggests that the intellectual reaction to change is more pervasive than at any time since the Enlightenment. Chapter 8 considers the collapse of the left-wing intellectual historical tradition. Its main thesis is that there is no longer a distinctive left-wing perspective on the questions of change, progress and history. With the erosion of this tradition, the closure of the historical mind is complete. The final chapter advances the author's own argument for the critique of history.

Mike Freeman, James Heartfield and Alan Harding have provided many useful criticisms which have been incorporated into this text.

Kirsten Cale, Joan Hoey and Ragni Miles consistently fed me new information and new ideas. Pluto Press was from the inception of this project supportive. My thanks to them all.

Frank Füredi
University of Kent at Canterbury
October 1991

1

History under siege

Somehow history has come alive. It has become a character in its own right; a kind of semi-divinity. We debate its meaning and appeal to its authority in both international affairs and domestic politics. Most of the time society looks to it for reassurance, as if to say 'it is still there, not much has changed.' History has become anti-change and reflects in its use a reaction to the unknown that lies ahead. This is what motivated the veteran Yugoslav dissident Milovan Djilas to comment in response to the outburst of ethnic warfare in his country that 'communism was just a temporary episode in our history.'[1] From East to West there is an overwhelming sense that our lives are subject to the dictates of the past. To introduce some of the influences behind the ascendancy of the past is the aim of this first chapter.

A sense of crisis

Optimism is distinctly out of fashion. Writers, playwrights and 'serious' film directors find 'happy endings' to be alien to their work. Intellectuals and politicians are also increasingly anxious about the future. As the year 2000 approaches, it appears almost as a caricatured imitation of the *fin-de-siècle* crisis of the nineteenth century. Friedrich Nietzsche has re-emerged as a modern cult figure on campuses throughout the West. Terms such as post-modernism, post-history, post-culture or post-industrial are used as a matter of routine in contemporary social thought. The mood of society is characteristically one of millennial doom. It almost appears that catastrophes are waiting to happen. Environmental disasters, nuclear proliferation, turbulence in Eastern Europe and the Third World, not to mention global economic upheavals, are just some of the themes that reoccur in what is often described as the 'second crisis of

1

modernity'. It is difficult to disagree with the statement that
'contemporary social thought has become dominated, if not obsessed
by the idea of crisis.'[2]

The prevailing sense of crisis in the West is all the more
extraordinary since the collapse of its main adversary, the Soviet
Union, ought to boost its confidence. In fact, the collapse of the Soviet
Union has served to heighten the sense of malaise in the West. A sense
of nostalgia often attaches itself to the Cold War past in contrast to a
feeling of anxiety about the future. From the standpoint of today, the
Cold War era was at least stable and predictable for many observers.
John K. Galbraith wrote that the 'hard intruding fact is that in the last
45 years, just short of half a century, no one has been killed, accidents
apart, in conflict between the rich or relatively affluent industrial
countries of the globe, this being true as between the capitalist ... and
those which have characterised themselves as communist.'
Galbraith's sentiments are widely echoed in the press. According to
the *Financial Times*, the 'West's relief at the ending of the Cold War is
history. It has been superseded by the fears of political instability and
an awareness that integrating eastern Europe, not to mention the
Soviet Union, into the world economy poses difficulties of a hitherto
unimagined complexity.'[3]

The Cold War may well be 'history', but uncertainties about the
present lead to a preoccupation with the past. For sections of the
American establishment, national self-doubt and a sense of decline
were caused by the humiliation of defeat in Vietnam. The invasion of
Iraq was not merely a war against the regime of Saddam Hussein but
also a way of settling scores with the past. One leading American daily
paper boasted that success on the battlefield 'will be the first step in
breaking the sour mood among the American elite, in building a new
mood that allows America to manage its own problems and play its
proper role in the world. It seems a strange and anachronistic notion,
we recognize, that a nation should seek its self-esteem on the
battlefield. But after all, that is where it was lost.' In case anyone was
in doubt what this editorial in the *Wall Street Journal* had in mind, this
was succinctly summed up in its forthright call for 'no equivocation,
no gradualism, no Vietnam.'[4]

The most curious feature of this editorial was neither its celebration
of American military glory nor its preoccupation with Vietnam.
Rather, it was its concern with an 'obscure professor's book' which
'became a best-seller because pages 514–535 discussed "imperial
overreach" and suggested American decline'. The obscure professor

under discussion is Paul Kennedy, whose book *The Rise and Fall of the Great Powers* became a focus for controversy during the late 1980s. At least subconsciously,the editor of the *Wall Street Journal* saw the war in the Gulf as proof that America was not in decline and would avoid the fate suggested by the historian Kennedy. This attack on an 'obscure professor' reflects the general unease that Western societies seem to have with their histories.

The systematic character of this anxiety is illustrated by the consistency with which ostensible victories seem to leave a bitter aftertaste. This reaction seems to reflect a loss of control over the direction of events. 'Historical change is happening in a way it was not meant to happen', observed an anonymous American defence expert at NATO headquarters in Brussels.[5] This loss of control over the direction of the future stimulates a tenacious affirmation of history.

Plundering the past

Anxiety about the direction of the future has stimulated a scramble to appropriate the past. Those most concerned with upholding tradition have initiated a series of debates with a view to revising history. Since their emphasis is very much on the revival of tradition it is not surprising that in general the debates first arose around the spheres of education and culture. The Japanese debate on the revision of school history texts illustrates the trend. Under the initiative of Takeo Nishioka, a former education minister, there has been a campaign to restore Japan's national symbols in the classroom. In early 1990 the Ministry of Education, under instructions from the ruling Liberal Democratic Party, ordered schools to display the Rising Sun flag and to sing the 'Kimigayo', the national anthem. This instruction came in the aftermath of a number of significant revisions made to Japanese history textbooks. For example in 1989 the ministry ordered a publisher to replace a section which described Japanese atrocities in Malaya during the Second World War with a story based on *My Fair Lady*.[6]

The measures taken in Japan to popularise nationalism through education have been widely criticised in the West. In many of the published Western accounts this reassertion of nationalist culture has been portrayed as a uniquely Japanese event. In reality it is only the symbols that are unique for more or less the same trend is evident throughout the industrialised capitalist world. American secretaries of education have been no less inhibited about interfering in the teaching of history than their Japanese counterparts. During the 1980s Secretary of Education William Bennett emerged as a WASP – White, Anglo-Saxon, Protestant – equivalent of Takeo Nishioka. Bennett argued that 'schools should foster a national consensus in support of the administration's policy in Central America.' In a similar vein, Gary Bauer, the Undersecretary for Education, attacked many of the textbooks used in schools. He insisted that 'textbooks should not read as if they were written by neutrals in the struggle between freedom and slavery.'[7]

The celebration of national identity through history schoolbooks has also been encouraged by the Conservative government in Britain. G. R. Elton, Regius Professor of Modern History at Cambridge, used his inaugural lecture to attack those who do not give 'English history a dominant role in English historical studies'. He insisted on the centrality of English history on the grounds that 'its people have contributed disproportionately to the stock of human invention and achievement.'[8] Elton's intervention is part of an intellectual programme designed to elaborate a coherent national identity for Britain. It has the support of leading Conservative politicians and involves the active participation of the establishment intelligentsia. The philosopher Roger Scruton argues that one of the main tasks of conservatives is to recapture history from the 'left establishment'.[9]

The campaign to popularise nationalism and national history in Britain has distinct similarities with developments in Germany. Obviously, embarrassing episodes concerning the German past make the campaign to revive German identity through history an intensely sensitive issue. But there is little qualitative difference between the German and the British nationalist projects. In the Britain of the 1980s the government has opted for celebrating anniversaries with military connotations while in Germany the emphasis has been on launching museums and exhibitions. The late Franz Josef Strauss, one of Germany's leading postwar conservative politicians, explained in the course of the 1987 election campaign:

It is high time that we emerge from the shadow of the Third Reich ... and become a normal nation again ... To idolise the nation is catastrophic and disastrous: but to deny the nation, to deny one's national identity, to destroy our national identity, to refuse to return to it, to a purified national consciousness, is just as disastrous.[10]

The issue of national identity has become something of a full-time obsession in the German press. During the decade prior to the fall of the Berlin Wall, mainstream West German periodicals were obviously preoccupied with this issue. Publications like *Criticon* and *Merkur* promoted an agenda organised around the construction of a past that could sustain German identity.

Plundering the past has become a highly respected enterprise. Former British Prime Minister Margaret Thatcher personifies this activity. Speaking on American television she attacked Germany and pro-unity Europeans by pointing to the past: 'we are 700 years old, Germany's parliament is only 40, Spain a dozen years old, Portugal even less.' In case anyone was in doubt about Britain's determination to stand up to German domination, she reminded her audience yet again that 'we were the people in Europe who stood alone when the whole of the rest of Europe collapsed, and the people who, with the United States, liberated Europe.'[11] Thatcher's views are far from eccentric, as anyone familiar with the British media will confirm. It is no exaggeration to state that the Second World War has become an almost permanent item of news on British television during the 1980s.

The confusion of the past with the present

The widespread concern with the past is often explained as the result of the re-emergence of old often unresolved problems. For example an article on the national question in the Soviet Union is titled 'History takes its revenge'. Another author notes that the Cold War has contained the old problem of European nationalism but with its end this danger will reappear. He warns: 'It will be a force for trouble unless curbed. The tendency of honest national history is especially important, since the teaching of false, chauvinist history is the main vehicle for spreading hypernationalism.'[12]

It is ironic that this author can see the problem of chauvinist history in Eastern and Central Europe yet ignore the issue in his own society, the United States. A recent study of 'How the American century ends' by a well-known US foreign affairs columnist begins with the statement that 'the accounts that history presents have to be paid' and suggests that what happens today is strongly influenced by the past.[13] No doubt the legacy of the past is important but there is a danger of self-deception if every conflict is explained away in this manner. Danger does not lie so much in the return of a troubled past but in the conflicts initiated today. Blaming the past represents a morbid fatalism and the rejection of the attempt to take responsibility for the control of human destiny.

Sometimes, on the other hand, the confusion of the present with the past takes the form of projecting backwards our contemporary concerns. The project of plundering the past is motivated by the concerns of today. Our view of the past is continually made and remade in response to the demands of the present. That is why changes such as the end of the Cold War lead to fundamental reassessments of the past. The growth of nostalgia for the certainties of the Cold War has already been mentioned. What for decades appeared as a fundamental danger to human civilisation is now perceived as a stable, orderly if tense state of affairs.

The questioning of identities, values and traditions inevitably leads to the reworking of the past. This is a matter of great concern for those committed to the maintenance of the status quo. Indeed, it is when the past is put to question that conservatives become sensitive to the problems of their time. In any case it is far easier to construct an idealised past than an ideal present.

Those who plunder the past are seeking authority and legitimacy for their actions. Every form of historical representation can become a resource when legitimacy or identity is contested. Thus the decline of the British film industry is seen as a blow to Britain's capacity to produce a usable past. Patriotic British film producer David Puttnam (of *Chariots of Fire* fame) has observed that there is no longer enough hard cash to promote a decent nationalist image, and warned that 'a nation that cannot celebrate its own heroes should start asking itself very serious questions.'[14]

A society which is suffering self-doubt is unlikely to celebrate its 'heroes' wholeheartedly for the simple reason that one person's hero may well turn out to be another's villain. This has been the sad experience of the traditional guardians of America's values. To take one controversial example: Allan Bloom's *The Closing of the American Mind*. The aim of this highly readable conservative polemic is to defend the 'traditional' values of America. In the course of attacking liberal and radical thinkers for undermining his idealised vision of American history, Bloom makes an interesting aside. He remarks that the 'bad conscience' these Marxists and liberals promoted, 'killed off the one continuing bit of popular culture that celebrated the national story – the Western.'[15] Bloom turns the issue upside-down. It was not the historical work of radicals that helped establish a sense of cynicism about the moral claims of the American frontier and the Western. Rather it was the questioning of the American way of life provoked by urban decay, racial conflict and the experience of Vietnam which disposed people to question the simplistic good-versus-bad imagery of the traditional Western.

A questioning of a way of life meant that films which projected that way of life into the past, that is the Western, became increasingly implausible. After Vietnam and the race riots, films about the Old West emphasised themes that reflected the times. Films concentrated on themes such as the loss of innocence, the death or the passing of the Old West. *Once Upon a Time in the West* or *Pat Garrett and Billy the Kid* are examples of this genre. Other films drew parallels with Vietnam and racial tensions. *Chato's Land* or *Ulzana's Raid* come to mind. Of even greater concern to moralists was the fact that it was no longer clear who was good and who was bad. This ambivalence was well expressed in Sam Peckinpah's *The Wild Bunch*, a film which reworked the traditional myths by looking at the passing of the Old West from the point of view of the outlaws. Bloom's concern with the Western is entirely understandable, for the passing of a national myth highlights a lack of cohesion in the present. Nor is Bloom the only traditionalist thinker concerned with films. In a major programmatic statement regarding the task of conservatives in the decade ahead, the editor of *Policy Review* boasts of at least one achievement in the 1980s: 'the movies of the '80s were much less radical than those of the '60s and '70s.'[16]

Of course Bloom is wrong. The Western has not died; only in its capacity as a national myth has it withered away. The Western, like all expressions of art and culture, continues to express the mood of the times. So does the capacity to imagine history. At the time of writing, the film *Dances with Wolves* was being acclaimed by the cinema industry as it made millions at the American box office. Dubbed a 'New Age' movie, this is an ecologically sound, racially enlightened portrayal of the Old West, where the Indians impart the profundities of folk wisdom and the American cavalry indiscriminately kills anything that moves. No doubt Bloom walked out before the end of the film. But like it or not it is a film that reflects some of the anxieties of a nation uncertain about its future. That those anxieties are very real was illustrated by the public furore that surrounded *The West as America*, an exhibition at the National Museum of American Art in Washington during the summer of 1991. The exhibition, which sought to challenge the myths of the West, was widely denounced by politicians as anti-patriotic. What gave this controversy a particular intensity was the widely shared view that the contemporary American identity was in some sense linked to a positive interpretation of the culture of the Western frontier.

Competing histories

It would be inaccurate to suggest that the contestation of the meaning of history is entirely due to the initiative of nationalist and conservative historians. That it has become an issue is a reflection of broad patterns at work in society. The absence of consensus about the past is a sharp reminder of disturbing disagreements about contemporary values. As always, the prevailing view of the past is one of the clearest indicators of popular mood. Conflicts about history suggest the absence of a shared tradition in many modern societies.

For a long time history has been a fragmented discipline. There is no history with a capital H; there are many competing histories. A lack of agreement about history reflects the absence of consensus today and vice versa. It has become increasingly clear that differences about the past express a lack of cohesion about the present. Many, especially conservative thinkers, believe that unless there is an agreed history there will be no future for society. One American conservative historian writes of a moral crisis 'so deep that it may signal the end of Western civilization'. She warns that only by re-establishing a continuity with the past 'can we prevent ourselves from being engulfed by a new "wave of the future" that is not our future at all.'[17]

The problem of continuity and of a shared past has also been at the centre of the *Historikerstreit*, the so-called historians' debate in Germany. This remark by the German historian Michael Sturmer is typical of the present concern with the recovery of History:

> When our neighbours observe Germans in relation to their history, they are confronted with the question: where is this all leading? ... there are signs that every generation now living in Germany has differing, indeed opposing pictures of the past and of the future ... The search for one's lost history is not an abstract striving after education: it is morally legitimate and politically necessary.[18]

Sturmer's concern with 'one's lost history' is by no means a uniquely German concern. The fear of losing the past and thereby also the future has a wide purchase on contemporary Western thought. In Britain it is never clear whether the discussion is about how to view the past or the present or what to think of the future. As the high Tory Ronald Butt has stated, a 'nation needs its history, without which its steps into the future will be hesitant and decadent, not to say barbaric.'[19]

Sturmer and Butt both seem to know what they are talking about when they use the word 'history'. In reality a nation's history is not unproblematic. The emergence of strongly contested and highly charged debates on what constitutes history in countries as different as Britain, France, Germany, Japan and the United States underlines the depth and breadth of the controversy. These debates about history indicate that there is no ready acceptance of common roots, origins or traditions. Thus Western societies appear to confront some disturbing questions about who they are, where they come from and what their future direction might be.

Particularly disturbing for the guardians of establishment values is the realisation that they can no longer assume that their version of the past will not be contested. The catastrophic consequences of this grim logic are all too evident in Eastern Europe and the Third World. If one group can gain legitimacy for its action through its interpretation of history, so can another. Intellectuals of the Georgian Republic of the Caucasus are appealing to their version of history to prevent the minority Ossetian population from enjoying any degree of autonomy. The Ossetians have replied with their own representation of the past. 'As with most national disputes', argues Jonathan Steele, 'history is a powerful part of the argument. Against the claim that the Ossetians are "newcomers", the Ossetians say they are descendants of an Indo-European people, the Alans, who settled the area in the fourth century AD.'[20] The same inexorable drive to conflict can be seen in the explosion of new histories in Yugoslavia. There is a mass proliferation of new history books which aims to stir up animosity against other ethnic groups. The Second World War is being re-fought between Croats and Serbs in a battle over numbers. The Serbian historian Veselin Djuretic claims that the Croat fascist movement, the Ustashi, killed 1.5 million Serbs. This is rejected as a lie by Croat historians who produce their own figures for atrocities committed by Serbs against their people.[21]

The dramatic and often violent consequences of competing histories in the Soviet Union or the Third World can easily obscure the more prosaic conflicts in the West. Yet are we certain that the history debates in the West and in Japan are devoid of the grim logic that we see elsewhere?

The controversies over history in the West and Japan have revealed societies that are deeply fragmented. The fracturing of official history has led to a free-for-all where different groups are all busy claiming their own distinct past. The scramble for identities seems to involve all sections of the political spectrum. It is as if the assertion of one identity unleashes a counter-reaction and leads to the emergence of another. Liberal and left-wing historians have encouraged 'hidden voices' and those 'left out of history' to claim their place. This has often led to competition between different constituencies. Competing histories represent an indirect way of staking a claim to society's resources. Since no one wants to be left out of history, the competition accelerates uncontrollably. This promotion of different histories and competing identities often leads to a stance whereby the exclusive and parochial is celebrated at the expense of the open-ended and the universal. Often these are understandable reactions to an insensitive official dogma. Unfortunately they too fall into the trap of plundering the past and often reproduce the narrowmindedness of conservative historiography.

A plurality of histories is acceptable to ruling elites within the confines of the classroom, but claims made on behalf of competing identities tend to undermine social cohesion. It is fine to talk about melting pots, pluralism or multiculturalism as long as no one questions which norms and values rule. However if there is no generally accepted view of the past this indicates that there is no common agreement about society's future direction. As one British intellectual, Jonathan Clark, who is in the forefront of the fight for a conservative ideological revival, argues: 'pluralism means more than interesting ethnic and cultural diversity: it means the clash of irreconcilable ideals in faith and morals.'[22] The implications of this argument are self-evident. Authority, morality and culture are not divisible. The very existence of rival cultures and identities calls into question the integrity of society.

A recurring tension between past and present identities, which influences all aspects of social theory, acquires a particularly sharp focus around the question of history. That is why this book is mainly devoted to the study of the relationship between perceptions of history and society. It is a work that began as an attempt to clarify key issues in historical sociology but which became increasingly a sociology of history – that is, about the relationship between society and views of the past, of change and by implication of the future.

The end of the Cold War highlights the persistence of ideological exhaustion, moral uncertainty and fear about the future in the Western capitalist world. During the era of superpower rivalries many of these sentiments were obscured by Cold War rhetoric or at least displaced by blaming problems on the Soviet threat. The speed with which Western celebrations of the triumph of capitalism have come to an end underlines a lack of direction about the future. Jonathan Clark's anxieties about pluralism and multiculturalism are symptomatic of defensiveness rather than of confidence. The same tone of resignation is manifest in Francis Fukuyama's hotly debated article 'The End of History'. For a statement that announces the triumph of the West and the defeat of Marxism this sounds positively downbeat about the future. He writes that the end of history 'will be a sad time' and that in 'the post-historical period there will be neither art nor philosophy, just the perpetual caretaking of the museum of human history.'[23] Fukuyama's speculations about the future may be somewhat tongue-in-cheek, but the overall mood he conveys is abundantly clear.

Fukuyama does not stand alone. Virtually the entire Western intelligentsia from left to right exudes a sense of despair. The fashion of post-modernism is illustrative of an era where terms such as progress and universalism are held in contempt in the academic world. The optimism of the Enlightenment is nowadays referred to only to show the distance of the author from such 'naive' and 'outdated' concepts. A collection of articles by sociologists on *Rethinking Progress* is introduced by an essay which finds it difficult to accept the relevance of reason to the solution of social problems. As for the concept of progress, it is treated as just about equivalent to bubonic plague in terms of its desirability.[24]

History seems to provide a mask for conflicting motives within society and in the relations between nations. Yet the emergence of the past and of history as the focus through which the problems of intellectual malaise and of legitimacy and identity are expressed and experienced has not been seriously considered by social scientists. This is surprising, since the past decade has seen the publication of hundreds of texts on topics such as the crisis of modernity, culture and progress. In general sociologists and related social theorists feel uncomfortable with history and have decided to ignore the subject. This is a shame since the subject is so wide that it covers virtually every aspect of social discourse, including that of culture.

Unlike social scientists, historians have taken a keen interest in the current debates about their subject. But the intervention of historians has been disappointing. Most of their contributions insist on isolating the problems of history as a profession from those of society. Consequently, when they speak of the 'crisis of history' what they have in mind are the specialist technical problems of their profession. As one American historian argued:

> Over the last twenty years American history has splintered. Indeed, the fragmenting has become so obvious that it is a commonplace in the discussions of the state of the American field. The principal source of that disarray has been an explosion of historical information, particularly in social history.[25]

This narrow conception of the crisis of history confuses cause with effect. The fragmentation that is the product of centrifugal forces operating at the level of society is interpreted as the outcome of forces generated inside the profession of history.

The indifference of social theorists towards history and the narrow technical approach of its practitioners means that important patterns, connections and themes are seldom considered. Thus there is a considerable body of literature on the German history debate, but this material is considered in an excessively German context without any reference to comparable discussions in Britain or Japan or in the United States. The important relationship between history and its uses in contemporary politics remains outside the framework of professional historians.[26]

An illustration of this professional myopia is a recently published collection of articles on the controversy over the teaching of history in Britain. This collection, which consists of 17 contributions, does not even bother to ask why the discussion occurred when it did. Only one contributor refers to anything outside Britain – an article by Alice Prochaska discusses a report on history teaching adopted by the California State Board of Education in 1987. None of the contributors considers why there is a general concern with history throughout Western societies. There is no attempt to relate the current debate to comparable controversies in the past. No explicit connections are drawn with current debates on history outside Britain; for example the German controversy is entirely ignored.[27] Many of these historians would have profited from reading E. H. Carr's *What is History*. Carr outlines as his purpose 'to show how closely the work of the historian mirrors the society in which he works.'[28]

In contrast, professional politicians have had no inhibitions about explicitly pronouncing on the subject, representing history as a political resource. History has become the small change of politicians interested in the upholding of special identities and traditions.

The themes

It is time to isolate some of the themes that will be considered in different contexts in the following chapters.

The overriding theme of our times is the fear of change. It is difficult to think of any film, novel or other production of art which shows the future in positive terms. In recent decades science fiction has become indistinguishable from the horror film. The world of Mad Max, which depicts survivalism in a brutal post-holocaust environment, strikes a resonance in the contemporary imagination, but a vision of a happy utopia does not. Society's views of the future, whether in the form of science fiction or statistical projections on demographic patterns, are above all statements about reactions to the present.

Fear of change has a deep popular resonance. It is a sentiment that needs to be explained. This negative orientation towards the future raises important questions about the interpretation of progress and development as concepts and as social processes. The pessimistic attitude towards change has important implications for the perception of history and for the ability to think historically. In this respect too Fukuyama is representative of the Western intelligentsia of the 1990s. On the right, the decline of socialism and disenchantment with the welfare state are seen as proof that the attempt to change society only makes matters worse. Left-wing and liberal opinion too has become sceptical about the future. Gareth Stedman Jones, a former member of the editorial board of the *New Left Review*, well expresses the profound scepticism towards history and change that unites all sections of the Western intelligentsia. He writes:

The once magical invocation of history's numinous and redemptive powers now looks either tawdry or sinister. From Passchendaele to Auschwitz, from the Gulag to Hiroshima, and so on to the Killing Fields, the twentieth century has remorselessly torn away from us all remaining vestiges of a simple nineteenth-century faith in progress.[29]

The apparent consequence of this almost pathological reaction to history is to deny the viability of progress and counsel reconciliation with life as it is. In this sense 'The End of History' in one variation or another summarises the mood of the late twentieth century.

A sense of terminus, which puts into question the project of social change, coexists with a major ideological problem. If this is it, if this is the end of history, then why is there no agreement on the fundamentals of society? This is the theme that haunts establishment ideologues and the conservative intelligentsia. There is a perceptible attempt to re-forge some kind of morality that could bind society together. For example the British conservative philosopher Roger Scruton fears a world 'without the sacred' where 'all is permitted, and where nothing has absolute value'.[30] The stress on 'absolute value' expresses a widespread concern with what is often described as 'relativism'. Relativism is an all-purpose concept that denies that any morals or values represent universal truths. This concept is also used to suggest that there are only subjective interpretations and no objectivity or objective truths. Insecurity about morality has stimulated the right-wing ideological project which upholds the 'sacred' and moral absolutes in order to attack the relativisation of values.

It is in this context that history becomes important. Despite the decline in historical thinking, there is a greater demand for History than ever before. At a time when the old absolutes are put to question and shared values appear conspicuous by their absence the question of social cohesion becomes critically important. Common roots and traditions can provide the means for the re-creation of consensus. That is why History is in such big demand, not history as a process of change but History as unchanging absolute identity that is common to all. As the German historian Hagen Schulze argued in one of the hearings for the Berlin Museum in November 1983:

Economic stagnation and new international constellations are giving the Germans a fright; unrest, anxiety, identity crisis and loss of direction are shaking society. The more uncertain the present and the darker the future, the stronger the need for direction from the past. The light that brightens the jungle of the present, reveals the path-markings and permits orientation, shines from the past, because there the experiences are rooted that make action possible today. For individuals just as for peoples, there can be no future without history; and what is not worked through in the memory will re-emerge as neurosis or hysteria.[31]

The intellectual orientation which looks for 'direction from the past' is the corollary to the declaration that history has ended. From this perspective the past becomes an indispensable resource for resolving society's problems. This will be an issue to which subsequent chapters will return time and again.

Finally, this book is concerned with examining the arguments and the mechanisms through which the construction of History is attempted and through which a sense of absolute values is refashioned. To anticipate one possible course of action: an attempt to build on the triumph of the West over the Soviet Union and Eastern Europe. It is true that for a brief period this victory seemed to provide capitalism with a sense of mission, purpose and direction. But not for long. Soon it became clear that the world was not a better place to live in than before. In any case the malaise experienced by capitalist societies had little to do with the Soviet Union. Winning the Cold War is unlikely to help solve the problems raised by Scruton or Schulze. The restoration of traditional and absolute values cannot proceed by simply repeating what worked in the past.

Almost spontaneously the advocates of History have sought to define a new tradition by attacking two targets. The first is the Third World. It is amazing how so many of the contributions which seek to reclaim moral absolutes and revive History lash out against the Third World. Defending the West seems to be more often then not an unconscious enterprise. Counterpoising the achievement of the West to the manifest devastation of the Third World is a simple way of claiming the mantle of history. That is why Fukuyama instinctively equated the end of history with the triumph of the West. In the same way appeals for the rehabilitation of national histories are often linked with cynical asides about the Third World. Elton's call for a 'History of England' is not unconnected with his arrogant dismissal 'of that curious extra-terrestrial place known as the Third World'.[32] Fukuyama has followed up his original article on history by claiming that the 'end of the Cold War has allowed us to debunk the moral pretensions of Third World tyrants.'[33] We shall consider later why Fukuyama and other writers seem curiously concerned with the 'moral pretensions' of the Third World. And why does the top-selling British quality Sunday newspaper predict that 'out of the Third World's arid soil monsters fully armed will spring for whom death and destruction are the only imaginable glory?'[34]

The second target is the 1960s. The 1960s are now held responsible for everything that is bad about Western societies. Everything from the breakdown of the family to the collapse of traditional values is held to be the responsibility of the 1960s. This sentiment has such strong emotional connotations that the very term 'the Sixties' immediately provokes an image of decadence and moral decay. According to the chair of the Adenauer Foundation, which is sponsored by Germany's ruling party, the Christian Democratic Union: 'The revolt of 1968 destroyed more values than did the Third Reich. To overcome it is therefore more important than trying to overcome Hitler once again.'[35] These are strong words indeed! Yet these sentiments are common currency within the current Western establishment tradition. By exaggerating the significance of the 1960s the problem of restoring faith in moral absolutes becomes manageable. It is almost as if, driven by instinct, conservatives are attempting to establish a coherence of thought through a critique of a caricatured version of the 1960s. When the 1960s are held out to be more destructive then the Third Reich than the term 'caricature' becomes something of an understatement.

A lot has been said about the past but almost nothing about the future. That resounding silence is probably the main theme of this book.

2

History in demand

Today the past enjoys unprecedented popularity. In every sphere of culture, from architecture and interior decor to the cinema and popular music, historical themes and nostalgic revivals predominate. While the public appetite for 'the old' seems insatiable, 'the new', anything modern or novel, is distinctly out of fashion. The contemporary cult of the past marks a dramatic shift in popular attitudes over recent years. In the early decades of the twentieth century public opinion celebrated novelty and innovation, new inventions and 'the latest' styles. The aspiration to be modern appeared to be the dominant influence on taste and the new was generally regarded as superior to the old. Now everything is reversed: 'modernity' is scorned on all sides and imaginative appeals to the past permeate popular culture.

It would be simplistic to suggest that the reversal of popular perceptions of the old and the new is either complete or that it took place at some precisely definable date. No doubt some people coveted antiques 50 years ago and some still favour steel and glass furniture today. Yet it is possible to make the general observation that whereas hostility to modern modes was a minority viewpoint in the first half of the century, in the second half it has become a mainstream attitude, at least in Western Europe and the USA.

By the early 1980s popular enthusiasm for the past had become so firmly established that it became a subject of widespread discussion. The American historian John Lukacs noted in 1980 that, whereas in the previous 25 years the circulation of most periodicals had declined, the only popular magazine that had 'earned its way without advertising' was *American Heritage*. Lukacs also drew attention to a 1976 survey of the Harvard class of 1968 which showed that more than 60 per cent of these graduates were engaged in restoring old houses.[1] Though not everyone is in a position to restore an old house,

17

a popular reaction against 'high rise' apartment blocks and other products of modern architecture is palpable throughout the Western world.

The prevalence of an outlook that prizes the old and scorns the new implies a negative judgement on contemporary society. Nostalgia for the past, for the 'good old days', suggests a degree of disenchantment or at least a lack of enthusiasm for life in the present. One observer has drawn a direct link between the British appetite for depictions of the days when 'British was the best' and Britain's decline as a world power:

> No wonder that present-day Britons show increasing interest in their past, whether through wartime or earlier dramas on televison, stately homes open to the public, historical novels, museums, or written history, scholarly or popular. The past is indeed another country, and some think it preferable to our own.[2]

It seems as if the attraction of the past lies in the conviction that it may provide something that is no longer available.

The popular affinity for the past should not be confused with an interest in the academic discipline of history. Indeed historians on both sides of the Atlantic have long been preoccupied with what they regard as the crisis of their subject. Their concerns about the fragmentation and lack of direction in the study of history have gathered momentum over the past two decades, particularly in the USA, where historians have faced declining job opportunities. At the 1970 meeting of the American Historical Association (AHA) there were 2,481 applicants for 188 posts; security measures had to be introduced to prevent applicants from destroying competitors' interview invitations.[3] In his 1981 presidential address to the AHA Bernard Baylin lamented the 'lack of cohesion' in the historical enterprise.[4] Historian James Turner noted that enrolments in history courses had plummeted and that faculties had vanished. He concluded that 'history appears headed for the garbage heap of history', placing the blame 'at the doorstep of its practitioners'.[5] Meanwhile in Britain Keith Robbins, president of the Historical Association, noted that many of the observations arising from the US 'crisis of history' discussion could be 'applied *mutatis mutandis* to the present problems of history and historians in the United Kingdom.'[6]

The sense of irrelevance experienced by professional historians indicates that the wider fashion for the past is quite unconnected to the academic study of history. Indeed there appear to be two distinct debates: one in the universities, which has little impact on society as a whole, and the other in the public sphere, the impetus for which comes from outside the academic world. Though the debates in historiography are of interest, our main concern is with the the discussion of history as a matter of public, often political, controversy.

The past under siege

The British historian J. H. Plumb has suggested that the entry of debates about history into the sphere of politics is itself a symptom of profound uncertainty about the direction of society. In *The Death of the Past* he observed that it is 'not accidental that great social crises, when secular authority or ancient belief are torn in conflict, bring forth a huge spate of historical writing and, indeed, historical controversy.'[7] Current attempts to restructure and extend the teaching of history in schools reflect the deep-seated insecurities of modern societies.

Indeed the very emergence of history as an academic discipline and a central feature of the school syllabus in advanced capitalist societies reflected the conviction of the ruling classes that history could act as a cohesive force against the destablising consequences of industrialisation. Authorities concerned with the maintenance of the established order have long placed great emphasis on history education. They regard it as providing vital moral inspiration and as helping to forge a sense of national identity in the face of disintegrative trends or subversive influences. For example Baron Kikuchi, Japanese Education Minister from 1901 to 1903, considered that history teaching helped to motivate his nation's soldiers to succeed in the Russo-Japanese war: 'I think that by this organised moral teaching we have prevented a great melting away of principle; we were drifting and seemed to be loosened from all solid ground of morality.'[8] The sense that old traditions and conventions are in jeopardy creates a demand for the teaching of history to provide an anchor in the past.

By the turn of the century leading educationalists in all the major capitalist countries were convinced that teaching history was a key aspect of national defence. It was not only the Japanese authorities who drew the link between military performance and history teaching. An early study, published in the 1920s, concluded that the education system in France was responsible for the exemplary performance of its soldiers in the First World War. It suggested that by keeping alive a desire to avenge the defeat at the hands of the Prussians in 1871, French history teaching helped the military effort four decades later.[9]

Nor was Kikuchi's concern with remaining on the 'solid ground of morality' a uniquely Japanese concern. Historians in other capitalist countries were equally concerned to define the function of their discipline as setting out moral examples and precepts. In the USA late nineteenth-century establishment historians such as Andrew D. White, the first president of the AHA, and Alfred T. Mahan emphasised the 'exemplar function of history'. In Britain history education developed at least in part in response to the painful perception of national decline. Sir John Robert Seeley, probably the most influential British historian in the late nineteenth and early twentieth centuries, regarded the shaping of public morality as his professional responsibility. According to one account, Seeley was concerned that since the days of Napoleon the English national character had decayed; this concern was widely shared within the British establishment.[10] Seeley's solution was to encourage, through the teaching of history, a new national morality. He set about rewriting English history as a series of morality plays. His 1881 lecture to his Cambridge students sums up his moralising perspective:

> It is a favourite maxim of mine that history, while it should be scientific in its method, should pursue a practical object. That is, it should not merely gratify the reader's curiosity about the past, but modify his view of the present and his forecast of the future. Now if this maxim be sound, the history of England ought to end with something that might be called a moral. Some large conclusion ought to arise out of it; it ought to exhibit the general tendency of English affairs in such a way as to set us thinking about the future and divining the destiny which is reserved for us.[11]

For Seeley, the 'practical object' of history is to reveal a purpose so that the meaning of life is clarified for all those whose fate is linked to the 'destiny' of England. History in this sense becomes a metaphysical entity, a kind of revelation of the human purpose.

It is not surprising to find that the sort of history that offers moral authority and national identity is in demand at times of social upheaval. Though this use of history rests on the dubious assumption that solutions to contemporary problems can be found by scavenging the past, it is always popular with those committed to upholding the status quo. Promoting the past and popularising its 'lessons' seems to provide an intellectual antidote to the moral drift brought on by social change. Writing in dread of the upheavals anticipated at the end of the First World War, the Earl of Meath proposed a number of steps which should be taken to encourage the 'cultivation of patriotism': 'every effort should be made in schools to explain to children the solid foundations on which British patriotism is founded' and 'greater attention should be paid in the schools to the teaching of the history and geography of the Empire.'[12] By inculcating a pride in a common past, defenders of the established order hoped to strengthen popular identification with the status quo and thus to weaken anti-establishment influences.

Success in using history to contain threats to social stability cannot be guaranteed. It may prove difficult to promote a pride in the past among those who are alienated from the existing order or demoralised by life in the present. In periods when society is gripped by a profound crisis of confidence, appeals to historical precedent may not be enough to restore faith in the established order. Nevertheless, at times when a particular society seems exhausted and there is widespread doubt about its future prospects, nostalgia for the past becomes widespread and history as a source of values and lessons can come into its own. Richard Hofstadter's *American Political Tradition*, published in 1948, captures the link between fear of the future and affection for the past:

Since Americans have recently found it more comfortable to see where they have been than to think of where they are going, their state of mind has become increasingly passive and spectatorial. Historical novels, fictionalized biographies, collections of pictures and cartoons, books on American regions and rivers have poured forth to satisfy a ravenous appetite for Americana. This quest for the American past is carried on in a spirit of sentimental appreciation rather than of critical analysis. An awareness of history is always a part of any culturally alert national life; but I believe that what underlies this overpowering nostalgia of the last fifteen years is a keen feeling of insecurity. The two world wars, unstable booms, and the abysmal depression of our time have profoundly shaken national confidence in the future ... If the future seems dark, the past by contrast looks rosier than ever; but it is used far less to locate and guide the present than to give reassurance.[13]

Though Hofstadter's eloquent analysis of nostalgia in postwar America shows his sensitivity to the popular mood, his attempt to differentiate between using the past as a 'guide' rather than as a source of 'reassurance' is problematic since in reality these motives are closely linked.

It is immediately striking that Hofstadter's description of America in 1948 would not seem out of place in a contemporary account. Although it is tempting to draw out the similarities, there is the danger of falling into the trap of reading history backwards and merely discovering the present in the past. In fact both fear of the future and obsession with the past exist on a far grander scale today than in the late 1940s. Except for brief episodes, Western societies have never recovered their optimism since 1945.

Since the 1970s long-standing concerns about the direction of society have been compounded by anxieties resulting from the gradual breakdown of the postwar world order. The decline of the USA's global hegemony, the collapse of the Soviet Union as a superpower, the rise of Japan and the re-unification of Germany – all these developments have undermined the balance of power established at the end of the Second World War, forcing all the main capitalist powers to readjust to the new circumstances. Such readjustments inevitably raise important questions about national identity and direction and create a corresponding concern to forge a domestic consensus on these matters in all the countries concerned. As the shifting world balance throws the status of every nation into question, every national ruling class has turned to history to provide identity and cohesion.

The breakdown of the old world order is the key to the crisis of history and all the controversies around history teaching. For example, Carol Gluck links the rewriting of national history in Japan to the changing international environment which 'compounds Japan's old dilemma of "proper place".'[14] The same forces which have revived Japan's concern about its 'proper place' have also affected Europe. 'The present condition of "Europe" has produced a crisis of historiography which matches the tensions and opportunities of the continent', writes one British historian.[15] This crisis of historiography is not simply an intellectual problem, but reflects a more pervasive ideological and political crisis in society. The current revival of history is an attempt to achieve in the late twentieth century what Seeley and others never fully succeeded in achieving 100 years ago. The project at hand is the construction of a past that can confer legitimacy on the actions of those who run British society (and its national rivals) today. To grasp this project it is useful to look more closely at how the demand for history has emerged in recent years.

The demand for tradition

Intellectuals and politicians professionally concerned with maintaining order and consensus have always been concerned to conserve links with the past and constantly fear the erosion of these links. They regard past experience and achievement, codified in tradition, as the most appropriate guide for human action. The main problem facing the traditionalists is that it is difficult to project a past that is both relevant and inspiring.

The recent histories of most countries contain embarrassing episodes which intervene to limit the scope for using the past, a problem that was widely recognised in the 1950s and 1960s. Speaking in New York in 1968, Plumb argued that 'there is little sense in any Western nation that their past is compelling them toward a certain future.'[16] Writing about the 'demise of the past', the trans-Atlantic French thinker Stanley Hoffman warned that 'through speed and the savagery of history, we have not simply lost touch with the world that is behind us; it also appears that this world said many things that turned out to be false and thus has nothing more to say to the average European.'[17] However, the awareness that the past had become marginal in modern society was a source of concern for mainstream conservative and even liberal politicians and intellectuals. Their anxiety was further compounded by the realisation that there was no longer any commonly accepted version of the past.

From the 1970s onwards a growing concern about 'moral drift' in society, articulated in terms similar to those of Kikuchi at the turn of the century, stimulated a renewed demand for the past throughout the capitalist world. This demand assumed a variety of forms but the call to reform education, and particularly the teaching of history, as a means of socialising the younger generation into the values of the past, was a common theme. In all major countries authorities expressed their concern about a 'decline of history' which, unless countered, would lead a new generation of citizens to become strangers in their own country.

Most of those demanding the reform and expansion of history teaching seemed unaware that this meant the creation of a politically expedient nationalist historiography. Hoffman is an exception because his assimilation of French history has sensitised him to the potentially chauvinist consequences of the project: 'are images of the past and visions of the future tied either to struggles for national identity or to the possibility of strutting on the world's stage?' he asks. Well aware of the answer, he opts for European unity as a way of avoiding the dangerous consequences of reviving past nationalist rivalries.[18] He still wants the past, but unlike others he wants a past that transcends the nation state.

Others are far less reluctant than Hoffman to draw out the nationalist themes of the history revival. In Japan in the 1980s there was mounting pressure for the revision of school texts and for the promotion of a strong sense of the past. Politicians have constantly sought to stir up Japan's public memory. When Prime Minister Nakasone came into office in December 1982 he announced that the time had come for the 'settling of accounts with the postwar period'.[19] In Britain and the USA the concern with the past is generally expressed indirectly through a discussion of the decline of history. The conservative historian Lord Elton attempted to kill two birds with one stone when he connected 'the decline of history' to the lack of cohesion of a subject that did not have as its 'central theme, the history of England'.[20] In the USA there is flood of literature bemoaning the 'decline of history', code for the approved tradition of nationalist history.

Robert Nisbet's *History of the Idea of Progress* is a coherent synthesis of the conservative ideological response to the perceived demise of the past. Nisbet self-consciously couples America's progress as a nation with its appreciation of the past. He evokes the good old days to show that it was the sense of the past that made America great:

> A respect for the past, nowhere more dedicated than in the United States, continued into the twentieth century. There were innumerable festivals, holidays and rituals, the purpose of which was a fusing of a people into a community ... There could not have been many homes in which elements of the past – political, military, and religious, preponderantly – were not frequently, even continually, brought to the attention of the young. How else to make children love country, race or nationality, and religion except through the incessant recreation of the past and its great events, heroes, leaders and prophets? No single subject in school or college was more honoured than history.[21]

Nisbet's romanticised representation of an America in which there 'could not have been many homes' that did not worship at the altar of the past, is meant to serve as a direct counterpoint to an era in which this religion is in decline. Nisbet presents his bleak historical vision in Manichean terms: 'not even in the Dark Ages has alienation from, lack of confidence in, and hostility toward fundamental institutions been as deep and widespread as in this final part of the twentieth century in the West', he warns.[22] Nothing less than the triumph of Evil over Good is the prospect Nisbet holds out for a society that does not respect its own history.

William Bennett, Education Secretary under the Reagan presidency, pursues Nisbet's theme in his discussion of 'why America's children are strangers in their own land'. According to Bennett the problem is the lack of good history in the nation's schools:

> Why should we be surprised, when many of our schools no longer make sure their charges know the long procession of events that gave rise to modern democracy? We offer our students the flag but sometime act toward it as if it were only cloth. We neglect to teach them the ancient texts sewn into its fabric, the ideas and endeavours of cultures whose own emblems in time lent us the designs for our own.[23]

Bennett's predictable solution is to call for more and better history teaching. He asserts that 'history is organized memory, and memory, in turn, is the glue that holds our political community together.'[24] Bennett's plea for more history is also endorsed by Allan Bloom who deeply regrets that the young know 'much less about American history and those who were held to be its heroes'.[25]

Bloom's reference to heroes indicates a recurring theme in the discussion about history. American historian William H. McNeill writes that 'a nation or any other human group that knows how to behave in crisis situations because it has inherited a heroic historiographical tradition that tells how ancestors resisted their enemies successfully is more likely to act together effectively than a group lacking such a tradition.'[26] According to McNeill, Britain's resolute resistance against Nazi Germany in 1940 illustrates the importance of a functioning heroic tradition. Thus what the history revival requires is not merely any past but a *heroic past*, one that can instil pride in a particular national tradition.

For the proponents of the history revival any form of history that does not extol the heroic legacy of a nation is worse than no history at all. This point was robustly affirmed by Margaret Thatcher in 1975:

> We are witnessing a deliberate attack on those who wish to promote merit and excellence, a deliberate attack on our heritage and our past, and there are those who gnaw away at our national self-respect, rewriting British history as centuries of unrelieved doom, oppression and failure – as days of hopelessness, not days of hope.[27]

Thatcher's angry reaction against a history which questioned the legitimacy of national traditions is shared by leading politicians in other Western states. Former West German Chancellor Helmut Kohl similarly insisted that in the 'long run no nation can live without a historic identity. If our German history was merely regarded as one single chain of crimes and failures, then our nation could be shaken and the future could be put at stake.'[28]

The promotion of pride in a heroic past is linked to another theme in the demand for history. Pride in the past means pride in individual and national antecedents and a preoccupation with 'roots'. According to this argument, the roots which are made conscious through history are vital to a secure society and if people lose an awareness of their national origins, all is lost. In his final address to the *Bundestag* another German Chancellor, Helmut Schmidt, warned that 'we are an endangered people, and God help us if we don't know our history well enough, if we ignore large parts of it.'[29] Just what it is about the past that is so essential for survival is seldom explained; its importance is generally asserted in an almost mystical way as a sentiment which is either self-evident or a matter of faith.

Invoking the past appears to endow with profundity statements that would otherwise be dismissed as platitudinous. Thus Lord Elton can preach that an 'era like ours, full of self-deprecation and envy, can do with the corrective of a past that demonstrates virtue and achievement.'[30] It is striking that the past conjured up by conservative historians always provides inspiration and encouragement while the present is depicted in pejorative terms. The promotion of histories of a virtuous past is based on the assumption that the past is a repository of moral instruction which can provide invaluble lessons for modern society. Yet when we look at the many attempts to explain these remarkable and mysterious properties of history, we find only cliches. Thus though Turner concedes that 'history can no longer pretend to give the answer', he still claims that it can supply a 'range of possible answers'. But there is more! The great value of history for Turner is that it 'teaches also respect for human limitations and possibilities'.[31]

The notion that history teaches specific lessons cannot stand up to serious examination. The fact that different lessons are drawn from the past at different times confirms that it is teachers who teach and that what they make of history depends above all on the shifting consensus about the past that changes with every generation. Turner's view that history contains answers to questions even before they are asked reflects a metaphysical perspective. This approach must assume either that nothing ever changes, so that it is necessary only to choose from an existing stock of solutions to the same endlessly recurring problems, or that history is merely a process of revelation of some predetermined truth.

The metaphysical premise of conservative historiography leads to conclusions which endow history with a sort of religious purpose or at least with a secular teleology. History gives direction and thus provides the key to the future. Michael Sturmer, one the leading conservative protagonists in the *Historikerstreit* expounded this outlook with devastating simplicity: 'in a land without history, the future is won by those who are able to harness memory, coin concepts and interpret the past.'[32] From this perspective history is not only metaphorically but practically a guide to the future. To confirm this proposition the British historian Donald Cameron Watt simply asks 'how do we know where we are going if we do not know from where we are coming?'

The sort of history that can provide direction for society is in widespread demand. But after the experience of Nazi Germany and Stalin's Soviet Union it is not so easy to demand the explicit subordination of history to political expediency. The idea of history as a revelation of some preordained purpose has been discredited by the catastrophes of the twentieth century. It is widely accepted that once history is established as a legitimate sanction of human action, the most sordid crimes can be enacted in its name. Hence the more subtle calls for the revival of history make no claims for the relevance of its lessons, emphasising instead the value of knowledge about the facts of the past, of history 'for its own sake'.

Despite the apparent differences between the view of history as a source of moral lessons and that of history as a collection of empirical facts, there is an underlying similarity. The latter view simply ossifies moral lessons and treats them as if they were incontestable facts.

Many advocates of a renewed emphasis on history teaching self-consciously distance themselves from the 'past as lessons' school. However, this approach raises the question of how history can be justified if it does not provide lessons. The familiar answer that history is important 'for its own sake' is no answer at all. The British Conservative ideologue and former Education Minister, Sir Keith Joseph, one of the key figures in the controversy about the teaching of history, expressed this sentiment when he argued that 'the knowledge, understanding and skills which the study of history can confer are of great value in themselves.' A pamphlet entitled *History in Peril*, published by the right-wing Centre for Policy Studies, argued in a similar vein that the past should be studied 'for its own sake' rather than as a 'source of lessons'.[33]

The argument that history contains intrinsic values and that there is something worthwhile in the study of the past for its own sake is simply a roundabout way of saying that it contains something to be revealed. It must be presumed that this something is more than a mere collection of 'facts' or a set of chronologies. Though Walter Bennett argues that 'history teaches respect for facts', it is not facts that he has in mind when he writes that if 'taught honestly and truthfully, the study of history will give our students a grasp of their nation, a nation that the study of history ... will reveal is still indeed, "the last best hope on earth".'[34] It thus appears that the value of history is not that it innocently respects facts but that it reveals values essential for the maintenance of society. The 'history as facts' school simply reintroduces the familiar moral lessons through the back door.

In method, if perhaps not in intent, the proponents of today's history revival follow the approach of nineteenth-century *historicism*. According to the historicist logic, truth can only be revealed through history by grasping the meaning of the tradition of the past. Without going too deeply into the psychology of contemporary advocates of historicism it appears that they are far more cynical than their colleagues in the last century. Many of those who are currently demanding more history teaching are quite indifferent to its content. Their sole concern is that it should provide a moral framework for cohering society. Hence they call for a style of history that minimises differences and highlights a common identity. They want a history that fosters myths about the past according to the needs of the present. Lest this be considered a harsh judgement or a polemical point, it is important to point out that many of the participants explicitly proclaim their apologetic purpose. To cite but one example:

Yet we cannot afford to reject collective self-flattery as silly, contemptible error. Myths are, after all, often self-validating ... Belief in the virtue and righteousness of one's cause is a necessary sort of self-delusion for human beings, singly and collectively. A corrosive version of history that emphasizes all the recurrent discrepancies between ideal and reality in a given group's behaviour makes it harder for members of the group in question to act cohesively and in good conscience. That sort of history is very costly indeed. No group can afford it for long.[35]

We have come a long way from a conception of historical studies as the collection of facts about the past, and indeed from the claim that history contains intrinsic values. Now history has turned into a kind of social or national fiction that is self-validating and confers the sanction of the past on all who invoke its authority.

It is easy to invent myths, but it is quite another matter to win popular acceptance of a particular version of a mythical past. Even if such a history is not intellectually contested there is no guarantee that it will inspire or influence the climate of opinion. There is also a further problem: any attempt to impose social cohesion may itself prove divisive. The celebration of a particular past may well represent the rejection of another. There is certainly little evidence so far to suggest that the current history revival has succeeded.

The terms of the debate

A country that needs to create and propagate a history that is a source of pride, providing the required lessons, roots and direction, also needs a past that is expunged of embarrassing episodes. The familiar phrase 'settling scores with the past' means the process of inventing a history that can lend legitimacy to contemporary society by downplaying disasters in the past and elevating the heroic. The motivation for the reworking of history is the desire to foster existing identities, and not simply identities in the abstract, but *national* identities. It also follows that what is in demand is not just history, but *national* history. Japanese Education Minister Takeo Nishioka justified the rewriting of school textbooks on the grounds that, since the country had 'improved its national strength and upgraded its position in the international community', it was important to 'enable children to have a proper awareness of the history of their own country by teaching them about historical facts.'³⁶

Nishioka's 'historical facts' are not randomly selected scraps of information about Japan's past. They are, he writes, facts that can be used 'so that children may foster a love for their own country'. Such calls for a revival of histories that promote patriotism are often accompanied by a rather forced distinction between 'national' and 'nationalist' history. Thus Keith Joseph states that 'I therefore see an element of national – which I emphatically do not mean nationalist – history as an inescapable part of any balanced school history course.'³⁷ Joseph may sincerely believe in the possibility of a non-nationalist British history, but experience shows that the drive to promote a national history cannot be separated from the tendency to extol an exclusivist pride and a particularist identity. Joseph's colleagues in successive Thatcher governments have certainly not felt inhibited about expressing their nationalist fervour. The distinction between national and nationalist history is as plausible as Nishioka's sturdy separation of teaching about Japan's past military glories and the encouragement of militarism. He protests, rather naively, that he 'cannot understand the argument that teaching about military or naval officers would lead to militarism'.³⁸

There are marked national variations in the form taken by the demand for history. Societies as different as Germany and Japan, Britain and the USA experience the problem of national identity in ways that are distinct and dissimilar. Each country's distinctive culture and unique experience of the past have important implications for the way in which the problem of history is interpreted. When it comes to rewriting their histories, it is immediately evident that Germany and Japan have the greatest problems, arising from their embarrassing roles in the Second World War. In their cases the challenge is to manufacture a past that can boost national pride at a time when memories of the offending episode are still very much alive at home and abroad. The thrust of national history in Germany and Japan is to portray their current economic success as the natural culmination of a tradition from which the era of fascism and war was but a transient and wholly uncharacteristic departure.

Britain and the USA face different problems. Both countries have successful pasts with only relatively minor embarrassing episodes. America's so-called Vietnam Syndrome and Britain's imperialist legacy are not national scandals of the same magnitude as the holocaust or the Japanese occupation of China and South East Asia. However, the Anglo-American establishment is painfully aware of its poor economic performance and of an apparently inexorable process of national decline. In these two societies the emphasis in the rewriting of history is on projecting a relatively positive past into the present, while dismissing current discontents as minor setbacks to the continued ascendancy of Western civilisation.

Although each country's history is constructed within a clear national framework there are inevitably points of interaction. The revision of Japanese history has attracted more international criticism than most. This is due to some extent to a clash of cultures and perhaps also to the ethnocentrism of Western critics. It is also because rewriting the history of Japan inevitably leads to the revision of the history of other countries, notably China, which resents the trend towards whitewashing Japan's conduct in the Second World War.

The attempt to sanitise the German past has also attracted some international criticism. The project of normalising Germany's recent historical record remains a source of concern to those who suffered during the Nazi era. One account of the German historians' debate concludes that the 'perfectly understandable desire of contemporary Germans to be absolved of guilt confronts the equally comprehensible interest of Jews and others in keeping alive the memory of the destruction of European Jewry.'[39] The British establishment plays a leading role in keeping alive the public memory of the Second World War, never losing an opportunity to remind Germany of its guilt and of Britain's moral superiority. The reaction of a group of right-wing Tory parliamentarians to a row in October 1990 between Margaret Thatcher, then Prime Minister, and other European leaders reveals a characteristic British attitude: 'If Europe is so stupid as to reject the one member which spilled blood to save her bacon in two world wars, then there is a clear lack of historic perspective in present thinking.'[40] The 'historic perspective' most favoured by many British conservatives would mean freezing time at around 1945.

For Britain the Second World War is very much in the present, as Robert Skidelsky observed in 1972:

> The Second World War was Britain's last heroic moment; it also established the contemporary British consensus. There has been no major new political or social thinking in Britain since World War Two merely a filling-in of detail. To challenge the existing interpretations is therefore to challenge in a sense everything that came out of the War – as well as to deprive ourselves of our last true moment of glory.[41]

The glorification of the Second World War remains central to Britain's political culture to this day. A recent survey of the British media showed that television programmes about the war, from documentaries to comedies, continue to flourish. The survey's author quotes a German commentator living in London who considers it 'rather curious' that 'the only comfort' for the English 'lies 45 years in the past'. In conclusion the author accurately sums up the role of the war in contemporary Britain:

> UK industry is dead, sterling's finished and the best the country can look forward to is the cheeky client relationship portrayed in *Auf Wiedersehen, Pet*. But in their obsessive trivialisation of the war, the British can still underline their inherent moral superiority.[42]

In a country preoccupied with national decline, images of Dunkirk and the Blitz help to sustain the memory of a heroic past.

The revival of nationalist historiography in Britain provides a mirror image to the history debate in Germany. Whereas the German establishment wants to forget the Second World War, its British counterpart wants to make sure that this is indelibly printed on the public memory. Nicholas Ridley, a Conservative government minister who was forced to resign in July 1990 after an anti-German outburst, was explicit about his concern to revive wartime memories. When asked 'aren't your views coloured by the fact that you can remember the Second World War', he replied:

> Jolly good thing, too. About time somebody said that. It was pretty nasty. Only two months ago I was in Auschwitz, Poland. Next week I'm in Czechoslovakia. You ask them what they think about the Second World War. It's useful to remember.[43]

It is not just one eccentric ex-cabinet minister who finds it 'useful to remember'. The fact that during the Gulf crisis of 1990–1, the Western media readily drew parallels between any softening of allied hostility towards Iraq and the appeasement of Nazi Germany in the 1930s confirmed that after 50 years Germany's rivals have no difficulty in remembering its past failures. No doubt this fact of life of international relations has not escaped the attention of conservative German historians who have long been trying to 'settle scores' with the Nazi period.

So far we have emphasised some of the variations in the revival of history among different countries and considered some of the difficulties and potential points of conflict that have emerged. These conflicts could be fruitfully studied further through a consideration of the changing character of international relations. However our main interest is on the domestic front, in considering the relationship between the revival of history and modern society. From this perspective, the variations in the form in which the concern about history has emerged are far outweighed by the similarities at the level of substance.

For example, whichever country we examine, the debate about history always takes place in response to what is described as an unpatriotic and intolerant left-wing or liberal intelligentsia. This attempt to establish a conservative intellectual hegemony uses a contemporary version of the German nationalist thesis that defeat in the First World War was not the result of military failure but of subversion by unpatriotic elements within the German ranks. According to the latest version of this 'stab in the back' conspiracy theory, society has suffered from a sense of guilt and doubt inflicted by groups of malevolent intellectuals, who have succeeded in assuming control over the levers of culture and education. In an intervention in the British debate the right-wing journalist Ronald Butt dramatically summons up this vision of betrayal when he exclaims that 'history has been derailed by a cultural *coup d'état*.'[44]

The campaign to restore nationalist history is always presented as a desperate eleventh-hour intervention to rescue a nation's identity and culture from imminent peril. Heaving a grateful sigh of relief that the Thatcher government had at last stepped in to influence the teaching of history, the Tory historian Norman Stone asked rhetorically: 'How did a Conservative government come so close to accepting the disintegration of a subject on which the whole Conservative philosophy is based?'[45] In Britain the image of the subversive intellectual is a recurrent establishment theme.

Conservative British historians blame the country's decline on intellectual sabotage rather than on economic and political failures. In their view a subversive history has eroded pride and confidence in the nation's traditions, thus lowering expectations and achievement. Thus the problem was not one of actual decline, but of bad history sapping national morale in schools and universities: 'the crisis of British History is a result not of the historical evolution of Great Britain but of developments within History faculties.'[46] In this flattering account of British history, all the problems of economic stagnation and declining international competitiveness were transformed into deficiencies in the conduct of courses by university history departments. During the Thatcher period of the 1980s, this perspective enjoyed at least the informal support of the government of the day. The Prime Minister herself applauded the establishment historian Lord Thomas for his 'powerful plea for restored pride in our past based on an understanding of its greatness and unique qualities.' For Thatcher, this plea was a 'reminder that a whole generation has been brought up to misunderstand and denigrate our national history.'[47]

The battle against the supposed denigration of national history was fought with equal enthusiasm elsewhere. In Japan the rewriting of historical texts, including such delicate modifications as the renaming of the 1937 Nanking massacre as a 'police action', was justified on the grounds that it redressed the balance against the distortions introduced by left-wing history books. The radical Japanese teachers' union provided a constant focus of attack for right-wing politicians and historians.

Whereas in the West conservatives tend to locate the cultural *coup* of left-wing intellectuals in the 1960s, in Japan it is pushed back to 1945. According to the emerging nationalist orthodoxy, since the end of the Second World War the minds of Japanese schoolchildren have been corrupted by unpatriotic teachers, a view vigorously argued by Yoshihisa Komori, London correspondent of *Sankei Shimbun*:

> Textbook-writing in Japan has a unique history. Immediately after the war, most authors, scholars and teachers were from the left, and backed by the powerful National Schoolteachers' Union, whose members taught students to boycott the national flag and national anthem. Many textbook writers presented non-communist countries in the harshest light while being uncritical of communist ones – criticising "Western imperialism" while glossing over Soviet oppression.[48]

For Komori the rewriting of history is a belated attempt to restore the balance: 'Japanese who support revision feel that since the pendulum swung to the left, it should be brought towards the centre.' But this balancing act is simply an attempt to justify whitewashing the role of Japanese imperialism during the Second World War.

In Germany the conservative or, as it preferred to style itself, neo-conservative offensive, *Tendenzwende*, explicitly targeted unpatriotic left-wing teachers and intellectuals. The drive to revise German history sought to counter the radical tradition's claim to offer the 'exclusive and indispensable means for coming to terms with the Nazi era'.[49] One of the earliest manifestations of the right-wing *kulturkampf* was a crusade in the early 1970s against guidelines for high-school curricula in the province of Hesse issued by the Social-Democratic administration, allegedly under the influence of New Left radicals. In West Germany as in Britain the campaign for patriotic history enjoyed at least informal state backing. Since 1982 the Kohl government has consistently promoted a history which does not 'exaggerate' the importance of the Third Reich. Kohl himself has taken an active interest in the subject and is advised by the historian Michael Sturmer, among others.

As a result of the more fragmented political system in the USA, issues such as the status of history and the way it is taught tend to be less politicised than in Europe or in Japan. Nevertheless, the theme that irresponsible intellectuals are to blame for the decline of history and thus for the erosion of American values is central to the conservative case.

Of all the major world powers the USA has fewest problems with its own past. Hence American conservatives are not concerned to revise, but rather to preserve and defend the traditional interpretation of the past. For them history means establishing what it means to be American, crucially by upholding one culture and identity at the expense of the rest. In the USA the 'stab-in-the-back' thesis often takes the form of a critique which combines a warning about the decline of history with the targeting of a threat to the American way of life. The familiar target is those unnamed liberal and Marxist professors whose carping criticisms have sapped confidence in American values, especially since the 1960s when, it is alleged, such treacherous academics took control over the university system. According to one account of Harvard in this period, standards declined because of 'the tolerance of plagiarists, loafers, incompetents, drunkards', leading to a virtual moral collapse: 'An affluent and indulgent society ... mistook flaccid permissiveness for tolerance. Everything went because nothing was worth defending, and the legitimate right to err became the disastrous obliteration of the difference between error and truth.'[50] The term 'permissiveness' has come to cover a wide range of sins: liberalism, relativism, indeed any questioning of what were regarded as the fundamental values of the nation.

While most conservative American commentators locate the great betrayal in the 1960s, some more ambitious right-wing intellectuals have traced the roots of radical treachery back to the interwar years when the American dream first came under serious scrutiny. For Allan Bloom, these early criticisms of the Founding Fathers provided the foundation for a more systematic assault that came in the 1960s:

There was even a general tendency to debunk the Founding, to prove the beginnings were flawed in order to license a greater openness to the new. What began in Charles Beard's Marxism and Carl Becker's historicism became routine. We are used to hearing the Founders charged with being racists, murderers of Indians, representatives of class interests.[51]

Like his colleagues in Japan and Europe, Bloom wants to reverse what he identifies as the subversive radical or liberal postwar tide. In this new history, one can be sure that events such as slavery in America, the carve-up of Africa, the rape of Nanking and the Holocaust will not be 'overexaggerated'.

The political terrain

The revival of history is not confined to the sphere of ideas. It is closely connected to developments in politics and ideology. Intellectuals may do most of the talking and writing, but it is the politicians who take charge when it comes to organisation and action. In recent years politicians have been busy trying to influence the public memory. In every major country the 1980s was a decade of anniversaries, centenaries and bicentenaries as governments seized on glorious events in the past to celebrate with parades and carnivals, and the opening of memorials, monuments and museums. It is not yet possible to assess the influence on public consciousness of such attempts to popularise national histories. The public memory is unpredictable and its evolution can often only be understood in retrospect. It is important to remember that popular moods and perceptions are more influenced by people's experiences of society and their quality of life than by official propaganda in the form of history. Thus debates about history should be regarded as symptoms of social trends rather than as fundamental determinants of society. With this proviso, we now turn to look more closely at the history debates in some of the world's leading nations.

The United States

As we have seen, the USA has few difficulties with its past and the conservative agenda emphasises the need simply to uphold traditional history. It has succeeded in minimising the potential embarrassment of the era of slavery by developing a nationalist presentation of the civil war. Unlike the German or Japanese ruling class, the American establishment has not felt the need to rewrite its history.[52] For example, the controversy that surrounded plans for celebrating the 500th anniversary of Colombus' 'discovery' of America was far less explosive than the debate in Germany around the meaning of the Holocaust.

Yet there is a striking contrast between the USA's relatively stable past and its currently fractured national identity. The growing scale of popular disenchantment with life in modern America, particularly among its multitudinous and diverse ethnic minorities, has led to increasing questioning of the validity of the much-vaunted American way of life for many of its citizens. This questioning of contemporary American society has led in turn to an interrogation of the past: if the promises of the American dream are exposed as fraudulent in the present, then why should anybody trust the traditional account of the past? Because American society is less polarised in terms of class than other capitalist countries, the debate about American identity takes a less politicised form. Hence disenchantment and alienation are seldom focused and the predominant symptoms of the problem of national identity are those of doubt and insecurity.

Linking the crisis of American identity to the humiliation of its defeat in Vietnam and the race riots of the 1960s has become something of a cliche. A closer examination reveals other important factors; in particular, the erosion of American global hegemony in the same period created a deepening sense of national decline. The cumulative effects of all these setbacks seriously undermined the self-confidence of the American establishment. In the 1970s the US political elite seemed to lose its grip over national affairs as it reeled from one scandal to another. In the America of Watergate, the ruling class clearly lacked the moral authority to contain the growth of cynicism and social malaise. It was the general loss of direction of American society in the 1960s and 1970s, rather than a conspiracy of liberal professors, which provoked a widespread questioning of national identities – present and past. A study of American school textbooks detected a significant change of tone in this period:

The late 1960s editions show that foreign policy has been a problem for years ... Urban blight, too, has long been a problem, and black Americans have historically been discriminated against. By the early 1970s these problems are running rampant through American history.[53]

The tendency to modify perceptions of the past in American textbooks went in parallel with the proliferation of evidence that modern society was not coping adequately with its problems.

The greatest ideological appeal of American capitalism was not its heroic past but its claim that everybody had a chance to make good in the land of freedom and opportunity. The depiction of the USA as a melting pot of immigrant ethnic groups and nationalities was always a compromise through which the WASP establishment was prepared to share out some of the abundant resources of American capitalism so long as it was recognised as the legitimate repository of authority. Pork-barrel politics, the provision of favours by WASP boss politicians to minority representatives in an essentially non-class, non-ideological system, was the appropriate expression of this political arrangement.

In the postwar decades the pluralism of pork-barrel politics led to an increasingly fragmented national identity. It was no longer simply a question of rival groups haggling over economic resources, but culture, history and identity were also thrown into the melting pot. In the field of professional history the result was a flourishing of diverse 'histories' and in wider society there was an explosion of claims made on behalf of alternative identities. The contestation of the traditional all-American identity and the call for its replacement by one which would include as equals those who had previously been left out, such as blacks, women, hispanics, native Americans and others, increasingly challenged the existing consensus. The fragmentation of American society has led to the emergence of a number of different interest groups all wanting to create a new past. Unlike in Europe, where the demand for a new history comes from the establishment, in the USA the call to rewrite the past comes from those who feel they have been excluded from the traditional version. Hence the history debate takes the form of a contest of values, of different interpretations of what is right and wrong.

From the point of view of American conservatives, the problem lies not only in the content of radical criticisms of historical orthodoxy, but in the very fact that they are criticising that which should not be questioned. The widely discussed controversy over the 'Western Civilization' course at Stanford University exposes the problem facing the conservatives. Their attempts to uphold the absolute values of Western civilisation are undermined by their formal commitment to the traditional pluralist perpective that denies ultimate authority to any particular point of view.

The American conservative intellectual offensive has been most successful when it has set out to mobilise patriotic public opinion. The objective of rallying popular opposition against those who represent non-Western and un-American values explains the often shrill and extravagant character of conservative campaigning rhetoric. Thus a feature in *Newsweek*, titled 'Thought Police', warned about the growing intolerance against Marxist and liberal academics in the universities.[54] In many local communities right-wingers have run campaigns against particular teachers and college courses. For example a Committee for Quality Education set up in 1989 in Brookline, near Boston, complained that 'our school system claims that European History is biased against women, minorities and poor people.' This complaint was taken up by Don Feder, a conservative columnist for the *Boston Herald*, who denounced the emphasis of history teaching on 'the contributions of Africans, American Indians, Polynesians, Eskimos and Aleuts.'[55]

The history debate in the USA, which takes the form of an argument between conservatives on one side and liberals or Marxists on the other, is singularly mystifying. A careful study of the terms of the discussion reveals that the differences are those of rival interests rather than of theoretical substance. The fact that all the protagonists share the ideological project of laying claim to a piece of the past explains the often melodramatic way in which the debate is conducted. A less charitable observer might suggest that different interest groups were merely trying to strengthen their claims for more resources through appeals to the past. From this perspective the debate appears more like a squabble between 'establishment conservatives' and 'conservatives excluded from the establishment', rather than a contest between true ideological opponents. However despite its non-ideological content, the history debate still has important consequences in the realm of ideas. The very questioning of the legitimacy of the established standpoint reinforces the problem of identity.

The close proximity to one another of rival or alternative US histories is revealed by their common desire to be included in the

American Way of Life. Following the precepts of conservative
historiography, all the minority histories look to the past to sanction
their status in the present. Thus minority histories too are obsessed
with heroic deeds and seek to cultivate pride in past achievements.
The approach of black history is characteristic:

> Black history emphasises African origins and the achievements of
> African societies while reducing the emphasis on the extent to
> which the black man was Americanised, insisting that the New
> World experience did not alter the self-conceptions of black men.
> Black history seeks black heroes who deny the universality of
> western values, who rebel against restrictive white society.[56]

The search for black heroes follows directly the procedure of
traditional romantic conservative historiography. Defenders of
American historical orthodoxy often accuse competing accounts of
the past of being anti-universal and *particularist*. This accusation is
undoubtedly a correct interpretation of the new histories. However,
the accusers must stand convicted not only of the same charge but
also of hypocrisy. Unlike their competitors, the establishment
historians present their particularism in the rhetoric of universalism.

It is ironic that the American right remains so oblivious to the
intellectual affinities it has with its opponents. One of the few
exceptions to this rule is Stanley Hoffmann, a commentator highly
regarded by American conservatives. More than a decade ago he
noted that the 'Marxist left and its intellectuals – the heralds of change
– have become the curators of the revolutionary museum.' Although
his use of the label 'Marxists' for those who turn to the past for
legitimacy was dubious, Hoffman was on the right track. He
perceived that some of the most radical rhetoric of the time was based
on a romantic attachment to the past. He recognised the trend for
minorities to seek 'after the past' and correctly concluded that as the
'majority grows distant from its past, these groups rediscover (or
invent) theirs. The present is the age of *their* romantic history.'[57]

The conflicts among different American histories cannot be
resolved as long as competing interests continue to seek to legitimise
their action by appealing to the past. Attempts by historians to
overcome social divisions by trying to reconcile conflicting claims on
the past remain unpersuasive. McNeill, for example, believes in the
possibility of creating a 'mythistory' which incorporates the
competing claims of all Americans in one pluralist narrative of the

past: This is not a groundless hope. Future historians are unlikely to leave out blacks and women from any future mythistory of the world.'[58] Diane Ravitch argues for a pluralistic multiculturalism as the cornerstone of a common history. She appeals for history to be removed from political pressure so that 'scholars synthesizing the best available research' can decide the subject's content.[59] Such optimistic speculations about the objectivity of scholars working in a political vacuum are unlikely to provide much of a solution.

As the American Dream has become increasingly tarnished, many Americans have turned back to their particular interest group as an avenue through which to try to move forward. As a result a kind of special-pleading discourse prevails which can only intensify fragmentation and division. Take for example the California state authority's attempt to provide multicultural history textbooks. Despite the fact that the authority, in a spirit of pluralism, sought to 'accommodate' every culture, its proposals were immediately 'attacked by black, Asian, Hispanic, Islamic, Jewish, Indian, Chinese, women's, gay and lesbian organisations, all claiming they had been slighted.'[60] It seems the melting pot is gone. All that is left is a shrinking pork barrel. Although in the USA history is not as politicised as it is elsewhere, the clash of competing identities and the defensive conservative reaction is set to continue.

Germany

Germany provides the ideal counter-example to the USA. Whereas in the USA the discussion is relatively unfocused, in Germany it is highly politicised. There is none of the pork-barrel type of discourse as the debate is not so much about what it means to be a German but rather about how to come to terms with Germany's past. Hence there is a remarkable unanimity on the need for a new history among all the protagonists, with differences largely of emphasis and of style, and only minimally of substance, about how the new history should be constructed.

The irony about the German *Historikerstreit* is that relatively minor differences have on occasion given rise to furious debate. The heated character of these controversies is to some extent due to their links with party political struggles. But there can be no escaping the fact that the highly charged atmosphere surrounding the German history debate is largely due to the formidable problems involved in rewriting a past that so recently includes the devastating experience of the Nazi era. The peculiarly painful and delicate issues raised by any reconsideration of the Nazi period mean that any attempt to forge a national identity with reference to the past is fraught with tension. As a result historical controversies have been highly politicised in Germany throughout the postwar period. For example, Fritz Fischer's account of the role of German imperialism in the genesis of the First World War sparked off a major controversy in the 1960s. The government withdrew a grant it had made available to him to lecture in America, and the press accused him of insulting the reputation of Germany.[61]

The intensity of the German history debate is directly proportional to the passions aroused by the enduring memory of the Holocaust. Whether or not this is stated, the discussion is always about how to come to terms with the experience of the Holocaust which remains a major obstacle to the reworking of a German identity. It is obvious that a past that includes such barbarism cannot be readily recruited to legitimise the existing order. Various factors, more international than domestic, make it impossible to pretend that the Holocaust was a minor event or that it never happened. Hence conservative German historians have been forced to adopt a strategy of either relativising the mass slaughter or blaming it on forces which were outside the control of Germany.

The project of rewriting the German past has been carefully pursued with an earnest desire not to offend international opinion. Nevertheless the obstacles are formidable. For example, many arguments routinely advanced by right-wing thinkers in other countries may cause a scandal when expressed by a German. Take Ernst Nolte's parallel between Hitler's genocide and Stalin's terror:

> Did not the National Socialists, did not Hitler perhaps commit an 'Asiatic' deed only because they regarded themselves and those like them as potential or real victims of an 'Asiatic' deed? Was not the Gulag Archipelago more original than Auschwitz? Was not the 'class murder' of the Bolshevists the logical and factual *prius* of the 'racial murder' of the National Socialists?
>
> Auschwitz is not primarily a result of traditional anti-semitism. It was in its core not merely 'genocide' but was above all a reaction born out of the anxiety of the annihilating occurrences of the Russian revolution ... It was more horrifying than the original because the annihilation of men was conducted in a quasi-industrial manner.[62]

Though Nolte goes a step further than many conservative historians in blaming the Russian Revolution for the emergence of the Nazi death camps, in substance his view is part of the German right-wing consensus. For example Joachim Fest develops Nolte's suggestion that it was the quasi-industrial aspect of the Holocaust that was so horrifying and argues that this was the only feature that distinguished the German from the Soviet camps.[63]

Though the way Nolte and Fest attempt to minimise the gravity of the Holocaust by blaming the Soviet Union may appear particularly crass and mendacious, their arguments are scarcely original. In substance they can be found in the highly respected international corpus of literature on totalitarianism. The thesis that there is a symmetrical relationship between Stalinism and Nazism is central to mainstream postwar political analysis in the West. Many non-German historians have sought to discredit communism by equating it with fascism. For example, at a recent symposium on the German history debate, many of the non-German historians present enthusiastically proclaimed the latest versions of the familiar analysis. Robert Conquest argued that a 'moral nihilism' was common to both National Socialism and Stalinism and concluded that 'they were of a type which put them apart from other atrocities in the past.'[64]

It is worth recalling how the revelation of the manifold connections between German capitalism and Hitler's regime put conservative opinion on the defensive in the 1930s and 1940s. In response to this embarrassment, many right-wing thinkers tried to shift the focus of the discussion towards blaming the Soviet Union for the tragedies of the time. Many of the leading figures of the postwar right first won their authority through their ability to redirect blame away from German capitalism towards Stalinist Russia. Hayek's *The Road to Serfdom* was written with the explicit aim of clearing up the misconception which prevailed among the 'parties at the Left as well as those of the Right' that the 'National-Socialist Party was in the service of the capitalists and opposed to all forms of socialism'. Hayek blamed the success of socialism for the eventual triumph of Hitler: 'It was the union of the anti-capitalist forces of the right and the left, the fusion of radical and conservative socialism, which drove out from Germany everything that was liberal.'[65] A similar argument can be found in Popper's *Open Society and its Enemies*, which depicts fascism as the product of the spiritual breakdown of Marxism.[66]

The intellectual precedents for the current revisions of German history can thus be found in long-established theories of totalitarianism. This confirms that there is little new in the case put forward by conservative historians in Germany today. That they provoke such furious controversy can only be attributed to the fact that these arguments are advanced by German historians who are determined to rehabilitate the German past. Thus German nationalist intellectuals work at a special disadvantage in attempting to forge a viable national identity in a country in which this project is particularly fraught with tension.

The other special feature of the German case is that the ruling class places a greater emphasis on the rehabilitation of its national past than it does elsewhere. This emphasis is understandable because the Nazi episode serves to weaken the legitimacy of the modern German state, making the use of the past as a basis of national identity deeply problematic. Hence since 1945 its authority has rested on the 'economic miracle' and on its success in projecting a positive alternative to the East German state. Though reunification will undoubtedly boost the legitimacy of the German state, in the long run there is no substitute for the authority conferred by a national identity based on a successful past. This is why the political elite, especially under the Kohl government in the 1980s, has been so committed to the recovery of the national past.

The campaign to normalise the German past first gathered momentum in the late 1970s during the conservative *Tendenzwende*. Earlier in the decade, despite a number of attempts to deal with the problems of the past, there was still a lack of confidence about tackling these issues. The Filbinger affair in 1978, when the Christian-Democratic premier of Baden-Wurttemberg was forced to resign because of revelations about his Nazi past, illustrated the heavy burden of the past that still weighed down the German right. Nevertheless, the past was gradually emerging into public view: a series of publications and exhibitions with historical themes attracted widespread interest.

Historical exhibitions have flourished in Germany over the past 15 years. High-profile initiatives like the Prussia exhibition in West Berlin in August–November 1981 were followed by a flood of articles in the conservative press on the subject of the Prussian identity. The fashion for promoting cultural representations of the past was clearly linked in the minds of conservative historians with the challenge of fostering pride in the German past. Plans to build two permanent national museums – a Museum of German History in West Berlin and a House of History of the Federal Republic in Bonn – were overshadowed by political controversy. At first the argument was between those who argued that the museums 'should provoke a critical confrontation with the past' and those who wanted to 'promote national identity'.[67] By 1983 and the return of a conservative coalition government the ideological commitments of the protagonists had become more apparent:

> At this point in the public discussion, which largely coincided with the return of the CDU/CSU to government, there was a definite shift from a rather open-ended reflection on the changing meanings of the national tradition, without any obvious political charge (as in the Berlin Historical Commission conference), to a more pointed emphasis on the problem of German *identity* in the present.[68]

Thus in the early 1980s there was a significant shift in the terms of the German history debate towards a more self-conscious promotion of national identity.

The Kohl administration actively encouraged the project of developing a more coherent German national identity. More than in any other country, the government in Germany openly sponsored the conservative ideological offensive, as one account described:

> Chancellor Kohl's conservative coalition is pursuing a systematic policy of placing its own men in charge of the country's radio and television stations; the press is heavily dominated by supporters of the ruling coalition; and state control over the curriculum, over history textbooks, and over university appointments is extensive.[69]

After 1983 the Kohl premiership gave conservative intellectuals a new coherence and confidence.

Kohl led by example, confidently projecting the image of a German no longer burdened by guilt, describing himself as the 'first federal chancellor of the post-Hitler generation'. He indicated his personal affinities by attending a convention of *Heimatvertriebene*, a group of far-right exiles from Silesia, once part of Greater Prussia and Hitler's Reich, but now under Polish rule. The first German chancellor to attend such a meeting, Kohl, by his very presence and by making a speech under the revanchist banner proclaiming 'Silesia remains ours', provided a moral lead in the campaign to whitewash Germany's past. In April 1985 the Bitburg affair provided another landmark in the drive to normalise Germany's historical record. President Reagan's visit to the Bitburg military cemetery – where there were 49 Waffen-SS graves – provoked an international outcry. But by persuading Reagan to state in public that those buried there were no less 'victims of Nazism, even though they were fighting in the German uniform', Kohl was able to establish an important precedent.

According to Eley, the effect of the Bitburg affair was to link a 'deep-seated complacency about the Nazi experience – a denial of its continuing relevance' with 'conservative desires for a "normal" national history'.[70] While Kohl set about settling scores with Germany's Nazi past, he turned up the volume of German anti-Soviet rhetoric. It seemed as though the more accusations that were made against the Soviet Union the more normal would the German past look in comparison. Kohl's casual parallel between Soviet Premier Mikhail Gorbachev and Nazi propaganda chief Josef Goebbels in an interview in *Newsweek* was symptomatic of this trend.

A growing confidence in reasserting a German national tradition in the early 1980s provided the background to the emergence of the *Historikerstreit* in 1986. This great debate among German historians was sparked off by an essay by Nolte entitled 'The past that will not pass away' and followed up contributions from fellow conservatives Klaus Hilderbrand and Michael Sturmer. The right-wing historians were soon challenged by the liberal social theorist Jurgen Habermas and a heated row ensued. The continuing debate has been extensively discussed and the relative intellectual merits of the rival positions are not our main concern.[71] The most significant feature of the debate has been the narrow framework within which it has been conducted. Liberal commentators in Germany and abroad have reacted to the more extreme pronouncements of the right-wingers. Yet on closer inspection, the liberal case often turns out to be no more than a qualified or moderately stated version of the conservative argument. It seems that even the most bitter opponents of Nolte and the rest accept that the project of developing a German national identity through history is a legitimate enterprise.

Any non-German observer is immediately struck by the limited and defensive character of the left's response to the conservative historians. It was after all, as Rabinbach recalls, the socialist Chancellor Helmut Schmidt who, upon returning from Israel in May 1981, declared that 'German foreign policy can and will no longer be overshadowed by Auschwitz.'[72] The intervention of Social-

Democratic Party secretary Peter Glotz at a forum on the *Historikerstreit* illustrates what almost amounts to a bipartisan approach to the quest to restore a German national identity through history:

> Is the search for one's own identity merely hocus-pocus? This is where I start to disagree with Jurgen Habermas. I doubt whether it is enough for democracy to base itself on a universalistic morality and a logical chain of reasoning, as for example in the text of our constitution. The need to take bearings and self-knowledge, but also self-confidence and pride from one's own history is not automatically right-wing.[73]

Two significant points arise out of Glotz's statement. First, he accepts the premise of the conservative case that 'self-confidence and pride' in German history should be part of the platform of the Social-Democratic Party. Second, in an attempt to occupy the centre ground, he self-consciously distances himself from the more universalistic stance of Habermas.

In fact Glotz has more in common with Habermas than he would let his audience believe. His accusation against Habermas is quite unfair – the liberal philosopher is as committed as the social-democratic politician to the recovery of a German identity. It is true that Habermas argues for what he calls a 'post-conventional identity' based on universalistic principles which can sanction a neutral 'constitutional patriotism'. This approach abstractly separates identity from history, but as a practical strategy it cannot avoid seeking to establish a link to the past. The logic of Habermas' standpoint is to use the 'constitutional' period since 1945 as an identity-creating past. Whereas the conservatives look back to the glories of Prussia and Bismarck, their critics accept the historical horizons of the postwar welfare state of Konrad Adenauer.

Mary Nolan's analysis of the German history debate shows that what distinguishes Habermas from the right is not the issue of national identity, but the question of what values that identity ought to express. She notes that, like the conservatives, Habermas and his supporters 'seek to instrumentalise history in the interests of identity creation': 'But whereas the right wants a uniform and emotionally felt national identity, Habermas, Wehler and Broszat strive for a calm reasoned acceptance of constitutional democracy, built on a critical understanding of Germany's recent past.'[74] Thus the key differences in the debate centre around the kind of history and the kind of identity required by modern Germany. Differences of temperament and of style, on the one hand a 'uniform and emotionally felt national identity', and on the other a 'calm, reasoned acceptance' of Germany's history-ordained destiny, are also important.

As in the USA, radical critics of the revival of history in Germany propose a makeshift pluralist identity as an alternative to the conservative conception. However, this strategy misses the key issue at stake: the aspiration for a national identity cannot be satisfied through many different identities. National identities are by definition exclusive (some more exclusive then others) and intolerant (some more intolerant than others). Thus the pluralist approach can at best offer merely a temporary compromise, but not a solution. The call for calm consideration of the question by Habermas and his colleagues is immediately undermined by their acceptance of the use of history for the purpose of identity creation. Appeals for reason are unlikely to be heeded once the passions latent in the process of forging a national identity are aroused.

The politicisation of history in Germany underlines the country's continuing problem of legitimacy. The persistence of this problem in such a highly successful capitalist economy indicates the recurring tension between history and contemporary society. It may also suggest that the strategy of plundering the past may not prove adequate to the task of solving such a deep-seated problem.

Japan

Though there are close parallels between Japan's relation to history and the German case, it appears that Japan is less burdened by its past. At the same time the drive to recover a national past is a key issue in Japanese politics, where it has been probably even more controversial than in Germany. Again the intensity of the history debate is partly a result of its relationship to party politics, which is even closer than in Germany. Whereas in Germany the two mainstream parties have sought to maintain a degree of consensus by restricting the terms of the debate, in Japan the restoration of a national history has become the particular cause of right-wing nationalists in and around the Liberal Democratic Party. As a result the opposition Socialist Party has been much more hesitant about supporting a consensus around the recovery of a national identity than the German SPD.

Some Western historians consider that Japan is more combative about reclaiming its national pride than Germany. According to Ivan Hall, an American professor of Japanese history at Keio University, the Germans have come to terms with their past much better than the Japanese. He maintains that the 'conservative forces here have not cleansed themselves', and that furthermore 'the leaders of the establishment of the postwar period do not really represent a change of heart or a real break in motivation and outlook, whereas in Germany they did.'[75]

Comparisons of degrees of German and Japanese contrition about the past are usually a roundabout criticism of the latter. American historian Arthur Schlesinger put this bluntly when he stated that Japan 'is even more mystical, portentous and humorless in its hyper-nationalist traditions than Germany and far more scornful of other countries.'[76] This contrast between a penitent Germany and an incorrigible Japan is drawn out in a rather exaggerated way by Ian Buruma:

> Why is there such contrast between West Germany ... and Japan? Why is it that one cannot open an issue of *Die Zeit* or *Der Spiegel* without finding at least one article painfully extracting yet another skeleton from the voluminous Nazi cupboard, while Japanese journals of equivalent quality publish article after article by revisionists, apologists and other *Alte Kampfer* for the Japanese cause? Why do West German textbooks painfully stress German Responsibility for the war, while the Japanese equivalents hurry through the war as quickly as possible to reach the much safer ground of Hiroshima and Nagasaki ... Why, in other words, does the majority of West Germans ... seem to have learnt its lessons, while most Japanese refuse to think about it?[77]

Buruma's questions suggest their own answers: the problem is that, lacking a tradition of Enlightenment values, the Japanese are less 'like us' than the Germans. Buruma's questions are not about Japan's relation to the past in general, but to a past created for it by the West, or more specifically by the USA. This is why he can dismiss the notion of 'white imperialist aggression' in Asia as an 'old nationalist canard' and why he expresses a barely concealed irritation that Japanese textbooks exaggerate the importance of minor incidents such as the dropping of atomic bombs on Hiroshima and Nagasaki.

It may well be that it is the intensity of Western ethnocentric hostility towards Japan that accounts for its distinctive attitude to its past. For Shinkaro Ishihara the racism of the West is the point of departure for his project of rewriting Japan's past. He warns his compatriots that the 'Japanese should not forget that Caucasians are prejudiced against Orientals', before launching into a paean to Japanese civilisation:

> Americans should know, as the early Portugese and Spanish missionaries wrote, that Japan had a highly advanced civilization by the mid-sixteenth century. In the Tokugawa period (1603–1867), more than 20,000 private schools throughout Japan taught reading and writing, a standard of school attendance and literacy without parallel for the time. Even townspeople could write the Japanese syllabaries and as many as 2,000 Chinese characters. An excellent mail service delivering letters, freight and cash extended from Edo (now Tokyo) to Kyushu.[78]

The tone of this celebration of the Japanese past is clearly one of frustration, of 'enough is enough'.

A sense of frustration at Western anti-Oriental prejudices is widespread among conservative Japanese thinkers. Many are astonished at what they rightly perceive as the application of a double standard. Shimizu Ikutaro personifies the changing intellectual climate in Japan. A professor of sociology, he has moved from the left-pacifist end of the political spectrum to the right. He maintains that Japan's conduct was no worse than that of any other combatant nation in the Second World War, arguing further that Japan adopted its militarist posture in response to Western imperialism: 'Japan had to do things that others would have done if Japan had not.'[79]

It is difficult to gauge whether in private the Japanese elite is more uncritical of its role in the Second World War than its German counterparts. In public the Japanese elite is certainly much less prepared to renounce the past. As far back as 1955 the ruling Japan Democratic Party attacked the liberal interpretation of the past offered in the schools in a pamphlet entitled *Deplorable Textbooks* that also accused teachers of feeding children communist ideas.[80] According to one account, since the 1950s government officials in charge of history texts have continually sent back manuscripts with comments such as 'descriptions of war are too gloomy', 'only Japan singled out as bad' or 'not suitable for children'.[81]

Despite differences of emphasis in relation to the war, the common features in the revival of history in Japan and Germany are much more striking. As in Germany, the conservative campaign to rewrite

Japan's national history gathered momentum in the late 1970s. The national history revival received direct encouragement from the Ministry of Education and gradually pervaded most spheres of intellectual life so that by the 1980s right-wing nationalism had acquired considerable influence. Retired history professor Saburo Ienaga, who fought a 20-year battle against attempts to delete embarrassing episodes from history texts, summed up the trend:

> In the 1970s I could write more freely on the massacre at Nanking. In 1980, the ministry suddenly wanted me to write: 'Many people died in the confusion after the battle.' They wanted me to deal with it as if it had been an earthquake.[82]

The nationalist revival soon reached beyond the educational sphere to influence the wider world of Japanese politics. According to Carol Gluck, the 'Japanese Bitburg' occurred in August 1985, when the Prime Minister 'decided to pay the first postwar official visit to Yakusuni, the shrine of the war dead, where not only the spirits of the common soldiers but also those of convicted war criminals are enshrined.'[83] Like Kohl, Nakasone claimed that he could make such gestures because he did not belong to the wartime generation. Such parallels between Japan and Germany have attracted widespread comment. The German historian H. Schulze has argued that 'although the Japanese inclination to harmonise their own history is certainly much stronger than the German, the chronological and thematic coincidences are obvious.'[84]

Nakasone declared that he was 'settling the accounts of postwar politics', a catchphrase he explained to a party study group in 1985:

> We are now clearing up, one by one, issues that have been left in abeyance all these years since the end of the war. We are dealing in a comprehensive way with matters that have been disparate before, that have not been squarely faced before. We are looking toward the 21st century and putting together a consensus, building unity as a nation, the Japanese nation; the Japanese people are walking in the world with our heads held high and contributing to the development of the state. We have reached a turning point. This is what I mean by 'settling the accounts of postwar politics'.[85]

Nakasone also let it be known that in his view there were no longer any taboo subjects and no question of Japanese guilt about the past.

However, in Japan as elsewhere, the drive to normalise the past has paid scant dividends in terms of forging an inspiring sense of national identity. History continues to be divisive. Even though the nationalists retain the initiative, the very fact that the attempt to create a national identity creates intense public controversy means that its purpose is undermined. Japan also faces criticisms from neighbouring countries, which experience its revision of history as an interference in their own. The West has its own reasons why it wants to sustain its version of Japan's past – at least in public. History is itself the battlefield for more than one conflict.

Britain

In comparison to other countries we have surveyed, the history debate in Britain appears a relatively restrained, characteristically gentlemanly affair. At first sight it appears be largely confined to the sphere of education, with much of the controversy arising from the practical details of the new national curriculum for schools. Most commentators on the subject carefully eschew an overtly political stance and even conflicting views seem to be largely concerned with technicalities. Thus *History Workshop*, which is subtitled 'a journal of socialist and feminist historians', includes a fairly neutral editorial which discusses the relative merits of right and left-wing contributions. The main burden of the editorial is to suggest that the battle lines are far from clear.[86]

One reason why the debate seems to lack the passion of the controversies in Germany and Japan is that the British past is *relatively* uncontested. There have been no major national humiliations or epochal atrocities. The British establishment has also succeeded in winning most of its domestic critics to accept at least part of its consensus about the past. For example, British imperialism has never received the sort of critical scrutiny experienced by US foreign policy after Vietnam. British left-wing historiography is itself imbued with a strong sense of nationalism and a deeply-held patriotic commitment.[87] The reaction of Christopher Hill, widely regarded as one of Britain's leading Marxist historians, to the Conservative government's attempt to revive national history is illustrative of the trend:

It would be nice if a new national curriculum created a more truthful patriotic histcry. If we just go back to national self-glorification, to painting the map red, history will be in danger of becoming the plaything of party politics, to be changed with each change of government.[88]

Hill has no objection to a 'patriotic' history, only to one that is not truthful and becomes a 'plaything of party politics'. The fact that a prominent radical historian clings in this way to the patriotic middle ground explains why the British debate remains relatively unpolarised.

The narrowness of the British history debate is partly a consequence of the incorporation of themes arising from the official labour movement into the British past. This is not merely the result of official recognition of Britain's long-established and highly respectable school of left-wing history writing. It is the consequence of a significant shift in British national identity in the 1940s towards an emphasis on Britain as a moral nation strongly committed to the welfare of its people. In the decades following the end of the Second World War, a spirit of national pride was fostered in the institutions of the welfare state, particularly the National Health Service.[89] Although this identity came under attack from the Conservative government in the 1980s it still serves to sustain a sense of attachment to a common past.

The dominant theme in the discussion of British history and national identity is that of national decline. This discussion has been running for so long, more than a century, that decline has come to seem almost a normal state of affairs. Indeed the central project of the Conservative government under Margaret Thatcher may be seen as an attempt to contain a deeply-rooted sense of national failure. As one observer has suggested, 'a revival of national self-esteem could not go hand in hand with historical self-deprecation'.[90] Hence the Thatcher regime constantly sought ways of celebrating the British past and made a political issue out of the school history syllabus. The discussion on the teaching of history is in fact less interesting than the wider issues it has raised but which are not formally subjects of debate.[91] Indeed by the early 1990s it was evident that the attempt to reconstruct a history of Britain's greatness was in danger of being overtaken by the accelerating pace of its decay as a world power. As one commentator remarked: 'more world history and less emphasis on the activities of English kings and queens are clearly desirable in what is now a middle-ranking, multicultural nation.'[92]

Britain's untroubled past can offer only limited solace to an imperial power evidently in terminal decline. A series of chauvinist anti-European outbursts by cabinet ministers has revealed a heightened sense of insecurity about Britain's position in the world. An editorial in an influential conservative newspaper in 1990 well summed up the predicament of the British establishment:

> Britain faces a world in which it can hope, at best, to play second fiddle to a regional superpower, which is a distinct demotion from running an empire or playing second fiddle to a global superpower (America). Even second fiddle to Germany is not guaranteed, since Britain is the poorest of the four big economies, behind France and even Italy, as well as Germany.[93]

Britain's relegation from 'playing second fiddle' is the driving force behind the conservative enthusiasm for history.

A deepening sense of doubt about Britain's role in the world has undermined the confidence of those who seek to promote a new account of British history. Insecure about the British identity, conservatives are ambivalent, if not openly hostile, towards the emergence of a multicultural society at home and to Britain's closer assimilation into Europe, developments which are both often regarded as a threat to the British way of life. Although it is rarely admitted in public, the object of the conservative campaign around the subject of history teaching is to uphold 'Britishness' against the influence of multiculturalism. The attack on multicultural education is central to the right's unspoken agenda. One historian, for example, counterposes 'ethnic history' to 'broad' history. His own preference is obvious: 'historians are the custodians of the national memory – which should be broad and general.'[94]

Ray Honeyford, the Bradford headteacher who provoked a political furore over his attack on multicultural education in 1987, has become the British right's favourite educationalist. He is one of the few who have openly questioned the validity of the multicultural project:

> Now ... [multicultural identity] appears to have no attachment to history, tradition, natural development or actual common experience – in other words, no attachment to those things which give the concept 'culture' real, human meaning. It takes its force rather from a bureaucratic attempt to impose culture from above, an attempt to wipe clean the slate of history and re-invent culture in accordance with official dictat. Such official multiculturalism is

not only offensively authoritarian; it is also both impractical and misguided.[95]

For Honeyford and his co-thinkers, multiculturalism undermines the uniqueness of the English/British identity. If other cultures are recognised as equal in worth to the British way of life then the special claims of history are undermined.

If it is to fulfil the requirements of today's establishment a British history must be *unicultural*. There can be no pride in the national past if a number of cultures are considered to have similar worth. This is why in Britain discussions of national identity inevitably open up the question of race:

> Barely a generation ago these islands were occupied by a single people, who despite differences of region, background and expectation were bound by common loyalties and affection, by a shared history and memory. Thirty years on and the English have become 'the white section of the community' and Britishness is something to be had from the bazaar.[96]

The argument is straightforward: an identity not rooted in history, one that can be purchased from a selection of others at 'the bazaar', is unlikely to be one that is highly prized. Far from inspiring pride, it can only discredit the past. Pursuing this argument further, reality is turned on its head and the breakdown of a usable past and a viable national identity is blamed on immigrants. This is more convenient way of grasping recent events than facing up to the fact that the 'shared history and memory' of the past could not indefinitely sustain pride in a nation experiencing the trauma of steady decline.

The British demand for history is ultimately an appeal for the legitimation of patriotism. Uncertainties about Europe, race and Britain's role have provoked a campaign to popularise patriotism which provides the main impetus behind the promotion of national history. The conservative philosopher John Casey justifies this posture on the grounds that 'British patriotism has always differed from the various *nationalisms* of Europe.' According to Casey, British patriotism was 'not expansionist or warlike' and it did not 'define itself *against* anyone else.'[97] This flattering portrait of British patriotism sits uneasily alongside the constant outpouring of chauvinist venom in the popular press.

The portrayal of a neutral or benign British patriotism is also inconsistent with contemporary initiatives designed to popularise patriotic history. Take, for example, an article entitled 'Why we should all be proud to fly a Union Jack', written by Oxford modern history professor Norman Stone to boost morale during the Gulf War:

> The Union Jack is a flag greatly to be respected. During the Second World War ... people stood up for *God Save The King* because it stood for survival. And not only *our* survival, but of standards of decency the world over. It is an element of sanity and decency in a bad, and sometimes mad, world. The British are now helping the Americans to see off a monster. We have done this before in the 20th century and sensible Germans are grateful for it. But there is more. Britain is a wonderful country. Its doings in history are way beyond its size. It invented most things to do with the modern world.[98]

Such eloquent statements are the distinctly British contribution to the philosophy of history.

The project of popularising a patriotic consensus based on the great British past has not only led to government intervention in history teaching but also to a reconsideration of what is of value in Britain's record. The old welfare values are being gradually replaced by themes of national and imperial glory. This conservative cultural challenge has been met by a defensive reaction from the left-wing and liberal intelligentsia, as in the USA and Germany. There has been a tendency to interpret the Conservative government's initiatives as merely to do with education rather than politics. Some liberal historians have even welcomed the renewed emphasis on history, with the qualification that 'it is vital not to create a climate of opinion in which British political history is all that is thought worth teaching in schools.'[99] Such calls for tolerance and pluralism in history teaching amount to an evasion of the central thrust of the conservative offensive. Thus a conference on 'History, the Nation and the Schools' in 1989, organised by *History Workshop*, succeeded in examining the subject outside the context of the political issues at stake.

The pluralist response fails to grasp that the promotion of the British identity cannot be conducted in a multi-history framework any more than in a multicultural one. National identity is never a problem when everything is going well: it only emerged as an issue in Britain when its world dominance came into question at the end of the nineteenth century. But once it becomes a problem then nothing seems to be able to resolve it. History has been called upon to perform a thankless task in Britain. As in the other national cases, the preference for the past testifies to a deep uncertainty about how to handle the present.

Conclusion

The quest for history is an ever-recurring sub-plot, that finds its way into most of the political and cultural debates of our time. Yet, although the revival of history is central to the conservative ideological project, it is seldom openly considered as a political issue. Of course, the very fact that the past is so furiously contested is itself revealing about society. The turn to history is a response to the perception of crisis; current anxieties and disillusionments are experienced as a loss of a relationship with the past, as the erosion of roots. Thus, although it is apparent that the problem lies in the present, society seeks a solution through the transformation of the past. The loss of direction is not blamed on society as such, but on those who question its structures and values and thus weaken the prevailing moral consensus.

Though the attempt to recover a usable past has not yet succeeded in confronting the problem of identity, the conservative ideological offensive has been successful in putting its opponents on the defensive. It can thus be argued that, even if the popular mood has yet to be won over, at least the intellectuals have been neutralised. Moreover as time passes the tone of acquiescence becomes more and more evident. For example, in 1984 Raphael Samuel challenged Lord Elton's call for a national history in the following terms: 'It is not the unity of national culture, but rather its unexplored diversities which provides the incitement to research. The patriotism – or sense of belonging – is local, regional and often familial rather than national in scale.'[100] Thus Samuel sought to slow the advance of national history through the advocacy of little patriotisms. It was a strategy of confronting one focus for identity with another, but at least it was an attempt to tackle the nationalist challenge. By 1990 he had shifted to adopt a more sympathetic view of the national 'scale' and exhorted his erstwhile comrades on the left to be more realistic:

Historians of the Left have shied away from the 'nation', either as a subject of study or as a symbolic category ... The announcement of a return to national history in the school curriculum filled many with alarm. For some it signalled a return to 'drum-and-trumpet' history, or the 'history of kings and queens'; for others, the idea of 'nation' was irretrievably associated with racism. Yet history, whether we like it or not, is a national question and it has always occupied a national space.[101]

More ominously, Samuel added that if the nation was 'expelled' from school, others, presumably even more xenophobic, would be happy to teach it.

The shift towards a general acceptance of national history indicates the common ground among most participants in the various history debates. This state of affairs marks at least a temporary triumph for the conservative philosophy of history. There are only competing claims for the past; little questioning of a mode of thought that seems to feel comfortable only when it is looking back. A vision oriented on the past and almost closed to the future is a testimony to the contemporary fear of change.

So far we have surveyed the relationship between history and society from the perspective of how it appears. Now we can move on to examine how this relationship has evolved historically.

3

History and society

Perceptions of history tend to fluctuate with changes in society. The demand for a particular type of history is symptomatic of the mood and intellectual influences that prevail at any time. In this chapter we examine how changing perceptions of the past reflect different responses to the changing character of society itself. In particular we distinguish between the conservative approach to history, which seeks to use the past as a bulwark against change, and the perspective of historical thinking, which embraces change as the dynamic principle of social development.

Historical thinking is the outcome of history: the very recognition that changes take place in society over time is itself the result of social development. Most serious modern thinkers, from across the ideological spectrum, agree that the emergence and advance of historical consciousness depends upon the development of specific forms of society. Moreover, it is also widely recognised that a sense of history requires a particular consciousness which is sensitive to the distinction between the present and the past. 'Man has in fact no past unless he is conscious of having one, for only such consciousness makes dialogue and choice possible', writes Raymond Aron, one of the most influential advocates of liberal pluralism in the postwar period.[1] Many of his intellectual opponents, including Marxists, would not disagree with this proposition.

Historical thinking, a sense of change and of development, is a prerequisite for the emergence of history as a distinct sphere of inquiry. People living in isolated small communities in antiquity, in a state of close dependence on their immediate natural environment, had a limited sense of change. An intimate reliance on the movements of the sun, the moon and the seasons restricted perceptions of change to notions of recurring cycles. In such societies people were likely to regard change as repetition rather than as development. Moreover,

59

living in isolated communities restricted the capacity of people to place their particular existence within a wider setting. Thus there could be no sense of a pattern to human existence as a whole nor the ability to conceptualise the relationship of one community with others.

The absence of a sense of history is typical of societies in which social relations are simple and there are only minimal variations in social organisation among neighbouring communities. According to one account, the need to theorise about history or the nature of society does not arise until civilisation is well advanced, and 'sudden, violent and far-reaching upheavals in social relations take place during the lifetime of individuals or within the memories of their elders.'[2] In a useful discussion of the 'Social function of the past', Eric Hobsbawm observes that for most of history 'we deal with societies and communities for which the past is essentially the pattern for the present.'[3] In such 'traditional' societies the past provides the point of reference for human activities. In these circumstances, change and innovation are minimal, though not impossible. Hobsbawn suggests that in what he calls the formalised social past, the collective memory is seldom so all-encompassing as to exclude all innovation. Nevertheless as long as the belief that the present should reproduce the past holds sway, there will usually be a 'fairly slow rate of historic change'.[4]

Once change becomes a familiar feature of society, the relationship between the past and the present undergoes a transformation. In such circumstances the force of tradition is weakened and its capacity to provide the standard for human conduct is significantly reduced. At this stage the 'past must cease to be the *pattern* of the present, and can at best become the *model* for it.'[5] But once the past becomes a model for action, its relationship to society alters: as Hobsbawn suggests, this 'implies a fundamental transformation of the past itself.' Now humans can begin to make statements such as 'we must return to our roots' or we must 'return to the old ways'. These appeals to go back to past traditions suggest that society has already abandoned these ways and that these customs therefore no longer have a direct relationship to society. The past 'now becomes, and must become, a mask for innovation, for it no longer expresses the repetition of what has gone before, but actions which are by definition different from those that have gone before.'[6]

When there is no way to go back to the past, an appeal to tradition means in practice a demand to alter the conduct of contemporary society. It generally implies projecting back in time values and rules; thus endowed with the authority of the past, they can be used to greater effect in the present. The invention of tradition is rarely consciously manipulative, but rather involves a semi-conscious process of selective remembering and forgetting.

The forces that weaken the links between past and present also provide the foundation for historical thinking. For people of a conservative disposition, an accelerating pace of change creates great insecurity. Paradoxically, for them the experience of rapid change creates a greater need for the past then ever before. As Abrams has observed, the unwelcome consequences of change stimulate the search for the certainties of tradition:

> Hitherto the past had provided the pattern for the present in quite straightforward ways. History had been an unproblematic matter of recording duration and succession. Neither duration nor succession had appeared to bring the nature of the principles of social organization into question. But that was just what happened in the mid-nineteenth century.[7]

Once change had transformed the nature of social conduct and rendered social organisation problematic, the past acquired a new importance. Conservatives turned to tradition to provide a source of certainty in a changing world.

On the other hand, those less committed to the existing order welcome change as an improvement on the existing state of affairs. A positive attitude to change leads to the evolution of *historical thinking*, a form of consciousness that regards all social arrangements as transient and therefore as susceptible to further improvement. As Hobsbawn suggests, once 'innovation is recognised both as inescapable and as socially desirable', in other words as *progress*, then it becomes possible to think in terms of making a decisive break with the old ways.[8] The repudiation of the past, the search for new, and by implication better, social arrangements and hence a generally positive view of the prospects for future – these are some of the characteristics of historical thinking.

Even after the development of a historical sense, society continues to evolve different perceptions of the past and develops different attitudes towards the question of change. In a sense the very demand for history has its own history.

With a capital H

Historical thinking should not be confused with history. There are different types of history, some of which embody a consciousness of change and some of which do not. Indeed, for many conservative theorists history is the antithesis of historical thinking, understood as the attempt to grasp in thought the dynamic character of social development. For them history expresses not change, but continuity, the reproduction of old traditions in new circumstances. For a conservative historian an intuition of what constitutes the essence of an unchanging past is comparable to a revelation, for it confers identity and meaning on the community concerned. To distinguish this apologetic type of history from genuine attempts to understand the movement of society over time, we designate it 'History'.

History with a capital H does not seek to understand change, but tries to recover a shared past in order to help forge a common identity. It uses the mask of the past to mobilise society for some purpose in the present. Such a History aims to legitimise current conduct and identities by elevating the authority of a particular past. This is the kind of history that is at the centre of all the controversies discussed in the previous chapter. As Robert Davies comments: 'remarkable efforts have been made by conservative politicians and historians to encourage confidence in the future by restoring patriotic British history to the centre of the historical curriculum.'[9] This observation could be made about the drive to create a nationalist history in any of the major industrialised countries.

The reduction of history to History has been widely endorsed even by prominent historians, many of whom accept that it is their professional responsibility to foster national identity or cultivate public memory. Take the following statement from a well-known introductory survey, *The Nature of History*:

> It is only through a sense of history that communities establish their identity, orientate themselves, understand their relationship to the past and to other communities and societies. Without a knowledge of history we, and our communities, would be utterly adrift on an endless and featureless sea of time.[10]

This statement can be interpreted in a number of different ways. In one sense it is tautological: it is through a sense of history that communities understand their relationship to the past. In another sense it is platitudinous: history provides an orientation to the future – but how? In yet another sense, it begs a crucial question: what kind of identity is at issue?

Communities have been known to survive without a sense of history, others with a number of competing identities. Thus when History is pushed forward as a creator of identity, it is not offering identity in the abstract, but a distinctive identity. Indeed the very purpose of identity-creation through History is to confer a sense of distinctness, to differentiate and exclude. The intensity of the passions generated by the process of forging any particular identity confirms that this cannot be achieved in a benign and neutral manner. The role of History is to provide the intellectual foundations of modern nationalism by helping to create a sense of national identity.

History as the signifier of identity depends on the presentation of constants, of characteristics that are supposed to be valued for the very reason that they never change. Such representations of identity amount to the *eternalisation of history*, as certain customs and forms of conduct are regarded as transcending any specific period in time. Both the past that is meant to inform a particular national identity and that identity itself derive their significance from their allegedly constant and unchanging character. The desire for certainties at a time of accelerating change encourages the drive to turn the past into a History that can service the needs of the present. Indeed History as an academic discipline emerged in response to such social pressures in nineteenth-century Europe.

Germany, in the early nineteenth century a nation yet to consolidate itself into a coherent nation state, led the way in establishing History as a sphere of academic and intellectual activity. The outstanding German historian Leopold von Ranke, like many of his contemporaries, regarded the nation state as the vehicle for carrying through 'the will of history'. Before unification in 1871 Germany was an idea, whereas Britain, France, Russia and the Austro-Hungarian empire were facts. As Joll observes, deep uncertainties surrounding German national aspirations stimulated the need to forge a national identity and the quest for History:

> While the underlying sense of continuity in British history has meant that British historians, whether Whig or Tory, have at least until recently never been in doubt that there was in some sense a British identity, German historians have repeatedly had to look for and define the nature of a German identity.[11]

The absence of a nation state called into question what it meant to be a German; the role of History was to elaborate and foster a sense of national identity.

In the absence of a unified nation state on which to found a sense of national identity, German historians emphasised the role of non-political, spiritual or cultural qualities in defining what it meant to be a German. This approach assumed that the central feature of German identity was the unique and unconscious development of national culture and that the task of the historian was to understand the soul and traditions of the people. Thus, despite Germany's national fragmentation, the mystical quality of being German provided the foundation for a unified and unifying identity. According to Ranke, this 'secret something' which 'we breathe in and out ... precedes all constitutions and quickens and fills all constitutional forms.'[12] In Ranke's view, constitutional and political developments were influenced by mysterious spiritual powers.

Despite the metaphysical tendencies evident in the writings of the German historians, they never lost sight of the fact that the traditions and spiritual qualities under discussion were *national* in character. Indeed the central impetus behind the development of German History was nationalism. As Marwick suggests, 'nationalism was a major impulse, but scholarship was a main outcome.'[13] If the German historians encouraged scholarship (in the sense of using primary sources), this was always subordinated to the imperatives of the nationalist programme. However it is invidious to single out German historiography as a special case, as for example the French writer Julien Benda does when he states that the nationalist intellectual is 'essentially a German invention'.[14] Though the German historians may have led the field, the discipline of History developed along similar lines in other advanced countries in the course of the nineteenth century.

In Britain too History emerged out of a clear commitment to nation-building. At Oxford, according to Soffer, the 'study of history began and continued as an epic illustration of the qualities required of England's governing elite.'[15] The aim of the leading Oxford historians was to trace 'the Divine purpose in the long evolutionary process which had ended in making England top nation'.[16] Thus the development of a History emphasising the unfolding through time of a divinely ordained spirit of the people cannot be regarded as an exclusively German preoccupation.

Though national Histories had a similar content, they assumed different forms appropriate to different national traditions. In the case of Britain, the emphasis was less on culture and more on the durability of political institutions. Thus, E. A. Freeman, the government-appointed Regius Professor of History at Oxford in the 1880s, believed that 'something very like the distinction between Whig and Tory can be traced as far back as the eleventh century.'[17] The eternalisation of nineteenth-century political institutions was a predominant tendency in British History: Macaulay boasted that 'in our island the regular course of government has never been interrupted.'[18] Yet British historians, including Macaulay, were not adverse to adopting the 'Germanic' custom of celebrating the moral and spiritual qualities of the British people.

In nineteenth-century France too the project of nationalising history proceeded with vigour. The university system was developed with the clear purpose of providing legitimacy for the relatively young republican regime. The teaching of History sought to establish a consensus around the principles of the 1789 revolution. At the same time, to strengthen the sense of continuity, historians were happy to integrate the glories of the French monarchy into a national tradition. Other republican historians found a continuity in the 'gradual emancipation of the masses from ignorance and oppression'.[19] French History was no less nationalist than those of other countries, but its distinctive feature was that it sought to represent French national identity through an association with the universalistic principles of 1789.

A recently published survey of French and German historians working between 1871 and 1914 highlights the similarities. According to Christian Simon: 'the two scholarly communities ... held similar views of their mission as educators of the nation.'[20]. In both cases historians were involved in fostering a tradition of patriotism.

In Germany, Britain or France History offered a distinctive national story as a basis for identity and thus became a mode of national self-perception. In the USA by contrast, a national identity emerged in large part as a reaction against the political values and institutions prevailing in Europe. The promotion of American exceptionalism became a central theme in creating a sense of American identity through History. According to the American 'consensus' historians of the 1940s and 1950s, national development was 'characterised by a degree of agreement and continuity which was remarkable when contrasted with the European experience.' In the absence of a feudal tradition, these historians argued that 'Americans had remained significantly free of deep-seated class and ideological cleavages.'[21] This flattering portrayal of the American past attempted to cohere an identity through a self-consciously constructed contrast with a decadent Europe.

But why was America so fortunate? How did it escape the fate of European decadence? Again History provides the answer, explaining that Americans possessed a special identity. Though there was some difference of emphasis about what constituted this, there was general agreement that it was special. According to Woodward, 'to define the distinctiveness of the American Character became the favourite pursuit of scholars.'[22] The American character, with its celebration of the pragmatic pioneer and the rugged frontiersman, seems to have little in common with its more soulful and spiritual German counterpart. Yet, though the character may differ, History follows the same procedure in all countries in the quest for national distinctiveness.

History with a capital H is a representation of a national myth through a selective re-ordering of the past. Its objective is to develop a sense of continuity so that contemporary insecurities may be allayed by the certainties of the past. Writing of the 'trauma of self-doubts' that prevailed after the First World War, Soffer suggests that 'the meaning of English history seemed one of the few remaining truths' to the generation educated at Oxford before 1914.[23] From this perspective History is something that we already know and the past merely illuminates what is familiar. Because links with the past are often established in the realm of culture, History is closely linked to the celebration of the cultural manifestations of a particular national character and mental outlook. Writing in the 1920s, Benda observed perceptively that 'patriotism today is the assertion of one form of mind against other forms of mind.' He noted that national tensions were often experienced as conflicts among rival cultures: 'Every nation now hugs itself and sets itself up against all other nations as superior in language, art, literature, philosophy, civilization, "culture".'[24]

In its capacity as an identity-conferring truth, History is closed to the possibility of change. The very survival of a distinct national character is held up as proof of the view that what really matters is beyond change. As a celebration of continuity, History can only assimilate change as a sub-plot to a national drama. But are other kinds of history possible?

The past, History and historical consciousness

The relationship between continuity and change is a central point of difference among competing interpretations of history. There is a wide spectrum of opinion, ranging from the fatalistic view that the past is merely reproduced in the present, to the voluntaristic perspective which endows human beings with the ability to make history according to their subjective inclinations. Here we discuss the relationship between History and historical thinking in order to explore the dialectic of continuity and change in different ways of looking at society past and present, and to clarify the different visions embodied in these approaches.

Historians have offered a variety of explanations of their discipline. Some have argued that history provides a picture of how things really were in the past; others contend that it is the search for the truth, while still others contend that it is merely the opinion of the historian. No doubt one of the reasons for the lack of consensus among historians is the existence of widely diverging views among them about the objectives of their work.[25] In the nineteenth century matters were more straightforward: historians openly proclaimed their ideological function in relation to the established order and often combined the roles of academic and civil servant. But after two world wars had exposed the dangers of nationalist ideology, cults of national identity and the apologetic role of national Histories, historians became more circumspect about how they defined their professional duties. The twentieth century has made questionable the authority of the past, leaving few national myths unscathed. As explicit Histories were discredited, historians were forced to find more neutral justifications for national identity and for their own discipline.

In his *The Death of the Past*, J. H. Plumb draws what he calls a 'sharp distinction' between the past and history. Although his discussion of this distinction does not resolve the issue, Plumb succeeds in elucidating the meaning of the past for the mainstream Western historian. He observes that the past is used in a 'variety of ways' to explain the origins and the meaning of life. It is used 'to sanctify institutions of government' and to 'invest both the individual human life or a nation's with a sense of destiny'.[26] Plumb conceives the past as something that confers authority and legitimacy on society in the present. Although he argues that the past was 'never a mere invention', it is clear that he would not want to apply the criterion of objectivity to it. Indeed at one point he concedes that the past is 'always a created ideology'.[27] When Plumb writes of the death of the past, what he means is that this ideology is no longer a source of unquestioned authority for society today. On the other hand Plumb argues that history is non-ideological. It is, like 'science', an 'intellectual process', trying to understand 'what happened' purely 'in its own terms and not in the service of religion or national destiny, or morality, or the sanctity of institutions'.[28] Thus Plumb distinguishes between a 'scientific' history and a conception of the past which approximates to what we have characterised as History.

Plumb's conception of 'scientific' history is less satisfactory than his treatment of the past. He says that the purpose of a historian of this school is to 'see things as they really were'. But this classically Rankian formulation simply amounts to a more 'objective' or 'truthful' variant of what he calls the past. Plumb's failure to fulfil his promise – that he will clarify the difference between the past and history – reflects his concern that any objective or critical history undermines the past.[29]

> The critical historical process has helped to weaken the past, for by its very nature it dissolves those simple, structural generalizations by which our forefathers interpreted the purpose of life in historical terms.[30]

There is a note of regret in Plumb's observations about the death of the past. It becomes clear that his objection is to simplistic attempts to use the past, rather than to the use of the past itself. Accepting that the functions provided by the past are still in demand, Plumb calls for a 'complex' past to be recreated around the themes of reason and progress. Instead of extolling a national character, Plumb wants to foster an identity that is not national, not 'black or white, rich or poor, but as man'.[31] In other words he would like a past that is cleansed of those nationalistic aspects that have been discredited by the extremisms of the twentieth century.

Plumb's difficulty in separating the past from history suggests that the two concepts are far from irreconcilable. If history is about 'what happened' in the past, then it is possible to conclude that this provides authority for our actions today. In this way 'what happened' is turned into an eternal principle; it becomes a society's officially sanctioned account of the events that contributed to its emergence. This is evidently what Plumb means when he states that there are 'human truths to be derived from history, and truths well worth telling.'[32] There is here no essential difference between this concept of the past and History. Plumb's version is a more sophisticated and less chauvinist version of what was previously permitted to represent the past.

Radical critics of mainstream representations of the past often object to the peculiar form in which national identity is presented, rather than to the legitimacy of the enterprise as such. In response to History they present a left-wing version of History, offering an alternative identity. Thus a left-wing French historian argues that 'what we know of the past can be of service either to the establishment or to the people's movement.'[33] The symmetrical relationship between an elitist history and a people's history reflects a shared methodology: whether the heroes are kings and queens or ordinary people, women and minorities, and whatever values are elevated, the past is the common source of authority. The personalities and the themes may be different, but it is all History.

Turning the past into History means using the authority of a series of myths to sustain a particular tradition in the present. For whatever purpose History is used, it ultimately *mystifies* and confuses. The retreat into the past in order to find self-justification reflects a desire to escape from the present and evade its challenges. The problem is not only that the past can always be manipulated, but that History is intrinsically an instrument of mystification.[34] This is why the attempt to use the past for radical purposes is an irrational project. Two radical British historians, Samuel and Thompson, justify their approval of the creation of a mythical past that represents minorities on the grounds that minorities suffer from mainstream images of the past:

> This is why for minorities, for the less powerful, and most of all for the excluded, collective memory and myths are often still more salient: constantly resorted to both in reinforcing a sense of self and also as a source of strategies for survival.[35]

The strategy of countering the myths of the powerful with the myths of the powerless, suggests that in their attitudes to the past there are no substantive differences between conservatives and radicals. They both seek legitimacy from the past; the dispute is over which past is legitimate.

The search for roots in the past implies an analogy between natural and social life. This orientation towards origins gives social development a fatalistic character: individuals and societies are what they are by virtue of their family and collective antecedents. Just as the roots of a tree determine the pattern of its subsequent development, so the human past determines its future. Human beings become the product of the past and have little influence over the determination of their future. The unique feature of human society – its capacity consciously to initiate change – is lost.

One of the ironies of the discussion of history in modern society is that the emergence of History generally reflected a hostility to historical development. This is why History became the natural discipline of nineteenth-century conservatism. By capturing particular versions of the past, History sought to negate historical thinking by minimising the effect of change and maximising the influence of tradition. Thus the past of History became detached from historical thinking and came to exist in a timeless and unchanging space outside the reach of human intervention. Conversely, a sense of history as change undermines the past and calls into question tradition and the identities based upon it. Historical thinking begins with the recognition that human intervention plays a key role in social development: from this perspective the present is no longer the product of an unchanging past but the result of the actions of human beings.

Historical thinking is directly antithetical to History. From the point of view of historical thinking, there are no eternally-fixed features of society, no features that are beyond transformation. The actions of human beings are decisive, not national characteristics, identities or past traditions. Instead of static traditions and fixed identities, historical thinking posits a dynamic relationship between human action and change. The early eighteenth-century thinker Giambattista Vico had already grasped the one 'eternal' principle – the responsibility of human beings for the making of history:

> In the night of thick darkness enveloping the earliest antiquity, so remote from ourselves, there shines the eternal and never-failing light of a truth beyond all question: that the world of civil society has certainly been made by man, and that its principles are therefore to be found within the modifications of our human mind.[36]

Vico had anticipated what was to become one of the great discoveries of the French Enlightenment. From Condorcet to Saint-Simon, the Enlightenment regarded history as a process of endless progress and therefore of endless change. The new world ushered in by revolution in thought and society was a world 'made by man'.

After the Enlightenment historical thinking could never be entirely suppressed. The rapid pace of global social development over the past two centuries has made it impossible to deny the reality of change, at least in the recent past. In response to the tumultuous consequences of the Enlightenment and the French Revolution, conservatives have not sought to abolish the concept of change, but rather to restrict the parameters within which it operates. By contrast, historical thinking embraces change, starting out from the assumption that the existing state of the world is transient and will soon undergo transformation. Whereas History argues that there is no escape from the past, historical thinking gives a decisive role to the subjective factor, to the potential for human action.

One of the main conservative criticisms of the French Revolution was that it attempted artificially to break with the past. As Sièyes noted, after 1789 'it was no longer France, but some unknown country to which the nation was transported ... The idea of the sovereignty of the people, uncontrolled by the past, gave birth to the idea of nationality, independent of the political influence of history.'[37] For anybody committed to the status quo, the attempt to conduct human affairs without the sanction of the past was an invitation to chaos. Thus the past became synonymous with control and restraint. Two centuries later the American sociologist Philip Rieff restates Sièyes' appeal to the past: 'How dare we dismiss the authority of the past as if we understood it? From the past we gain our regulatory weight, to hold against the lightness of our acts.' He warns grimly that, 'released from all authoritative pasts, we progress towards barbarism, not away from it.'[38] In this schema 'the lightness of our acts' is the puny counterpoint to the 'authority of the past'. Moreover in Rieff's gloomy scenario a society that is not prepared to respect its past is doomed to decadence.

Marx provided the classic counterpoint to the conservative world view. He reversed the conservative conception of the relationship between human 'acts' and the past: the struggle for social liberation meant freeing society from the domination of the past:

> The social revolution of the nineteenth century cannot draw its poetry from the past, but only from the future. It cannot begin with itself before it has stripped off all superstition about the past. Earlier revolutions required recollections of past world history in order to dull themselves to their own content. In order to arrive at its own content, the revolution of the nineteenth century must let the dead bury their dead.[39]

To Sièyes' ideal of a life controlled by the past, Marx counterposed a life of struggle to win freedom from the past. From the perspective of History, the past is a repository of lessons; from the perspective of historical thinking seeking solace in the past means squandering the human potential to influence the course of events in the present.

Historical consciousness points towards the negation of History. Consistent emphasis on the potential for change cannot be reconciled with the worship of continuity with a stable past. Marx forcefully expounded the combative logic immanent in historical thinking:

> *History* does *nothing*, it 'possesses *no* immense wealth', it 'wages *no* battles'. It is *man*, real, living man who does all that, who possesses and fights; 'history' is not, as it were, a person apart, using man as a means to achieve *its own* aims; history is *nothing but* the activity of man pursuing his aims.[40]

It is not surprising that historical thinking provoked a conservative backlash in the nineteenth century. Conservatives rightly recognised that the rejection of the past would inevitably lead to the questioning of every aspect of the existing state of society. The genesis of History was directly inspired by the determination to tackle that danger.

History as anti-change

We have seen how History emerged as a distinct discipline in response to the social turmoil of early nineteenth-century Europe; its form was given by its role in the general conservative *reaction* to Enlightenment thought. The terms 'reaction' or 'reactionary' mean strictly a retrograde tendency to go back to pre-capitalist society, a point of view motivated by the impulse to turn back the wheels of history after the cataclysmic events of the French Revolution. Conservatism as a distinct modern standpoint acquired its shape as the 'doctrine defending the institutions and values of the old order in Europe against the ideas and political movements of the Enlightenment and the French Revolution'.[41] We use the concept of reaction here in a wider sense, to imply an aspiration to conserve the past so as to legitimise the present. As we shall discuss further in Chapter 8, by the late twentieth century it was not only politically committed conservatives who were reacting to historical thinking. Today's identity-oriented Histories share the same intellectual assumptions, if not the political objectives of nineteenth-century conservative reaction.

The new ideas thrown up during the Enlightenment were a fundamental challenge to the accepted wisdom regarding the relations between the past, present and future. For medieval thinkers texts such as the Old and New Testaments underpinned the consensus that the future of humanity was fraught with difficulties. Not only was there no golden age ahead, but on the contrary any change meant a move further away from the lost perfection of the Garden of Eden. The Enlightenment challenged the pessimistic Judaeo-Christian tradition which located perfection in a primeval past and projected a future of gloom.

Enlightenment thinkers insisted that progress was the development of human reason. Furthermore they regarded change as positive, since it reflected the process of applying reason to the problems of humanity. Whereas medieval scholars looked to the glories of the past, the eyes of the Enlightenment were turned resolutely towards the future. 'The golden age', wrote Saint-Simon, 'which a blind tradition had always placed in the past, lies ahead of us.'[42] By reversing the relationship between the golden age and the present, the Enlightenment put everything to do with the past in question.

To counter the Enlightenment's emphasis on change, conservative thinkers emphasised the resilience of tradition; against the Enlightenment's universal themes they upheld the particularist values of the past. This stance was most coherently elaborated by German historians, who looked upon the Enlightenment as a French plot. Except for a few isolated individuals, such as the Freiburg historian Carl Rotteck, by the second decade of the nineteenth century the German intelligentsia had been converted to a vigorous anti-Enlightenment stand:

> Educated opinion now agreed that all values and rights were of historic and national origin and that alien institutions could not be transplanted to German soil. Moreover, they saw in history, rather than in abstract rationality, the key to all truth and value.[43]

German History affirmed a sense of continuity and imparted a sense of exclusiveness in values and traditions. Such traditions, deeply rooted in the past, fostered an identity which could provide security against change.

The historical thinking popularised through the Enlightenment was now confronted with History as created by the conservative reaction. As Zeitlin observes, throughout the nineteenth century the conservative anti-historical impulse sought to marginalise change and to affirm the past as the overriding influence on the day-to-day affairs of society:

> Increasingly, the nineteenth century turned to the investigation of the origins of existing institutions rather than to their transformation according to rational principles. An historical attitude emerged in which more than ever before institutions were regarded as the product of slow organic development and not of deliberate rational, calculated action.[44]

The conservative spirit, expressed in the works of Louis de Bonald and Joseph de Maistre, and even by an ostensible liberal such as Edmund Burke, reasserted the role of transcendental forces in the movement of society. This *historicist* perspective replaces the human agent with God. History becomes a process of revelation of some divine purpose.

Since the early nineteenth century conservative history has polemicised against any programme of social change on the grounds that it naively underestimates the sturdy qualities of the past. The French Revolution and its claim to express the march of progress provided the object of the first wave of the conservative attack. Although later joined by other revolutions, it still features prominently in the conservative critique. As Elton puts it, the 'three well-attested revolutions of modern Europe – the English, French and the Russian – all demonstrate the inability of revolutions to eliminate the past.'[45]

For conservative thinkers the failure of revolution, or indeed of any far-reaching programme of change, results from the limits of human reason and human action. While the more pious historians point out the futility of challenging divine omnipotence, the more secular opponents of change emphasise the marginal role that human beings can play in the making of history. This standpoint is clearly articulated by the conservative historian Sir Lewis Namier:

> Conservatism, of which Metternich was an exponent, is primarily based on a proper recognition of human limitations and cannot be argued in a spirit of self-glorifying logic. The history of the French Revolution and of Napoleon had shown once more the immense

superiority which existing social forms have over human movements and genius, and the poise and rest which there are in a spiritual inheritance, far superior to the thoughts, will, or inventions of a single generation.[46]

Thus if human action fails to develop in accordance with the spirit of the past, the past will take its revenge and expose the futility of human pretensions.

The limited potential of a single generation is a recurrent theme of conservative historiography. Since most generations play a rather undistinguished role in history, this observation appears simply commonsensical. Yet there have been times when a single generation has changed the course of history so irrevocably that there could be no return to the past. This was the case for example after the French Revolution. George Steiner has argued that the changes unleashed by 1789 were so overwhelming that the subsequent counter-revolution could do little to reverse them: 'the counter-revolution prevailed neither in action nor in its critiques'.[47] At key moments in modern times the drama of human action has overwhelmed the plain commonsense of conservative historiography.

The limits of Reason

The relegation of the human factor in favour of the influence of tradition is often justified by the argument that the legacy of the past is far weightier than the possible contribution of a single generation in the present. Many conservatives also believe that the past is a much safer guide to human conduct than reason, which they regard with suspicion as an unnatural motive for human action. Whereas the past requires only to be obeyed, reason is likely to be overwhelmed by elemental human passions that are deeply rooted and irrational.

Some conservatives have argued that historical thinking uproots people from their past and leaves them in a spiritual vacuum. Writing in the 1880s, Nietzsche pushed the irrationalist mode of thought to the most extreme conclusions. Ruminating over the unhappiness caused by a sense of ceaseless change, he noted that the most 'extreme case' was a man 'without any power to forget', in other words, a man lacking the capacity to feel unhistorically. 'Such a man', he wrote 'no longer believes in himself or his own existence; he sees everything fly apart in an eternal succession and loses himself in the stream of becoming.' According to Nietzsche, the 'historical sense' threatened to destroy human culture.[48]

More restrained thinkers questioned the rationalist claims of the Enlightenment without necessarily celebrating the irrational, but all agreed that any attempt to implement a programme based on reason meant destroying what bound society to its roots. According to this view, the very application of reason threatens to detonate an explosion of irrationality. Thus Isaiah Berlin represented the fear of change as a legitimate concern with the irrational:

> The French Revolution was founded on the notion of timeless truths given to the faculty of reason with which all men are endowed ... It preached a peaceful universalism and a rational humanitarianism. But its consequences threw into relief the precariousness of human institutions; the disturbing phenomenon of apparently irresistible change; the clash of irreconcilable values and ideas; the insufficiency of simple formulas; the complexity of men and societies; the poetry of action, destruction, heroism, war; the effectiveness of mobs and of great men; the crucial role played by chance; the feebleness of reason before the power of fanatically believed doctrines.[49]

Berlin extends this list into a veritable political manifesto against the pretensions of reason. It seems that any strategy to achieve rational change must upset the existing precarious balance and inevitably make things worse.

A friendly critic of Berlin, Conor Cruise O'Brien, takes his argument several steps further and finds the Enlightenment guilty for the subsequent emergence of totalitarian states. According to O'Brien, the Enlightenment created an 'emotional vacuum' which was filled by nationalism. The bitter Europe-wide war which ensued was therefore the 'indirect responsibility' of the Enlightenment, and, before even a plea for mitigation can be entered, he insists that 'the responsibility, though indirect, was real, through the creation of that cosmic emotional vacuum'.[50] Like most proponents of the 'spiritual vacuum' thesis, O'Brien does not pause to explain why the application of reason should lead to totalitarianism. The only conclusion to be drawn from the conservatives' 'cosmic' statements is that once traditions and identities are confronted by the demands of change, then anything goes. Nietzsche wrote of a 'malignant historical fever' to describe the condition of those plagued by the emotional vacuum.

Clearly the risk of provoking such maladies is itself an eloquent argument against change.

Sceptics about the potential of rational action not only questioned the role of rationality in altering society, they also accepted the view – at least implicitly – that irrationality was more typical of human beings than behaviour motivated by reason. Thus the critique of historical thinking inevitably led to the forceful imposition of strict limits on the potential for rational action. In minimising the role of reason, the role of purposeful human action in the making of history was fundamentally questioned.

The mystique of the particular

The conservative rejection of reason was linked to the view that particular identities were not susceptible to rational analysis. Proponents of History believed that imagination, feeling and intuition were necessary to grasp the essence of particular communities. As Barnes has argued, the romantic historical style of nineteenth-century writers such as Jules Michelet, James Anthony Froude or Thomas Carlyle attempted to bring the reader into a direct relation with the sensations evoked by the events of the past.[51]

German idealist philosophers and historians considered that sensitivity to the inward life and an intuitive feeling for culture were more important than rational analysis. Thus Justus Moser argued against extracting meaning from history. He suggested that 'historical and rural life were, in some sense, mysterious, awe-inspiring, and for that reason incapable of rational analysis.'[52] Since communities and cultures all possessed their own special inward life, general explanations would be of little use in throwing light on processes that were highly particular. Particular identities had to be understood in their own terms and not as part of some abstractly conceived universal pattern.

The elevation of particularism boosted the case for a nationalist historiography which could take an aggressively anti-universalist form. Thus Hans Kohn has argued that German nationalism was 'animated by a fervent and self-righteous rejection of the West, of the Enlightenment, of rational reasonableness and universalist objectivity'. He adds that it expressed a 'boundless hatred of the French and the alien.'[53] History promoted a sense of national mystique which defined the spirit of a people.

The mystique of the particular elevated differences and celebrated the characteristics associated with the spirit of a particular people: inevitably it tended to idealise a particular race. Though the racism of nineteenth-century German historians has been most widely recognised, the racial version of History was by no means peculiar to the Germans. For example, the anti-French themes that are identified in German History can also be found among certain schools of Anglo-American History.[54] More conspicuously, the race theme dominated British imperial historiography in the same period. Fryer writes that most of the 'respected names in British nineteenth-century historiography were racists, and most of them reflected in their writings one or other of the central tenets of racist ideology.'[55] It is worth recalling that at the time a racist outlook was not regarded as socially unacceptable within Western societies. The celebration of race was an essential component of the mystique of particularism.

Around the turn of the twentieth century it was not unusual for the particular essence of a nation to be expressed in the language of race. For the British Social Darwinist, Karl Pearson, history could be reduced to the struggle between races: 'History shows me one way, and one way only, in which a state of civilization has been produced, namely, the struggle of race with race.'[56] The idealisation of the particular did not necessarily lead to Pearson's racially aggressive stance, but it always tended towards an overdetermined sense of difference – whether ethnic, communal, cultural or racial. The growing interest in race and other national or cultural characteristics reflected a tendency to uphold the legacy of the past in the face of threatening trends towards change. The more self-conscious thinkers linked the affirmation of the past to an explicit rejection of historical thinking. They loathed what Nietzsche scathingly dismissed as 'the unrestrained historical sense'.[57] Though not all nineteenth-century Western historians were racist or irrationalist, in their common reaction to the Enlightenment and their commitment to national identity few could resist the demand for History.

Those Histories that had emerged in the nineteenth century as a reaction to the threat of change became focused at the turn of the century on the maintenance of the national status quo. The use of History to justify the nation state was common to European states, as the liberal German-Jewish historian Hermann Kantorowitcz noted in 1929:

For in Germany – and indeed all over the Continent – it is by no means considered sufficient that an historical work should tell the truth in accordance with the convictions of the author. In a work dealing with higher policy it is held to go without saying that the author shall enter upon his investigations in the interests of his own nation and against its antagonists, and that his work shall be 'patriotic', and the outcome of 'national feeling'.[58]

By the early twentieth century History had become an ideological resource in geo-political conflicts.

The evident manipulation of History in the decades leading up to the Second World War finally provoked a reaction against it. After the experience of Hitler's Germany the project of creating a mythic past as the basis of national identity was fatally compromised. There was even a widespread tendency to locate the roots of Nazi Germany in the deliberations of nineteenth-century History. Kohn for one argued that 'German romanticism and historicism, fusing with Prussian concepts of the authoritarian power-state, coloured much of German thinking in the War against the West, which started around 1812 and reached its climax after 1933.'[59] Of course Germany was not the only nation to propagate tendentious History, Hitler was just more explicit than most of his rivals. However once the catastrophic consequences of the Nazis' racist project became widely known, nationalist historiography fell into disrepute. Indeed until the recent re-emergence of the demand for History, the history profession has explicitly eschewed nationalist history.

The disgrace of History did not lead to the revival of historical thinking. The sense of change, which was so enthusiastically articulated during the Enlightenment, did not reappear after 1945. Indeed it was not so much History, but rather its nationalist excesses that became the subject of concern. Any History that came close to nationalist propaganda could not survive the Hitler episode, creating at least temporary difficulties for right-wing nationalist historians. But because the anti-historical assumptions of official History were never questioned, the defeat of the nationalist standpoint was more apparent than real. It could only be a matter of time before History made a comeback.

The decline and rise of nationalist history

In a widely discussed article published in 1973, the historian Paul Kennedy examined what he took to be 'one of the most interesting developments in twentieth-century historiography' – the 'decline of

nationalistic history writing in the western world.'[60] Nearly two
decades later things look much different: while there has been no
return to the unrestrained patriotic literature of the nineteenth
century, the national has become an increasingly acceptable focus of
historical writing.

Two world wars certainly put History on the defensive.
Barraclough wrote that 'after 1914, as they broke apart into warring
factions, each interpreting the "facts" of history in the light of its own
national traditions, it was hard to think of historians as an international band of disinterested scholars, all striving for "objective"
truth.'[61] Already in disrepute, History appeared to suffer a fatal blow
as a result of the Nazi experience. As Kennedy notes, the rejection of
the 'myth of racial superiority' was a 'direct result of the universal
abhorrence at the excesses of the Nazis – excesses which were only
taking the Darwinist, racialist and atavistic writings of the earlier age
to their logical conclusion.'[62] The Second World War undermined
right-wing nationalism and conservative patriotic history, especially
in Germany. During the subsequent Allied occupation of Germany,
history textbooks were rewritten according to the guidelines of the
're-education' programme.[63] While those on the losing side faced a
major rewriting of their history, nationalist historiography everywhere was tarnished by its association with fascism.

Though History went into retreat everywhere, it did so differen-
tially. For example British history faced less of a critical re-
examination than those of most other Western nations.[64] At the same
time all Western nations faced a crisis of confidence in the immediate
postwar era. The growth of Third World nationalism and the eruption
of anti-colonial revolts further called into question the special claims
of Western nationalisms. Even British diplomats realised that
circumstances had changed and that a new vocabulary was required,
as one Foreign Office expert on Asian affairs noted in 1950:

> Intense nationalist propaganda during the last year has led to a
> strong bias against Colonialism of all sorts. Any suggestion of racial
> discrimination even against the black African, for whom a certain
> scorn was felt, led to indignation. Words like 'Colonial', 'Asiatic'
> and 'Native' were unpopular.[65]

When racial discrimination 'even' against the African was no longer
acceptable the old imperial language could no longer be preserved
intact.

As the language changed so too did the representation of the past. Kennedy's thesis on the decline of nationalist historiography was part of the consensus among professional historians. By the late 1960s and early 1970s the view that the 'new history' had triumphed over the old was almost an article of faith in the specialist literature. Barraclough for one was optimistic that there had been a 'major shift of focus from the particular to the general'. Though others were more circumspect, even an astute critic of German nationalist historiography could exaggerate the transformation in the intellectual climate prevailing in West Germany in the 1970s. Thus John Moses' study of the Fischer controversy – a debate about Germany's responsibility for initiating the First World War – concluded that Fischer's liberal historiography had helped 'to explode any historically based moral claim for reunification'.[66] The editors of a comparative study of history textbooks also testify to the decline of nationalist history. Berghahn and Schissler's survey concludes that the 'decline of political and diplomatic history with its emphasis on the national past continued after 1945 and by the 1970s the earlier balance *vis-à-vis* social and economic history had seen a marked change.'[67]

With the advantage of hindsight it appears that the decline of nationalist history was not as complete as it may have seemed at the time. The retreat of History was more an instinctive reaction to the extreme consequences of nationalism rather than a reasoned rejection of the fundamentals of this approach to the past. The method of using the past to evoke a sense of authority and tradition was not seriously questioned. What was questioned was the explicitly chauvinist purposes for which this historical tradition was used.[68] Nor was the anti-Enlightenment impulse behind the development of History put under serious scrutiny. Commentators were inclined to argue that the reaction of historicism to the Enlightenment had gone too far, not that this reaction was essentially wrong:

> Too deeply bound to its origin in the eighteenth-century conservative revolt against the forces of modernity represented by the Enlightenment and the French Revolution, historicism was unable to come to grips with the great social transformations that have occurred in the modern world. It showed understanding for the role of the irrational, the spontaneous and the unique in history, but it underestimated the elements of rationality and regularity.[69]

Such an even-handed balance between historicism and the Enlightenment could not challenge the assumptions of History. If it is accepted that historicism had a legitimate case against the Enlightenment, then it becomes a problem only when it is presented in an extreme nationalist form. In the same way nationalist historiography was only identified as a problem when it began to appear aggressive to others. Thus what was widely perceived as the decline of nationalist historiography was in fact merely the demise of one of its forms.

Waiting for a come-back

Many commentators have interpreted the proliferation of different types of histories in the 1950s and 1960s as marking the marginalisation of the nationalist approach to history. This reaction is understandable since, in terms of sheer output, the impact of the so-called new history was overwhelming. But it is unlikely that the decline of nationalist history was the result of forces internal to the history profession. Rather it seems that the demise of History after the experience of two world wars encouraged the fragmentation of the subject. To some extent the existence of a wide range of competing specialities may be said to reflect a continuing lack of consensus about the meaning of history as a subject. As we have seen, the decline of nationalist historiography was a pragmatic response to the Second World War and to the far-reaching changes that occurred in the Third World in its aftermath. It is necessary to emphasise that the response was pragmatic: while the nationalist excesses of History were repudiated, its underlying assumptions were rarely considered.

Pragmatism was also evident in the selective way in which the question of national identity in History was tackled. Thus although explicitly nationalist historiography had lost much credibility in professional circles it lingered on in school texts. One study of American and British school texts in the 1960s found that nationalist bias still existed, though in a more subtle form than previously.[70] English history texts have been criticised on the grounds that they promote a 'narrowly national outlook'. German scholars have also suggested that English school texts provide a negative image of the German identity.[71] No doubt research would reveal that from the 1960s onwards, school textbooks modified their nationalist prejudices. Nevertheless, whatever the message of school texts, it is undeniable that the new history never vanquished the old in popular culture and popular consciousness. Nationalist literature may have become discredited in professional circles, but elsewhere – as the popularity of historical biographies testifies – it remained essentially unchallenged.

Concern with the representation of a national identity remained an important theme throughout the postwar years. In the USA in the 1940s and 1950s consensus historians projected a national identity in more subtle terms than in the 1930s:

> Historians were prepared to respond to appeals to render patriotic service in their writing so long as the contradiction between norms of detachment and objectivity on the one hand, and of mobilization and usefulness on the other, were not posed too sharply; so long as the requirement for doublethink was not made too manifest. When calls for the mobilization of historical consciousness made explicit the extent to which they entailed the abandonment of scholarly norms, they were angrily rejected.[72]

This was indeed pragmatism in action. On occasions, when the Cold War demanded, even this pragmatism was abandoned in favour of an explicit veneration of the American dream. Thus in 1949, Conyers Read used his presidential address to the American Historical Association to call the profession to take up arms: 'Total war, whether it be hot or cold, enlists everyone and calls upon everyone to assume his part. The historian is no freer from this obligation than the physicist.'[73]

In the USA History continued to expound traditional historicist themes throughout the Cold War. The American historian David Fischer wrote in 1970 that 'German historicism is dead, or dying, but the same ethical version of the genetic fallacy appears in other forms':

> Something of the fallacy of ethical historicism appears in the absurd and dangerous idea that America's rise to power and prosperity is a measure of its moral excellence – that the history of the Republic can be seen, in short, as a system of morality.[74]

However in its American form nationalist historiography was rarely noticed in the postwar period.

Americans were not alone in their concern to promote national identity through history. The programme of re-education imposed on Germany and Japan by the Allies received only token acceptance from significant sections of the intelligentsia. The wider population was even more hostile to what was perceived as outside meddling in education. In relation to the German experience Berghahn and Schissler observed that 'just as this programme generated great resentment among the West German population in general most of the country's professional historians found it impossible to accept the underlying assumptions about the German national past as consisting of nothing but a series of disasters and wrong turns.'[75] It is not surprising that in West Germany it was difficult to find historians who were prepared to pay even lip service to the anti-nationalist cause. As a result it was not until the 1960s that the values embodied in German national historiography were explicitly challenged.

In Britain the resentment of establishment historians at the decline of nationalist history was palpable. They would often lash out against Third World thinkers who were still allowed to be nationalists. In 1963 the Regius Professor of Modern History at Oxford, dismissed African history as the 'gyrations of barbaric peoples in insignificant corners of the globe.'[76] As usual Elton led the way in the reassertion of the conservative tradition. In 1968 he bemoaned that 'we are no longer patriots' and that 'we are no longer parochial'. With a touch of sadness he remarked that 'we are more ready to believe in China and Peru than in Runcorn and Southampton.' The point to which all this was a prelude was that the 'historian's task consists among other things' in a 'crude re-kindling of a certain respect for a country whose past justifies that respect.'[77]

Elton not only sought to uphold nationalist history but also to justify the particularism of anti-Enlightenment thought. He did this not by unequivocally defending particularism, but by suggesting that the balance had shifted too far in favour of a universalistic perspective. He wrote:

> To suppose that those who attack historians for being too parochial and too much concerned with the details of political history and such-like are right is to suppose that what is wrong with the world at present is an excessive concentration upon one's own country and nation and an excessive concentration on the particular, an absence of general theories, an inability and unwillingness to read large, to look large, to think large. I don't believe this is true.[78]

Elton's rather defensive version of nineteenth century anti-cosmopolitanism amounted to a plea to come home, get to know the parochial and experience the mystique of the particular. The arguments were all there – it merely required a more receptive public mood to give History confidence and with that a semblance of coherence.

Second time farce

Within a couple of years of the publication of Kennedy's essay on the decline of nationalist historiography, the outline of a nationalist revival was taking shape. By the late 1970s a concerted counter-attack was under way and History was once again on the advance, its survival greatly assisted by the insubstantial critique that nationalist history had received during the postwar years. The worldwide resurgence of historicism today seems more impressive than it really is because it was generally assumed that it had ceased to exist. In fact nationalist history has always had an important existence. What has changed is that today conservative thinkers are more confident about their project and it is their intellectual opponents who are now on the defensive.

Berghahn and Schissler have surveyed the state of affairs in Britain, Germany and the USA:

> Striking parallels can be discerned in all three countries, however, in respect of the influence of politics and ideology and in respect of major long-term swings of pendulum. The United States, West Germany and Britain have recently experienced a counter-movement to the tide of social and economic history that swept through them after the Second World War. This counter-movement has revived the importance of national political history and values, and with it has revived the problems from which this type of history has suffered in the past.[79]

The authors are right to suggest that the new nationalist historiography will prove no less problematic then the old. But are we merely seeing a swing of the ideological pendulum as they suggest?

In terms of substance and analytic orientation the new conservative History has much in common with nineteenth-century historicism. But the creation of national identity in the late twentieth century is a much more problematical project than it was in the nineteenth. At that time nations were in the process of coming into existence in an era of confidence and expansion. Today the mood is much more defensive.

Davies' comments on the revival of nationalist history are apposite. 'These events', he notes, are 'symptomatic of a sick society' which seeks comfort in the 'recollection of a glorious past.'[80]

The revival of nationalist history also has to contend with the problems of neutralising the legacy of the Second World War and the demands of competing identities. These concerns are implicit in Hirsch's call for a 'national' American culture:

> Although nationalism may be regrettable in some of its worldwide political effects, a mastery of national culture is essential to a mastery of the standard language in every modern nation. This point is important because educators often stress the importance of a multicultural education. Such study is indeed valuable in itself; it inculcates tolerance and provides a perspective on our own traditions and values. But however laudable it is it should not be the primary focus of national education. It should not be allowed to supplant or interfere with our schools' responsibility to insure our children's mastery of American literate culture.[81]

Nineteenth-century historians did not have to proceed so tactfully. This semi-apologetic plea for 'national education' indicates that the attempt to construct a national identity now faces considerable difficulties.

Today a straightforward nationalist history may even prove embarrassing to conservatives. For example a discussion on British national identity in the conservative weekly *The Spectator* in 1989 was critical of the 'outbreak of nationalist mysticism' and questioned the manipulation of history for the purpose of developing a 'national identity or national values'.[82] Appeals to the past are as likely to throw up new problems as solve old ones. Whatever the problems that face the revival of History, the project will not be abandoned. The attempt to resolve contemporary problems through the revival of traditional values continues to dominate the conservative imagination. In a sense reality is reversed: conservatives believe that the 'neglect of the past' is responsible for the problems of society. In reality perception of the problems facing society in the present tends to undermine traditional versions of the past.

The attempt to emulate the nineteenth-century intellectual reaction to the Enlightenment in the late twentieth century is unlikely to result in the production of viable national identities. The second time around, this enterprise becomes even more artificial then previously.

Ironically, although its prospects look uncertain, in the absence of any dynamic tradition of historical consciousness it can still influence contemporary thought.

History does not repeat itself. The very demand for an identity-creating history only draws attention to the extent to which circumstances have changed since the initial conservative assault on the legacy of the Enlightenment. Those who want to uphold identity and resist change have to take account of their highly compromised heritage. In the next three chapters we examine the specific issues that preoccupy those in the forefront of the conservative intellectual offensive in order to clarify the character of the new demand for History. Our aim is to provide a sociological analysis of the history of the demand for History.

4

The moral impasse

The notion that modern Western societies are undergoing a profound moral crisis has become something of a platitude. The prevalence throughout the 1980s of 'moral panics' over issues such as Aids, abortion, child abuse, hooliganism and delinquency in virtually every advanced country reflects a widespread sense of a loss of consensus concerning basic values and beliefs. It is difficult to pick up a book about contemporary society that does not express serious concern about its lack of direction and cohesion. The combination of a sense of moral decay and an acute anxiety about the future has led to a preoccupation with the past and to a tendency to romanticise history.[1]

The collapse of the 'Red Menace' and the suspension of Cold War rivalries in the late 1980s has brought to the fore problems of legitimacy which were previously obscured by the intensity of highly ideological superpower conflict. For 40 years it could be argued that progress in the West had been delayed by the exigencies of containing the enemy in the East and that Western societies had to stand together against the threat of communist subversion. Once the external focus of unity was removed, the lack of social and moral coherence of the advanced capitalist nations stood exposed.

Instead of boosting confidence, the West's triumph in the Cold War merely revealed its lack of dynamism and vision. The quest among leading Western politicians for a 'big idea' to replace the anti-communist crusade of the postwar decades reflects the exhaustion of the established order and its lack of a credible programme for the future. As one contributor to the *Foreign Affairs* discussion of the 'Winds of Change' put it, a 'plausible vision of the common good remains stubbornly elusive'.[2] Such a vision, which could provide the foundation for a new consensus and a positive identification with society, has yet to be elaborated.

The externalisation of domestic problems, along the lines of the

Cold War model, is unlikely to provide a substitute for a genuine programme for the future, as leading military historian Michael Howard has observed:

> The events of the past decade however suggest that the fundamental problems of the twenty-first century will not be those of traditional power confrontations. They are more likely to arise out of the integration, or disintegration of states themselves, and affect all actors on the world scene irrespective of ideology.[3]

According to Howard the long-term challenge facing the West is that of 'maintaining cohesion in increasingly heterogeneous societies'. Growing social tensions and mass immigration have 'eroded the cultural cohesion of older communities.'[4] The problem of legitimacy, which Howard characterises as a lack of 'cultural cohesion', explains the pervasive pessimism of the Western world. As he concludes: 'we are left with a West whose wealth provides no relief from anxiety and turbulence.'

Concern about social cohesion and moral crisis is by no means a novel phenomenon. We are witnessing today the cumulative effects of a process that has been under way for decades. Even in the USA, where a sense of optimism persisted more strongly than elsewhere in the postwar period, a lack of direction gradually became widespread. Even at the height of the booming 1950s, American thinkers of virtually all shades of political opinion were deeply concerned about the absence of any positive vision of the future. 'No one could ignore the avalanche of works with such titles as "whither modern man?" or "good-bye to the West", or the "destiny of European culture"', wrote Judith Shklar in 1957.[5]

Fears for the future were guided by the insight that America had lost touch with its past traditions and traditional values. Christopher Lasch observed in the mid-1970s that 'we are fast losing the sense of historical continuity, the sense of belonging to a succession of generations originating in the past and stretching into the future.' For Lasch, the distinctive feature of the 'spiritual crisis' of the 1970s was the 'waning of the sense of historical time – in particular, the erosion of any strong concern for posterity.'[6] While Lasch's description of the symptoms is no doubt accurate, his diagnosis of America's malady is somewhat superficial. For the erosion of concern for posterity was itself a symptom of an underlying loss of confidence in the present and the absence of a perspective for the future. This malaise, which was not specific to the 1970s, has become universal in the 1990s.

Now that the end of the Cold War has removed the last excuses, the sense of foreboding about the direction in which society is moving has become more widespread in the USA than ever before. William Pfaff's *Barbarian Sentiments: How the American Century Ends* projects an image of a nation paralysed by its uncertain identity:

> The political rhetoric of the United States has continued to employ the old vocabulary of American exceptionalism, national mission, American pre-eminence. Yet there is no longer an intellectually responsible ruling idea of Americanism, a fully acceptable formulation of this justificatory national purpose – to say nothing of a national policy to advance it. There no longer is a clear ethnic identity.[7]

Pfaff's main concern is that the old institutions and conventions have ceased to be effective. This emphasis on the divergence between the traditions of the past and the expectations of our times is a recurring theme among postwar American writers. If the USA, the most optimistic of the Western powers, is so beseiged with doubts and insecurities, then we may expect to find comparable concerns among the other major capitalist societies.

The demand for cohesion

Pfaff's portentous aside, that in. America there is no 'clear ethnic identity' identifies one aspect of the problem of social cohesion. Another important aspect is the absence of commonly shared views about the future, reflecting the difficulty establishment forces throughout the West are having in developing a sense of positive identification with the institutions and values of the system. In one form or another this problem has been one of the main concerns of social thought over the past two centuries. According to Giner the 'search for community' is an attempt 'to reconstruct the lost primeval bonds either by theory or by doctrine'.[8] Yet another factor is the pervasive sense of intellectual and ideological fragmentation. Conservative thinkers are always the first to point out that one of the central defects of our times is the conviction that nothing is sacred, that no values or attachments are beyond question. The sociologist Carlo Mongardini argues that the 'preconceptions of every cultural form have been called into question' and therefore 'nowadays, no religion, no moral values or knowledge can be funded on undisputed premises and certainties.'[9]

Parallels between today's crisis of values and the *fin-de-siècle* malaise of the 1890s are now commonplace. Are these comparisons valid? There are undoubtedly similarities between the emergence of nationalist histories in the nineteenth century and today's conservative reaction. However, emphasising similarities may well obscure the distinctive features of both periods. Let's briefly compare the two.

The nineteenth-century conservative reaction was a response to social problems that were perceived as indicating a crisis of tradition and of values. The declining influence of traditional beliefs and the weakening of religious faith were experienced as a crisis of morality. According to Emile Durkheim, the old values had disintegrated, and in the absence of any replacement that could bind society, a moral vacuum resulted. Earlier thinkers such as Edmund Burke and Louis de Bonald had argued that the moral order was based upon sentiments and values nurtured over the centuries. Burke concluded that it was not only 'material interests but spiritual ties and sentiments' which 'bind the members of the community together'.[10] Conservatives such as Joseph de Maistre were obsessed with the attempt to find a focus around which to unify society. They believed that the conservation of society and its continuity depended on developing its sense of moral unity. According to Zeitlin, their ideal was the Middle Ages, when social unity was guaranteed by Christianity, a faith universally accepted in Western Europe.[11]

Not only conservative thinkers were preoccupied with the problems of moral breakdown. Liberals, radicals and even social democrats recognised that without a consensus built on a system of values and beliefs, social stability could not be guaranteed. In his later years even Saint-Simon, formerly an upholder of the Enlightenment, proposed a New Christianity to enforce the 'spiritual and moral unity of men and nations'.[12] Left-wingers and conservatives disagreed only about the forms through which moral unity could be achieved. Whereas right-wingers proposed the revival of old-style Christianity, radicals considered that traditional religion had been discredited or had become irrelevant to modern times. They advocated new secular faiths, often closely linked to science, as an alternative. Thus while Saint-Simon advocated various secular religions, Auguste Comte shifted from ardently defending positive science to an equally robust advocacy of a positive religion.

Both conservatives and radicals focused on issues of *social solidarity* because of their common concern about the breakdown of communities and the potential threat posed by the masses, who were no longer restrained by old conventions. Scientists and philosophers who were themselves hostile or indifferent towards religious faith were reluctant to allow their scepticism to undermine the faith of the masses, fearing that this might contribute to the erosion of the social stability ensured by superstition. For example, as early as the eighteenth century the mechanical materialist Holbach had argued that ordinary people should not be informed about the non-existence of God because of the danger this might cause for social order.[13] The same point was echoed by the Social Darwinist Benjamin Kidd, whose 1894 work *Social Evolution* emphasised the importance of religion and other non-rational factors in enhancing social cohesion.[14] What now appear as bizarre combinations of piety and science were a familiar feature of nineteenth-century bourgeois thought.

Liberal thinkers now re-interpreted freedom to mean *security*. As Giner suggests, security required that the masses 'should be protected from coming into contact with the great truths of science and philosophy'.[15] Conservatives were even more enthusiastic about promoting religion since, unlike the radicals, they actually believed in it. Yet even they were not as concerned about the content of faith as they were with the links between religious tradition and the murky mythical past, as de Maistre explained:

> Man's cradle must be surrounded by dogmas and when his reason awakens, he must find all his opinions already made, at least those concerning his social behaviour. Nothing is more important for man than prejudice.[16]

In the conservative imagination, prejudice and dogma were directly linked to the enforcement of order and the maintenance of cohesion.

The most extensive analysis of the nineteenth-century decline of religious forces and the resulting moral vacuum is to be found in the writings of Durkheim. Though his emphasis was different from that of conservative thinkers, Durkheim's conviction that 'moral remaking' was essential for social stability brought him into line with the anti-Enlightenment tradition. At the same time he regarded conservative attempts to revive traditional religion as anachronistic. For Durkheim only *the need for religion* was eternal – its specific forms could change as society evolved:

Thus there is something eternal in religion which is destined to survive all the particular symbols in which religious thought has successively enveloped itself. There can be no society which does not feel the need of upholding and reaffirming at regular intervals the collective ideas which make its unity and its personality.[17]

For Durkheim religion was simply a process through which people 'reaffirm in common their common sentiments': a secular celebration of the French republic could play a role analogous to that of medieval Christianity:

> What essential difference is there between an assembly of Christians celebrating the principal dates of the life of Christ, or of Jews remembering the exodus from Egypt or the promulgation of the decalogue, and a reunion of citizens commemorating the promulgation of a new moral or legal system or some great event in the national life?[18]

Though Durkeim's pragmatic approval of any set of rituals or doctrines which might help to promote a degree of moral unity in society appalled religious traditionalists, they shared the same preoccupations and objectives.

Durkheim's conviction that there was 'something eternal in religion' coexisted with an acute sensitivity to the vacuum left by the decline of religious faith and the resulting sense of moral decay. He regarded the late nineteenth century as an era of 'moral mediocrity', as a 'stage of transition' between the passing of traditional Christianity and the emergence of a new religion. He was certain that there could be no return to the past but less clear about the shape of the future:

> The great things of the past which filled our fathers with enthusiasm do not excite the same ardour in us, either because they have come into common usage to such an extent that we are unconscious of them, or else because they no longer answer to our actual aspirations; but as yet there is nothing to replace them.[19]

This sense of loss, and the recognition that there was nothing to replace the old certitudes, became a central motif in Western thought in the new century.

Durkheim's work expresses an underlying conservative sensibility that is only superficially contradicted by his pragmatic attitude towards religion. The common feature in the late nineteenth century concern about the past is the commitment to enforce social stability through promoting moral values. In the conservative imagination, the conviction that society is based on a moral code is transformed into the notion that sound morality precedes a stable social order. The logical primacy of the moral order is thus understood in temporal terms: the past provides the framework for moral remaking. Durkheim insists on both the logical and temporal priority of morality, observing that 'nearly all the great social institutions have been born in religion.'[20] If for Durkheim religion is merely a vehicle through which society can become acquainted with the past, then History is merely another form of religion.

Durkheim's observation that modern society has nothing to replace the 'great things of the past which filled our fathers with enthusiasm' has a contemporary ring. Indeed in the postwar decades, Durkheim has emerged as one of the major influences on Western social thought. Although the recent revival of conservative historiography has been closely linked with the issue of moral unity, anxieties about social cohesion go much further back. For much of the twentieth century History and moral remaking have come together in a familiar reaction to the decline of old traditions and institutions. This Durkheimian synthesis is well articulated by Daniel Bell:

> If religion is declining, it is because the worldly realm of the sacred has been shrinking, and because the shared sentiments and affective ties between men have become diffuse and weak. The primordial elements that provide men with common identification and affective reciprocity – family, synagogue, church, community – have become attenuated, and people have lost the capacity to maintain sustained relations with each other in both time and place. To say, then, that 'God is dead' is, in effect to say that the social bonds have snapped and that society is dead.[21]

For Bell, the weakening of the past, of the 'primordial elements' of society, leads to a loss of cohesion. Without collectively shared beliefs, society dies since it lacks legitimacy.

Bell and Durkheim both emphasised the need for moral consensus to counter the problems of social disintegration. Is it therefore legitimate to consider today's revival of History as a 'second crisis of modernity'? Many of the contemporary subjects of debate – identity, morality, values – bear a striking resemblance to the themes at issue in the 1890s. But it would be inappropriate to present the two discussions as one eternal debate. It is the difference between the two debates that helps us put the current preoccupation with moral unity into perspective.

It is first important to point out the relative social weight of those concerned with the moral impasse facing society. Today the perception of moral crisis is virtually universal. By contrast, the nineteenth-century reaction to the Enlightenment was very much a minority affair. Conservatives appalled by the collapse of tradition and social scientists worried about what would replace the old institutions were both unrepresentative of mainstream thought. Throughout most of the Western world, this was a period of rapid economic and technological advance and a time of unprecedented intellectual optimism. This outlook remained generally dominant until after the First World War, and in the USA it continued into the 1940s and 1950s. As H. Stuart Hughes insists, the significance of thinkers like Durkheim, who were ambivalent about modernity, was not that they were representative of their period but that they anticipated subsequent trends. In his authoritative survey of European thought between 1890 and 1930, Hughes writes of 'certain periods in history in which a number of advanced thinkers' have 'proposed views on human conduct so different from those commonly accepted at the time' that their work constitutes an 'intellectual revolution'.[22]

The conservative reaction of the nineteenth century was subordinate to the prevailing sense of dynamism and progress. Today's conservative revival takes place in a context of economic stagnation and a climate of all-pervasive pessimism. The moral crisis of the late nineteenth century was strictly circumscribed. Conservatives were painfully aware of the decline in religious observance, but there was no crisis of faith in general. The wider sense of confidence in society generated new secular faiths, in science, the national mission, racial superiority or imperialism. By contrast, the late twentieth century has witnessed the demise of both sacred and secular convictions and has yet to find anything to replace them. The difference between the two periods is articulated by Cyril Garbett, a former archbishop of York:

> The loss of faith has been followed by moral chaos. The agnostics of Victorian days were confident that the Christian ethic, which they reverenced, would remain unshaken even if the faith with which it had always been associated should be abandoned.[23]

Garbett's distinction between 'loss of faith' and 'moral chaos' implies that the decline of Christian worship in the nineteenth century was not a disaster since it did not undermine faith in many of its values. Today, when society has ceased to believe in anything, the result is 'moral chaos' and social problems of a qualitatively different order.

There is no straight line between the original conservative reaction in the nineteenth century and the moral impasse of today. Although Victorian confidence never existed without a sense of doubt, it did exude a quality of certainty about the future, which would strike the contemporary reader as naive. This was so more or less up to the turn of the century. One of the main arguments of this text, which will be developed at greater length, is that it is precisely the breakdown of the new faiths which evolved as alternatives to medieval Christianity that underlines today's moral impasse.

Themes and arguments associated with the confident mood of a century ago have also become compromised. For example many of the most dynamic nineteenth century thinkers were confidently Social Darwinists. After the experience of fascism, Social Darwinism is no longer an acceptable point of view. 'The social theorists of the late nineteenth and early twentieth century were as anxious to claim the epithet "Darwinian" as some modern social theorists are to disclaim it', writes Greta Jones, the author of a valuable contribution on this subject.[24]

Let us take another example, the imperialist mission. In the Anglo-American context this functioned as a viable faith that cohered the political elites and inspired a wider social strata, including a section of the working class. Lord Curzon's 1908 speech in Birmingham illustrates this synthesis of faith and optimism for the future:

> I speak of Empire ... because I am a convinced and unconquerable imperialist, who by the accident of events has been called upon to spend the whole of his working manhood in the study or service of Empire, and to whom it has come to be a secular religion, embodying the most sacred duty of the present, and the brightest hope for the future ...
>
> In Empire we have found not merely the key to glory and wealth, but the call to duty, and the means of service to mankind. Empire can only be achieved with satisfaction, or maintained with advantage, provided it has a moral basis ...
>
> To the people of the mother state it must be a discipline, an inspiration and a faith.[25]

To be sure, Curzon's presentation of the moral foundation of imperialism was primarily propaganda. Nevertheless it did function as a secular religion. By providing material benefits alongside moral fulfilment it successfully encouraged social cohesion.

As a result of the upheavals in the two decades that followed Curzon's speech, imperialism became a less credible doctrine. In the eyes of many, the imperial ideal appeared as an apology for greed and overseas plunder. Its discrediting along with the other faiths of the late nineteenth century has deprived Western societies of their previous moral certitude. To put matters most starkly, that which gave faith and inspiration had by the middle of the twentieth century become an embarrassment! With the idea of imperialism so compromised, it became increasingly difficult to extricate a past and a tradition that was usable in the new circumstances. To this day none of the Western powers has succeeded in finding any vision that approximates the confidence-boosting qualities of the American Manifest Destiny or the British imperial ideal.

The problem of today's moral impasse is that the recent past is not reusable for the purposes of shaping a viable identity. The question mark which hangs over the past raises queries about what is to be the foundation of moral unity. The conservative response to this is simply to suggest that the past is not problematic, there is little to be ashamed of, it is best to get on and revere it.

Perceptions of the problem

A crisis of legitimacy is seldom experienced as such by the ruling classes. It is rare that a ruling elite has the self-consciousness to admit that its system of values has become exhausted. It is far easier to blame the media, social workers, teachers or lax parents.

Throughout this century the most consistent expression of the problem has been the ever-recurring crisis of education. Blaming the messenger for the bad news – by holding teachers responsible for the decline in authority – is a persistent conservative attitude. The reaction of the British Colonial Office to the negative image that imperialism acquired in the late 1930s and early 1940s is paradigmatic in this respect.

A committee set up by the Colonial Office to plan long-range propaganda designed to defend the empire swiftly isolated the teaching profession as the main culprit. The report, completed in May

1942, noted that the attitude of teachers towards the empire was 'not mere indifference', there was 'often an attitude of suspicion amounting in extreme cases to a feeling that our national record in the Colonial field is not one of which we can we proud.' This came as a shock to a class that had hitherto routinely regarded the empire as the highpoint of human civilisation. In subsequent discussions around the report, the 'defeatism' and 'sense of shame' that the teaching profession ostensibly possessed regarding British imperialism were explained away as character defects. According to one official, 'teachers suffered from an inferiority complex which made them historically "anti-gentry" and they somehow associated Imperial matters with this complex.' Women teachers, unlike their male colleagues, 'led a segregated existence and their ignorance and indifference to Colonial matters' was 'understandable'.[26] Throughout this and subsequent deliberations, there was never a suggestion that imperialism had itself become discredited. Teachers were seen as trying to discredit what was otherwise held in esteem by the rest of society.

Concern with the state of public morality itself indicates an unwillingness or inability to go beyond symptoms, in order to tackle the problems facing society. Although much of the discussion about the moral climate is driven by emotion and influenced by prejudice, it provides useful insights into the intellectual outlook of those concerned.

Reservations about the moral climate of society are always linked to new attitudes towards the past. Any questioning of society is held to be the result of a lack of respect for the past or for accepted conventions, institutions and values. The questioning of custom and of the role assigned to the individual has been depicted as the recipe for moral chaos by conservative thinkers since ancient Greece. Hesiod connected the danger of chaos and social decay to the breakdown of the bonds between parents and children, when 'the father will no longer resemble his children nor the children their father'.[27]

In an embryonic form this upholding of family bonds anticipates the arguments of nineteenth-century conservatives regarding the naturalness of eternal morals and values. Smith notes how 'reconstructions of the national past' in the nineteenth century aim for a kind of 'naturalism':

> The past that they seek to unfold should be as organic and natural as conceivable, and our histories interpreted as if they were

extensions of the natural world in which communities obeyed similar kinds of 'laws' to those governing the natural world. In other words, societies were subject to the same laws of birth, growth, flowering and decay – and renewal – as plants and trees, and fed by analogous elements. Lack of any of these nurturants spelt decay, and it was the task of nationalist educators to re-supply them.[28]

Thus the wisdom of the past can be communicated only through intermediaries. Therefore whenever the past ceases to motivate society it is the intermediaries that are held to blame. In capitalist societies the most prominent intermediaries are the teachers, which is why one of the first symptoms of moral impasse is the crisis of education.

Education

Even a superficial glance at American, British or German periodicals shows a concentration of intellectual concern with yet another 'crisis' of education. *Time* magazine warns that 'in US classrooms, battles are flaring over values that are almost a reverse image of the American mainstream' and that as a result 'a new intolerance is on the rise'. *The Sunday Times* complains that 'widespread ignorance of science and technology has already made Britain a laughing stock among its industrial competitors.'[29] The major texts calling for the moral remaking of society have education as their main focus. Bloom's *The Closing of the American Mind* is appropriately subtitled 'How higher education has failed democracy and impoverished the souls of today's students'.

The education system, as the main institution for representing society's wider traditions and values, is intimately bound up with the question of authority and legitimacy. This relation is often trivialised, for example by blaming permissive teachers for crime and the breakdown of authority, but even more sophisticated condemnations of the education system have as their self-flattering supposition the view that otherwise impeccable customs and values are improperly communicated by teachers.

In some cases the failure to communicate society's sound values is assigned to the *malevolence* of teachers. According to Roger Kimball, the conservative author of *Tenured Radicals*, the generation of the 1960s conspired to take over American campuses so as to turn them into engines of social change. Roger Scruton accuses the British New Left of similar conspiracies.[30] This witch-hunting of educators has a long and respectable record. The frustrated bureaucrats in the Colonial Office are not alone. Listen to Representative George Dondero of Michigan raising the alarm in 1946:

> This country is being systematically communized, perhaps unconsciously, through its educational institutions. These institutions are instruments through which left-wing theories and philosophies may be and are taught to large groups of young Americans by persons whom they respect and trust – their instructors. That process has been going on for years, in an insidious manner. As a consequence, we now have an entire generation of voters who do not appreciate our Constitution, or our national history.[31]

Dondero's statement would comfortably fit into the current discussion in Britain, where conservative ideologues berate the 'pinkish educational establishment who have dominated school education for the past 20 years.'[32] In Japan the teachers' union has faced vitriolic denunciation from conservative forces during the postwar years.[33]

The concern that conservatives express over the system of education indicates their heightened sensitivity to the problem of social cohesion. This is an almost instinctive reaction, guided by the recognition that traditionally the main institutional framework for popularising nationalism and for instilling a particular moral outlook was the system of education. From this perspective, moral unity is determined above all by the character of education. Bloom argues that every educational system has a 'moral goal', since it wants to produce a 'certain kind of human being'.[34] Thus if society has too many of the 'wrong' type of people, it must be due to a flawed system of education.

The traditional view of education is akin to its approach to religion. Education should convey *truths* about the national purpose and uphold a moral code. When teachers diverge from this task of propaganda, there is a danger that questions will be asked about things that ought to be beyond question. Thus the traditional conservative critique of education is that it fails to ensure that the fundamental values of society are conveyed to its students. Today this critique argues that education is too pluralist and multicultural.

Walter Moberly's *Crisis in the University*, published in 1948, anticipates the reaction of the late 1970s and 1980s. As head of the

British university system, Moberly's main fear was that many students were not receiving proper Christian guidance. He took strong exception to the 'morbidly exaggerated call of neutrality', and he wished to replace this with a robust campaign on behalf of traditional values. According to Moberly, the West was to achieve reconstruction after the Second World War 'not by abandoning our tradition but by rediscovering and reinvigorating it.'[35]

Moberly's standpoint on education is unequivocal. Tradition and morality are not divisible and teachers cannot remain neutral about a subject so crucial to the future of a nation. In the aftermath of the Second World War Moberly's views sounded like a defensive plea. By the 1970s such views were very much part of the Western mainstream consensus. The equivocating, value-free and neutral educator returned as the prime target of the late twentieth-century conservative ideological offensive. Bloom clearly echoes Moberly in his critique of the 'education of openness'. Bloom argues that an education system that fails to uphold values as truths beyond question leads to a neutral stand on what is right and what is wrong.[36] The implication is that the affirmation of tradition and values by the system of education will create the conditions where moral unity can thrive.

Most of the contributions to the 'crisis of education' discussion tend to be shallow and unwilling to consider the social causes of moral impasse. Hannah Arendt is one exception to this trend. Although she would eschew the label conservative, many thinkers of that persuasion express admiration for her work. Arendt, like the conservative critics discussed above, recognised the key role of education in the provision of socialisation. She, herself is also concerned with the problem of moral incoherence. But unlike many other contributors, Arendt argues that the 'crisis' of education is merely a symptom of more deep-seated concerns. More than three decades ago she observed:

> In America, one of its most characteristic and suggestive aspects is the recurring crisis in education that, during the last decade at least, has become a political problem of the first magnitude, repeated on almost daily in the newspapers.[37]

Arendt recognised that the problem was not the school system but the absence of consensus on the basic values of society. There had to be agreement about the past before a system of education could extol its virtues. 'The problem of education in the modern world lies in the fact that by its very nature it cannot forego either authority or tradition, and yet must proceed in a world that is neither structured by authority nor held together by tradition', she wrote in 1961.[38] In other words the education crisis is merely a symptom of the more fundamental breakdown of authority and tradition; the erosion of legitimacy is experienced as a problem *internal* to the system of education.

Arendt also grasped the fact that ultimately the erosion of authority and of tradition was connected to the collapse of the past. In this sense her arguments anticipate those who seek the revival of History in the 1980s. There is a difference in that Arendt is far more pessimistic about the prospects of reviving the past. It is worth quoting her at length on this point:

> The real difficulty in modern education lies in the fact that, despite all the fashionable talk about a new conservatism, even that minimum of conservation and the conserving attitude without which education is simply not possible is in our time extraordinarily hard to achieve. There are very good reasons for this. The crisis of authority in education is most closely connected with the crisis of tradition, that is with the crisis in our attitude toward the realm of the past. This aspect of the modern crisis is especially hard for the educator to bear, because it is his task to mediate between the old and the new, so that his very profession requires of him an extraordinary respect for the past.[39]

This clear statement of conservative sensibility, whereby authority, mediated through education, acquires its shape through its relation with the past, is unusual in that it also recognises the real source of the problem.[40]

Today the controversy surrounding education is far more extensive than it was 30 years ago. Shor's study of the American education system shows how debate which focused on vocational issues during the years 1971–5 gave way to a 'literacy crisis', during the years 1975–82, which then culminated in a crisis over discipline and the pursuit of 'excellence'.[41] The same series is evident in Britain. Its resilience must be a testimony of the unending search for a solution to the problem of authority.

Tradition

The term 'lack of respect' for some traditional value or institution, recurs time and again in the conservative literature. This is the common-sense perception of the problem of moral unity. The failure of education to sustain authority is blamed on a lack of respect for tradition. Upholding the 'authority of the past' is the role assigned to teachers, for example, by Philip Rieff:

> As teachers, we must be at war with the culture 'lifestyle', with the endless order-hopping of the questing young, often formatively encouraged by their still questing parents, for whom the quest is an escape from the untaught authority of their own past. Authority untaught is the condition in which a culture commits suicide.[42]

In this, it is difficult to separate where the past ends and authority begins. It is clear only that there are some truths that can be mobilised for a war against the 'endless' questioning of the feckless. These truths, which are sanctified through the past, constitute *tradition*.

Tradition is one of those ill-defined terms that can be used to include just about anything. It usually involves projecting into the past values that one wants to uphold, recasting them as a tradition. Often matters are as cynical as just that. For example writers who are concerned by lack of moral and social coherence often complain about the absence of functioning myths. One account of British intellectual life during the period after the Second World War observed that half the contributors to the periodical *Horizon* complained about society's lack of a 'prevailing myth'.[43] As the present-day history debates show, myth-making remains an essential element in the assertion of national traditions. Enoch Powell, the leading figure on the right wing of the postwar British Conservative party argued that 'the greatest task of the statesman ... is to offer his people good myths.'[44]

Some writers have reservations about the mysticism and irrationality involved in myth-making. But in the end their commitment to social stability and moral order outweighs such reservations. This is the point of view of Allan Bloom, who sees the need for an unquestioned tradition that can contain the momentary passions of the vulgar masses. He reasons that:

> Some kind of authority is often necessary for most men and is necessary, at least sometimes, for all men. In the absence of

anything else to which to turn, the common beliefs of most men are almost always what will determine judgement. This is just where tradition used to be most valuable. Without being seduced by its undemocratic and antirational mystique, tradition does provide a counterpoise to and a repair from the merely current ... The active presence of a tradition in man's soul gives him a resource against the ephermal, the kind of resource that only the wise can find simply within themselves.[45]

Bloom recognises the undemocratic and irrational mystique of tradition but reckons that it is a small price to pay for the enforcement of a moral order. From this elitist standpoint only the wise can be relied to make the right choices; the rest need myths and traditions to guide their actions.

Bloom and his co-thinkers instinctively grasp that there exists an unresolved tension between their commitment to reason and their aspiration for the unreason of a functioning tradition. This tension is invariably resolved in favour of the latter. Reason becomes a negotiable commodity that will always be bartered away for moral order. When the situation appears to call for drastic solutions, conservative social scientists are prepared to trade away their secular pretensions altogether. Daniel Bell, brooding about the 'cultural contradictions' of capitalism, has no hesitation on this point:

What holds one to reality, if one's secular system of meanings proves to be an illusion? I will risk an unfashionable answer – the return in Western society of some conception of religion.[46]

Bell's advocacy of religion explicitly pays its respect to the legacy of Durkheim. There is however an important difference between the two. Bell is no fervent believer in anything. His pragmatism or, less charitably, his cynicism is illustrated by the phrase 'some conception of religion'. Not this or that religion but *any* religion is preferable to the secular uncertainties facing society. In contrast, Durkheim had a far more positive approach: his support for French republican nationalism was driven by wholehearted conviction.

The problem of tradition thus tends to be pragmatically translated into that of faith, religion or morality. It involves the invention of some kind of a religion. Arthur Koestler, whose writings have strongly influenced post-Second World War conservative thought, insisted on the centrality of finding a solution to the 'craving for Faith'. In his novel *The Age of Longing* one of his characters, Julien, argues that the only 'hope' of preventing extinction is the 'emergence of a new transcendental faith'. This had to be a 'new religion, of a cosmic loyalty with a doctrine acceptable to twentieth-century man'.[47]

Koestler and Bell's pragmatic attitude towards the invention of a new faith is not acceptable in its entirety to tradition-oriented conservatives. The problem with a 'new' religion is precisely that it is *new* and lacks the sanction of the past. Newness implies change, whereas what is wanted is continuity. That is why the use of the past is in the end indispensable. To modernise a tradition is legitimate, so long as it is fashioned from the past. The problem of moral unity therefore requires the recreation of links with the past through the sanctifying of tradition.

Ortega y Gassett argued back in the years between the two world wars that the old cannot be exchanged for the new without damaging the moral order. He warned that 'Europe has been left without a moral code' and observed: 'Europe is now reaping the painful results of her spiritual conduct. She has adopted blindly a culture which is magnificent, but has no roots.'[48] No matter how magnificent, a culture without roots is doomed to wither away. A viable moral code requires roots in the past. Tradition is important precisely in order to resist the seduction of society by new ideas.

The reaction to historical thinking discussed previously in relation to the revival of History has its parallel in the sphere of morality. Rieff's attack on 'endless order-hopping' demonstrates a gut reaction against the acceptance of change and of new solutions. The Cold War American theologian Reinhold Niebuhr directly equated the spiritual impoverishment of his time with the belief in progress through historical change. He informed readers of his *Faith and History* that 'we are seeking in this treatise to understand how modern culture could have arrived at so dubious a conclusion that history is the solution to all human problems.'[49] The process of change, rather than providing a solution, is seen as constituting the core of a spiritual crisis. For Niebuhr the breakdown of tradition was but a prelude to moral collapse. Individuals, 'freed from the disciplines of the older organic communities, were lost in the mass and became the prey of demagogues and charlatans who transmuted their individual anxieties and resentments into collective political power of demonic fury.'[50] In this Hobbesian nightmare only tradition stood between humanity and retrogression into barbarism.

The overexaggerated emphasis by conservatives on the question of tradition and morality is based on the recognition that while it is not possible to revive the 'older organic communities' it is always possible to mobilise the past through imagination. In this way it is hoped that traditional values can recreate the moral unity of the no longer existing organic communities. Ironically as the breakdown of communities in capitalist societies has intensified, public discussions of moral concerns have accelerated. In the course of this process many conservative thinkers have become self-consciously anti-secular – and many prominent liberal intellectuals have become increasingly disposed to accept religious and morality-related options.

Religion has been an important terrain for the project of reviving tradition, particularly in the United States and in Britain. In addition to the 'pinkish education establishment', British conservatives have strong objections to the do-gooders in the Anglican Church. The British New Right thinker Paul Johnson is vitriolic against the 'embarrassed and apologetic tone of voice which has become perhaps the most striking characteristic of up-to-date Anglicanism' and its 'periodic orgies of self- abasement'.[51]

Johnson and others seem to crave for the certainty of a medieval dogma. There is even a hint of envy in some of the Western discussions about Islam: at least *their* religion carries conviction and provides certitude. Western conservatives, despite some recent intellectual triumphs, can only dream about a functioning unquestioned tradition.

There are still too many choices and too many values and too much change for the conservative imagination. Roger Scruton, a fervent champion of the conservative cause, almost sounds like everyone's defeated grandparents when he fears for a world 'without the sacred' and where 'all is permitted, and where nothing has absolute value'.[52] Absolute values require that there be absolutely no change, or at the very least the denial of historical thinking. Even meaningless superstition is to be preferred to the demystification of the sacred. Leading British Conservative ideologue Digby Anderson celebrated the medical problem of Aids as the vindication of 'arbitrary and senseless' religion over the old morality:

> The old wisdom, displaced by progressive gospel, no longer looks quite so *passé*. Its adherents did not question everything but followed religious and social conventions even when these appeared arbitrary and senseless ... Desires were repressed by inculcated habit and deterrence. Repression was not then viewed

as a bad thing. And a necessary corollary of the rules was guilt, fear, scandal and stigma so denounced and derided by 'rational' progressives. They do not appear so obviously ridiculous today.[53]

This enthronement of prejudice indicates just how strong is the search for certainty in the conservative consciousness.

The discussion of tradition, which almost always leads to a consideration of religion, morals or values, is clearly motivated by the erosion of belief. Lack of belief in the values of tradition and the institutions associated with it, such as the family, have become the dominant concerns of the West in the past two decades. The social causes of new patterns of human relations are seldom explored. Instead an unproblematic tradition is counterpoised to a society in decay.

The suggested inference is that this fall from grace is a punishment for abandoning the values sanctioned by the past. Aids is the divine punishment for unnatural practices. The multiplication of moral panics in the postwar period represents society's difficulty in dealing with the problem of moral unity. The discussions of morality always return to the past. To substantiate their perception of the problem they need to point to communities which were morally coherent, where the doors could be left open without acting as an invitation to criminals, where everyone respected the sacred, where there was no family breakdown, where women had no abortions and where no one questioned the basic conventions except for a handful of hardened deviants.

Anxieties about tradition and morality are allowed considerable latitude. The conservative imagination is spontaneously drawn towards moral concerns because social problems redefined as moral problems invite a return to the 'tried and tested' values of the past.

Insecure cultures

It is widely recognised that issues such as education, tradition and morality are central to the conservative perception. However there are other issues, less often reflected on in public, which touch centrally upon the subject of our discussion. One of the most widely discussed in the West is that of race. Because of its sensitivity, it is more often than not discussed in a coded or at least guarded manner. But the issue of race, immigration or of the ethnic is never far away from the debates on national identity, history and education. Thus the major historical controversies over French history and identity are fundamentally about what it means to be French. Perry Anderson is very much to the point when he suggests that 'immigration and education, as one would expect, lie at the centre of these exchanges.'[54] Through the elaboration of a common race and culture a link is established with the past, a past entirely exclusive to the people concerned. Culture delineates a common past for some and excludes others.

Culture is one of those ambiguous terms used to convey distinct values and traditions. It is often portrayed as a sacrosanct inheritance of a community. It implies language, religion and customs – through which a distinct identity is established. It involves the selective appropriation of the past so as to establish a select and homogeneous community. By sharing a culture, communities may be established. The relevance of culture for identity formation is most striking where people possess nationalist sensibilities but who do not have nation states. According to Nipperdey, 'it is virtually obvious that language, culture and history constitute the nation and not popular sovereignty of the political will or the constitution, as in the case with nations that have a common state.'[55]

Culture is society's cumulative inheritance of the past. For conservatives, the past is lived through culture. This legacy of the past establishes natural sentiments, loyalties and emotions. This naturalising of culture is essential for the enforcing of a working identity, for culture, like the past, tradition, or morality, must be above question. If culture expresses natural impulses it becomes a fact of life rather than a subject for debate. The lived results of these impulses are national and racial characteristics.

Since the experience of Nazism, the presentation of culture and of race as natural has become a sensitive subject. This is explicitly discussed mainly by intellectuals of the far right. The French far-right think-tank *GRECE* depicts the *rootedness* of France in almost biological terms:

> If France is merely a concept, totally removed from the realities of soul and blood, patriotism then becomes ideological and contains in itself all the germs of universalism: he who wishes to be French is French.[56]

If Frenchness has a natural foundation, then it becomes an incontrovertible quality – exclusive to those who inherit it. This is seen by conservatives as what really binds society into a coherent unit. The emphasis is on exclusiveness; culture and identity do not become objects of negotiation. As one conservative Cambridge don argued: 'although the British have a tradition of according citizenship to foreigners, in reasonable numbers, they have always assumed that membership of the nation is characteristically inherited rather than simply chosen – as one might choose to join a club.'[57] The converse of this position is that the cultural identity through which roots are established with the past is not a matter of choice but of 'blood and soil'.

The celebration of race and culture is far more muted in the United States than it is in Britain, France or Germany. The reason for this is that the United States has promoted itself as a melting pot for different groups of immigrants. Moreover the delicate aspects of race relations have led to a political agenda which is self-consciously multi-ethnic. Even in Europe, where there has been no advocacy of the melting-pot tradition, the dominant trend in the postwar period has been to make concessions to multi-ethnic and multicultural attitudes. This has been evident in the British education system and to a lesser extent that of France. However the conservative campaign to uphold national identities finds it difficult to handle the realities of a multicultural society. As a result culture has become an important area of controversy.

The crisis of confidence contained in the moral impasse discussed previously is almost tangible in relation to the conservative revulsion against multicultural society. This reaction follows from the recognition that if cultures are held to be equivalent, then one's own national culture is no better and no worse than the next. National culture loses its uniqueness. The specific traditions and values associated with it no longer have that sacred binding quality. The attempt to consolidate a national identity contradicts a functioning multiculturalism. That is why the attempt to revive a nationalist historiography has coincided with a campaign against multiculturalism.

The treatment of different cultures as equally valid calls into question the claim of absolute loyalty made by any particular one. For those interested in social cohesion, culture can be no more a subject for debate than morality. Conservatives have coined the term cultural relativism to express what they consider to be a betrayal of identity. According to this point of view, relativism, be it in the sphere of morality or culture, fails to take sides between good and bad. Bloom's widely discussed text is designed above all to counter cultural appeasement. 'History and the study of cultures do not teach or prove that values or cultures are relative', he argues.[58]

The reaction against cultural relativism exposes deep insecurities about the coherence of the moral order. Once the special dignity with which culture has been customarily treated is removed, there is little left with which to build a moral community. Professor Arthur Schlesinger at City University of New York equates cultural relativism with the collapse of History. He has warned that if 'we repudiate the quite marvellous inheritance that history has bestowed on us, we invite the fragmentation of our own culture into a quarrelsome spatter of enclaves, ghettos and tribes.'[59]

Throughout the West moralists and conservatives have reacted virulently to claims that their culture is no better than those of others. In Britain Bryan Appleyard, a regular columnist for the *Sunday Times*, denounces cultural relativism as if it was a mortal threat to the nation. This 'instinctive belief' of the 'entire educational establishment', he says, has destroyed Britain's capacity to 'celebrate what we are'. His strident polemic barely hides a profound unease with the state of his culture. A harmless television commercial which portrays a young Englishman going off to the exotic Third World to discover himself manifestly touches a raw nerve. Appleyard lectures his readers:

> There is one final layer of intellectual corruption that needs to be exposed – cultural relativism. This is the most deeply hidden of all because it is the deadening conviction that all cultures are equal and that therefore, ours is of no special value. It can even be glimpsed in the current moronic Nationwide Building Society television advertisement in which dancing natives carrying spears are unquestioningly characterised as springing from an 'older, wiser' culture.[60]

Clearly no one remotely confident in his or her culture would react with such emotion to a commercial soliciting business for a building society.

The very discussion of culture is symptomatic of unease and insecurity. Ruling elites that are confident of their societies need not express concern that dancing natives with spears are about to subvert their youth. Appleyard is even concerned about the corrupting influence of Teenage Mutant Ninja Turtles on the British way of life. According to Appleyard what makes these turtles 'objectionable' is the assumption that 'society is in disarray and the authorities are too corrupt and incompetent to do anything about it.' To make matters worse, the heroes represent non-Western culture in their use of alien martial arts. Appleyard's explanation for favouring British boxing over Eastern martial arts represents a *tour de force* in contemporary culturalism:

> There is ... a critical difference between boxing and the martial arts. Both impose a regime of austerity, health and a degree of puritanical rectitude on their practitioners. But boxing feeds back into the culture; the martial arts oppose it – and it this opposition which is exploited by the Turtles film. It says Western values have failed, only those alien systems can protect us.[61]

The cultural anxieties that this statement expresses are significant. Appleyard is saying that one's culture is weakened if positive qualities are attached to the cultures of others. From this it follows that the assertion of one culture must be at the expense of another; multiculturalism necessarily represents the denial of a particular culture. This conclusion is based on the premise that culture cannot yield anything of itself to another without losing its quality as a unique special inheritance. Multiculturalism thus at the very least implies competing identities. Worse still, the very term 'multi' deprives culture of a capacity to confer identity.

Multiculturalism confers an element of choice which directly contradicts the immutability of a tradition based on the past. Consequently conservatives experience multiculturalism as an attack on *their* culture and a negation of national identity. Enoch Powell, the leading political thinker of the British right, expounded these concerns in his 1981 speech to the Thurrock Conservative Association:

> The presence of a common status where there was no common nationhood had produced in the cities of England a concentration of other nationals who asserted the contradictory claim to belong – and yet not to belong – to this nation ... So far our response has been to attempt to force upon ourselves a non-identity and to assert that we have no unique distinguishing characteristics: the formula is "a multiracial, multicultural society". A nation which thus deliberately denies its continuity with its past and its rootedness in its homeland is on the way to repudiate its existence.[62]

Not everyone concerned with the representation of national identity would put the argument with such force. But it is Powell's merit to have drawn out the intellectual consequences of the logic of national identity creation. Multiculturalism destroys the carefully nurtured singularity of national identity. It also calls into question the carefully crafted unique past of British History. Nineteenth-century historicists and opponents of Enlightenment thought would have instictively empathised with Powell's warning.

Even the free-market pretensions of the liberal and libertarian right cannot evade Powell's logic. Their common concern for stability and order leads to a common commitment to uphold an exclusive identity and hence an exclusive culture. So the old Cold War liberal Daniel Bell is more worried about the reaction to racism than racism itself. He seems to yearn for the good old days before race was a hotly contested issue and notes:

> Since no group can now claim explicit superiority, each group can emphasize its own language, religion, and culture as of intrinsic value and can assert a pride in the aggressive declaration of one's own ethnicity.[63]

Bell of course is happy to uphold the 'superiority' of his own nation, which he says is patriotism, not aggressive ethnicity. It is interesting to note that whenever Bell uses the term 'racism' in connection with white America, he puts quotation marks around it, to scare off the reader.[64] Even a self-professed liberal and opponent of state control such as Friedrich Hayek, the leading postwar theoretician of free enterprise, seems prepared to compromise when the issue of race is at stake. David Edgar has shown that Hayek justified support for strict immigration controls in order 'to prevent an unpleasant reawakening of primitive instincts'.[65]

Culture is a particularly acute problem for the American establishment. The breakdown of the melting-pot model and the growth of particularistic and ethnic-based claims to culture ensure that the question of identity becomes a permanent issue on the political agenda. In the United States more then anywhere in the West there is a manifest absence of intellectual consensus of what constitutes national culture. The debate on Western Civilization courses at Stanford and other universities in the 1980s illustrates this problem.

In America the question of culture does not pertain only to education. The very meaning of American is contested. In addition there are major linguistic conflicts, whereby ethnic groups demand language rights. An article in an American conservative publication warns: 'The spectre of linguistic diversity in turn has sparked insecurity about national cohesion and fostered a movement to designate English as the official language of the United States.'[66] The highly charged atmosphere of this debate shows the fragile foundation on which the American identity is built. The very attempt to use education to promote a particular tradition and culture has the effect of exposing the absence of a collective identity.

Finally, some of the more subtle attacks on multiculturalism suggest that the celebration of one culture need not be at the expense of another. This contention of culture neutrality, however well-meant, misses the main point of the controversy. At the end of the day *culture is a euphemism for nationalism.* Culture is not about ethnic food or music or literature. It is above all a representation of nationalism. The projection of culture coincides with the development of nationalism. Benda is right to draw the connection between this development and the 'war of cultures'.[67]

The clearest connection between culture and national conflict is to be found in the archives. A memorandum written by the British Ministry of Information and Political Warfare Executive during the Second World War spells out the implication of the cultural war. Culture was to be mobilised to contain American competition:

> In striving to hold our own as a World Power in competition with America – and it is as well to admit quite frankly that, however excellent our relations with America, the element of competition will never be altogether eliminated – we enjoy a peculiar advantage in the cultural field; an advantage which people in many parts of the world, such as Latin America and the Iberian peninsula, would be only too glad to see us exploit.[68]

Culture was also to be used as a weapon against France. Since its military defeat by Nazi Germany, the 'cultural and intellectual leadership which France formerly exercised is no longer accepted', argued the memorandum. Self-flattery was the order of the day. The memorandum hyped up the advantages that British culture had over the rest:

> Many of the peoples, both in Europe and outside it, who formerly looked to France for leadership in this sphere are now looking to

Britain; and it is essential that we should respond to this challenge, and prepare ourselves to accept such a position both in Europe and further afield. In undertaking this task, we have certain definite advantages over both our potential rivals ... Over Russia we have the advantage that English is a more universal language than Russian, and that British culture is not linked to a suspect ideology. Over America we have the advantage of a superior indigenous cultural tradition, and of greater proximity, both physical and spiritual, to Europe.[69]

No doubt similar documents are to be found in the archives of all the other main powers.

The intimate connection between nationalism and culture continues to this day. The reaction against multiculturalism is motivated by fears that it restrains the consistent projection of a nationalist identity. William Bennett's assertive stance on Western culture has nothing to do with his love for Plato, Voltaire or Freud. As he states: 'the West is under attack', so it must be defended. He adds boastfully: 'those who attack Western values and accomplishments do not see an America that – despite its imperfections, its weaknesses, its sins – has served and continues to serve as a beacon to the world.'[70]

Defending the West

No treatise on the need for history or calls for the affirmation of traditional values and morality is complete without at least an aside which celebrates the West. At first sight it would seem difficult to justify the West as an appropriate subject in a discussion of the moral impasse. Yet for all that it is one of the most systematically discussed concepts in the writings of those concerned with reviving History.

As a concept, the West is almost never analysed nor defined. It seems to have more of a philosophical than a geographical existence. Sometimes Japan is included under this rubric. At the very least it stretches from Australia to Austria. The lack of definite content seems to confer advantage: its meaning fluctuates between a way of life, a civilisation, a tradition and a political outlook. Its plasticity allows it to be pragmatically deployed. The West has been defined in relation to the Soviet bloc and also in relation to the Third World.

In the field of identity creation, the main use of the term 'the West' has been to evoke a long and successful tradition, associated with Judaism, Christianity, Classical Greece and Rome as well as the industrial spirit of capitalism. During the Cold War, the West had an important legitimising role. Stories of the past which emphasised the continuity of the Western way of life – what Albert Soboul has aptly characterised as 'NATO History' – were an important ideological resource. This type of history equated lofty values such as democracy, freedom, reason and progress with the essence of Western civilisation. Novick has commented that this 'reification "of the West", and the identification of its heritage with the struggle for freedom, was no small contribution to American ideological mobilization.'[71] This mobilisation was pursued as a clearcut ideological crusade. It was in this vein that David Owen, a professor of history at Harvard, described a course on Western civilisation as helping to discredit 'facile generalizations' such as those of Marxism and other 'ideologies'.[72]

The West and the celebration of its civilisation has been particularly prevalent in the United States. The reason for this is the relative brevity of the US past and tradition. A more usable tradition has been constructed by anchoring the American identity in the virtues and achievements of Greece and Rome. High points in human achievement were brought together into a process – Greece, Rome, Western Europe – which was shown to culminate chronologically in the American way of life.

The celebration of the West was by no means restricted to the United States. As will become clearer, it has been central to the ideological discourse of all Western capitalist societies. Although the ideological role of the concept of the West is manifest, it would be wrong to reduce its mobilisation to a cynically manipulated propaganda.

The West as signifier of a tradition and as focus for identification has been under discussion throughout this century. There is a considerable body of literature dating from around the beginning of the century which deals with issues like the decline of the West or the future prospects of the Western way of life. This literature often tends to combine an upbeat account of the virtues of this civilisation with a sense of resignation about its future. Spengler's work *The Decline of the West* provides the prototype. Most works on the subject contain a warning to the West. For example Chirol's book *The Occident and the Orient*, published in 1924, warns about the 'revolt of the Orient' and the 'dangerous issue of racial conflict between the white man and the colored peoples who constitute the vast majority of mankind'. Chirol hopes that conflicts between Western nations will disappear since 'broadly speaking' they all belong 'to the same type of civilization'.[73]

This common bond which binds all members of the 'same' civilisation together becomes important in the History created in the period after the Second World War.

After 1945 the projection of the West repeated many of the old themes, such as anxiety regarding decline. But the terms of the discussion had changed and the motives behind the elaboration of the concept had altered. Western liberal and conservative intellectuals were now concerned with the negative consequences that the growth of anti-imperialism and the assertion of the Third World could have for the moral claims of the West. The negative connotations that Western expansion acquired in the post-1945 period coincided with attempts to claim a moral authority on behalf of the Third World. The sensitivity of the Western intelligentsia to these claims is shown by the sheer volume of their replies. Often books authored by conservative and liberal thinkers on ostensibly domestic concerns contain an obligatory defence of the West. Let us take a few examples.

Daniel Bell's *Sociological Journeys* invites the reader at several points to dismiss Third World ideology, which plays on 'liberal guilt about racism and imperialism' and its 'moral claims for redressing poverty and exploitation'. By associating anti-imperialist sentiments with that of guilt, Bell is able to dismiss this standpoint as unworthy of an objective social scientist. In any case, says Bell, there is nothing to feel guilty about since America at its worst is more virtuous than the Third World at its best:

> For all the domestic ills or foreign 'crimes' of the United States, its record as a civilized society commands respect – especially compared to the savageries of the Soviet Union or Germany or the newer states of Rwanda, Burundi, or Uganda – and we need not be apologetic on that score.[74]

This prototypical manipulation of national pasts has become a standard formula for rehabilitating Western domination of the rest of the world.

There are a variety of arguments used to defend the special claims of the West. One of the most common is the association of the promotion of the individual and of individual rights with Western civilisation.[75] In contrast Bloom is of the view that only in the West is there a concept of good that is separate from individual interest.[76] Many writers claim that the past itself is proof of the special character of the West. Western civilisation thus becomes synonymous with the only past worth having.

For the British conservative historian there are no 'new ideas on the horizon which could effectively challenge ours in a free encounter' as long as 'the West still has leaders with a sense of historic past'.[77] Upholding this past has become something of a sacred duty for Paul Johnson, who insists that 'civilisation not only has a right but a positive and imperative duty to defend itself' for 'we are the beneficiaries of the past and, more important, the trustees of the future.'[78] From this viewpoint, the West becomes a distillation of the major past achievements of humanity.

For some conservatives the worth of the West is established on mystical and quasi-racial grounds. Roger Scruton makes clear his dislike for fashion when he observes that 'it is unfashionable to say that Western civilization still lives, that it is nobler, better and more worthy of survival than its rivals, and that we ought to cease our childish lamentations and give ourselves to its defence.'[79]

The constant repetition of the theme of guilt by the advocates of the West reveals their own insecurities about the Western tradition. It is analogous to the uncertainties about culture. There is one important difference between the West and the other traditions discussed in this chapter: right from the end of the Second World War, the West was the one tradition constantly expounded by all sections of bourgeois thought. Liberals, social democrats, conservatives and others could disagree or have different emphases on culture, morality, the nation or interpretations of the past. The one tradition that they all held in common was that of the West. As a result this tradition acquired a central position in the subsequent evolution of bourgeois thought.

The postwar bourgeois consensus concerning the West cannot be dismissed as simply a reaction to perceptions of a challenge from the Third World. Those perceptions were widespread and help explain the sheer quantity of defensive literature, but other important motives also prompted the glorification of the West. To put it bluntly: *the Western idea became the last refuge for the expression of a sense of superiority and of uniqueness.* In the aftermath of Nazism and the Holocaust, racism and even nationalism stood intellectually discredited. Moral unity and collective confidence could no longer be constructed on the old basis. The West not only provided a tradition that was not soiled by previous experience, it could also offer an alternative to the ideological challenge posed by the Soviet Union. So the idea of the West can convey a sense of superiority because it does so in a

philosophical form. For the editor of *The Times Higher Education
Supplement*, 'the idea of Europe' is a 'civilising principle', a 'model of
modernity', an expression of 'universalism'. At a time when all 'Big
Ideas are compromised', we are reminded that 'Europe was, and is,
a Big Idea'.[80]

The importance of the West is illustrated through the writings of
liberal intellectuals who were bitterly hostile to nationalism and the
tradition it embodied but who were fervent propagandists for the
Western cause – particularly a number of prominent Jewish
intellectuals who were deeply alienated by what they perceived as
nationalist excesses. This trend is personified by Hans Kohn, an
eloquent foe of nationalist historiography. Kohn was deeply
concerned to encourage a liberal tradition that could counteract the
danger of the revival of German nationalist history.[81] At the same time
he stridently sought to boost confidence in a non-national and liberal
tradition, which he associated with Western civilisation.

Kohn's polemic against the pessimism expressed by the historian
Arnold Toynbee in his writings on Western civilisation indicated the
importance Kohn attaches to this tradition. He interrogates Toynbee:

> Why does he emphasise so much the fact that Western civilization
> is not the only one, that it does not tower as fulfilment over all
> others, and that no civilization is final or immortal?[82]

Kohn's incomprehension of Toynbee's lack of commitment to the
West is based on an unambiguous belief in the superiority of Western
principles. 'I cannot share Mr. Toynbee's overcritical attitude to
modern Western civilization ... modern Western civilization has set
new and to me higher standards of respect for the individual, of social
responsibility, and of critical inquiry, than any preceding civilization.'[83] It never occurs to Kohn that his own approach to Western
civilisation is not dissimilar to the approach to the nation which he so
strongly objects to in nineteenth-century German historians. Western civilisation provided a mask for the representation of particularist
interests. The interests of Western governments were conveyed
through what had previously been an anti-particularist intellectual
programme.

Kohn is by no means alone. Virtually all the main theoreticians from
both the liberal and conservative camps expressed this standpoint
during the Cold War. The high priest of individualism and the free
market, Ludwig von Mises, ominously reported how 'other races take

pleasure in plotting white man's destruction.' His support for
Western civilisation was unequivocal because of the 'sphere of
spontaneous action it secures to the individual'.[84] The transatlantic
French intellectual Raymond Aron took strong exception to the
suggestion that the West was finished. He wrote:

> Europe has two reasons for refusing to regard itself as decadent. It
> was Europe's achievements, and later its military follies, that
> brought humanity to the threshold of the universal age. In an age
> in which men no longer need to tyrannize each other to be able to
> exploit natural resources, Europe can still be great if it conforms to
> the spirit of the new age by helping other peoples cure themselves
> of the childhood diseases of modernism.[85]

By setting the standards, and teaching others to solve their problems,
the superiority of Western civilisation is almost casually reasserted.

As the next chapter will show, the assertion of the West has gradually led to the adoption of a stridently anti-Third World posture.
Uncertainties about culture have led intellectuals from Europe and
America to justify their way of life by extremely negative comparisons
with the Third World. Not all would go as far as the editor of the
Sunday Telegraph, who chillingly reminded his readers that 'an ugly,
evil spirit is abroad in the Third World and it cannot be condoned:
only crushed, as Carthage was crushed by the Romans',[86] but on the
substance of this warning there is an impressive consensus. Pro-
Western civilisation and anti-Third World sentiments are common
among those who argue for the revival of nationalist history in the
major capitalist powers.

Absolutes and relatives in history

The uncertainties expressed concerning social cohesion, culture, tradition and morality are often represented as a debate between absolute
and relative values. In historiography and other fields of intellectual
endeavour, the conservative agenda characteristically aims to legitimise absolute values. The object of conservative scorn is variously
described as relativism, cultural relativism, moral relativism or value
relativism.

The reaction against relativism encompasses all shades of thought
committed to the defence of the status quo. This reaction is motivated

by the fear that scepticism has gone too far. It is argued that openness and criticism has destroyed the consensus around social values: the denial that any values are intrinsically superior to others has led to the erosion of the distinction between right and wrong. An intellectual posture which equivocates on these questions is held by conservatives to be morally corrosive.

Bloom's reaction to the education of 'openness' illustrates the reaction against relativism. Bloom objects to a form of thought that critically questions everything, especially the past, as it 'pays no attention to natural rights or the historical origins of our regime'. If even the national past is not above questioning then new generations are left with nothing to believe in, according to Bloom, who warns: 'Thus openness has driven out the local deities, leaving only the speechless, meaningless country'.[87] Without an unproblematic tradition to uphold, the nation loses its meaning, leading to moral chaos. This theme is also pursued by Newt Gingrich, the right-wing Republican party whip. Gingrich claims that the moral relativism of the liberal establishment is sapping the nation's will, akin to the way the moral collapse of the French Third Republic led to the humilation of 1940.[88] Gingrich's extravagant claims are an acceptable part of right-wing discourse in the United States, where relativism is often attacked as if it was a kind of moral treason.[89]

Other objections to relativism stress that if everything is put to question then, logically, nothing can make sense. Gellner attacks 'permissive relativism' as a 'charter for dismissing intellectual coherence'.[90] Scruton is concerned that relativism threatens the 'sense of the sacred'; he fears a world 'without the sacred' where 'all is permitted, and where nothing has absolute value.'[91] The corollary of this proposition is that without absolute values there is no sense of restraint, no moral sanctions or codes. This represents the intellectual expression of moral impasse.

One of the ironies of history is that the growth of relativism, to which the right so vehemently objects, has as its intellectual origins the conservative reaction to the Enlightenment. At the intellectual level this reaction took a strong exception to the claims of objectivity, rationalism and universalism put forward by the Enlightenment. It sought to preserve tradition by claiming that individual and cultural values could not be assessed by any objective criteria; they were either the product of divine intervention or the prejudice produced through the experience of time. As Burke put it: 'instead of casting away all our old prejudices, we cherish them to a very considerable degree ...

and the longer they have lasted, and the more generally they have prevailed, the more we cherish them.'[92]

The defence of tradition thus coincided with the endorsement of the particular against the universal and the subjective against the objective. Although this response characterised the conservative reaction in Europe as a whole, the German historicist school elaborated it most clearly. This philosophy denied the possibility of a rational and objective consideration of history. Stressing the particular and individual, it questioned the common/universal process. This led to a deeply relativistic, almost arbitrary, representation of the historical process. As Iggers wrote, this standpoint 'assumes that there are no universally valid values'. At the same time, however, all values are culture-bound and since all 'cultural phenomena are emanations of divine will' they represent 'true values'.[93] This recognition of particularistic truths existed within a broad relativistic framework. Above a specific culture there could be no universal values.

In the case of German conservatives the relativisation of values did not lead to scepticism regarding the status of tradition. Values were relative but they were also true for the culture or people concerned. In this way a strong sense of faith could coincide with a relativist view of values. Iggers points to a contradiction in the 'historicist attempt to base a positive faith in a meaningful universe on historical relativism.'[94] He suggests that at the time this contradiction was resolved by the deep attachment of the German conservatives to a moral world: 'What preserved them from ethical and epistemological relativism was their deep faith in a metaphysical reality beyond the historical world.'[95] Hughes confirms this point: 'the problem of the relativity of individual judgments troubled Ranke scarcely at all: he had his religious faith to sustain him.'[96]

Nevertheless there is an inescapable conflict between relativism and faith. When faith gives way to questioning then relativism can lead to a total breakdown of coherence. Relativism, even when qualified, necessarily has a corrosive effect on faith. What the Hungarian Marxist Georg Lukacs characterised as the 'outbreak of a bottomless relativism and agnosticism' is evident in the writings of Nietzsche. In his preface to *The Will to Power*, Nietzsche sees only a future of 'nihilism'.[97] Nietzsche attacks conventional faith in the old morals and Christianity not because he is against faith as such but because that faith did not work. What now remains is the relativism but not the faith. This shift can be seen in the development of historicism. The nineteenth century historicist characteristically expressed the sentiment of faith. In the twentieth century, historicists often self-consciously became sceptics. With the twentieth-century American historian Carl Becker the relativity of all historical judgements is fully established.[98]

The growth of pessimism with the Enlightenment in the late nineteenth century, often described as the 'revolt against positivism', did not work entirely to the advantage of conservative thought. It led to the growth of relativism but not to the strengthening of faith. There was a growing tendency to question the objective view of history, but after the experience of the previous century faith in tradition could not be restored. Max Weber's fact / value distinction can be seen as the most sophisticated attempt to respond to the twin questioning of the objectivity of science and the faith in tradition. When he argued 'that it is one thing to state facts, to determine mathematical or logical relations or the internal structure of cultural values, while it is another thing to answer questions of the *value* of culture and its individual contents', Weber established a framework where objectivity in science could coexist with the most irrational prejudice in the realm of values.[99] As Istvan Meszaros argues, Weber's 'extreme *relativization of values*' is coupled with the 'glorification of arbitrary *subjectivity* and of its dubious accommodation to the "demand of the day", as required by the established order.'[100] Weber, concerned with the problem of social order, provides an intellectual defence of tradition. By separating the question of objectivity from the consideration of value, tradition can be defended simply on grounds that are entirely arbitrary.

Weber's reconciliation of objective facts with the relativisation of values did not restore the appeal of tradition. Rather the relativist perspective which the conservative had used as a stick with which to beat Enlightenment rationality was now turned on the claims of tradition and absolute values. In the nineteenth century cultural relativism could shield tradition against the claims of universalism. Not so this century. In an age of scepticism the view that all values are true gave place to the perception that no values are absolutes.

In the field of history, the scepticism of the early twentieth century led to the questioning of the authority of the past. The least traditional of all capitalist nations, the USA, led the way. According to Hughes:

No European historian of the early twentieth century was willing to throw in his hand and confess to total relativity of historical judgements. It was an American, Carl Becker, who finally had the bravery – or the sense of intellectual defeat – to affirm that 'everyman' was 'his own historian'.[101]

According to Novick's excellent study of American historiography, a sense of disillusionment and disorientation was widespread in the profession. Novick indicates that during the first half of this century, cultural and ethical relativism became increasingly influential in American history.

Historical relativism became a growing intellectual phenomenon throughout the West. It took an extremely pessimistic posture in Germany. Karl Heussi, in *Die Krise des Historismus*, wrote of a collapse of belief in the objective study of history.[102] The experience of the Second World War gave a tremendous boost to a relativist interpretation of history. Nationalist history, with its special claim to represent the truth, was palpably in retreat. At the same time the optimistic belief in progress and science were rudely shattered by a barbaric war. Cynicism about objectivity and truth was coupled with a dense scepticism about old articles of faith.

Cultural relativism, which in the nineteenth century was part of the conservative ideological baggage, thus became associated with the postwar left's assault on absolute values. A History which purported to proclaim the truth was increasingly characterised as propaganda. The following dismissal of objective history by Dance characterised the mood of the 1960s:

In fact, there can be no such thing as objective history. Historians (honest or dishonest) are no more objective than witnesses (honest or dishonest) in a law-court, no two of them give the same account of the same thing.[103]

The widespread questioning of objectivity was coupled with criticism and even ridicule of tradition and of absolute values. It is to the prevalence of this trend that the conservatives of today so strenuously object.

The return of the absolute

Until recently there was little serious intellectual effort to recover the legitimacy of absolute values. Throughout most of this century, bourgeois thought has been concerned to challenge what it considered to be the absolute faith and determinism of Marxism. To counter this threat, it was necessary to challenge any notion of objective laws of history and to restrict the field for rational human intervention.[104] As Hughes argues, the revolt against positivism was above all a reaction to the appeal of Marxism. 'To come to terms with Marxism, then, was the first and most obvious task confronting the intellectual innovators of the 1890s', writes Hughes.[105] The attack against Marxist 'determinism' led to the encouragement of scepticism.

In an intellectual climate of scepticism, conservative thinkers, as indeed liberals, felt distinctly uncomfortable. Except for a few isolated figures, they abandoned the project of restoring tradition. In the 1950s and 1960s those concerned with social order sought to limit the damage caused by extreme scepticism. For example Judith Shklar was concerned that the cynicism that prevailed in the 1950s might turn into social despair. Her solution was to offer a 'reasoned scepticism' for even 'scepticism is politically sounder and empirically more justifiable than cultural despair and fatalism.'[106]

Damage limitation through controlled scepticism was one option, but it still provided no answer to the problem posed by Shklar of the 'absence of permanent attachments' – the problem of tradition.

One of the most coherent attempts to tackle this is to be found in the writings of Isaiah Berlin. Berlin yearns for the days of nineteenth-century liberalism when the contradiction between the spirit of science and faith in absolute values could be easily resolved. He writes that 'rights described as "natural" or "inherent", absolute standards of truth and justice, were not compatible with tentative empiricism: yet liberals believed in both.'[107] Berlin is aware that the main alternative proposed against Marxist 'determinism' has been relativism, but the cost of this is too high, since it can lead to the renunciation of all moral values.

Berlin's solution is to reintroduce values into the facts of history. He does this by the affirmation of a moral order where rational value judgements can be made. His criticism of the absurdity of the relativisation of values, however, is far clearer than his solution. 'We are told that it is foolish to judge Charlemagne or Napoleon or Genghis Khan or Hitler or Stalin for their massacres, that it is at most a comment upon ourselves and not upon the "facts",' he states with irony.[108] However he is not able to provide a logical foundation for making judgements of value. Despite his liberalism Berlin is forced to recover the transcendental values from the historicist reaction to the Enlightenment.

Berlin's riposte to what he takes to be the standpoint of determinism indicates that he feels most comfortable with the conservative reaction to the Enlightenment. He writes:

> To accept this doctrine ... [determinism] ... is to do violence to the basic notions of our morality, to misrepresent our sense of the past, and to ignore some among the most general concepts and categories of normal thought. Those who are concerned with human affairs are committed to the use of moral categories and concepts which normal language incorporates and expresses.[109]

We are back with morals that are 'basic' and 'normal' because they correspond to 'our sense of the past'. The only ground for the affirmation of a commitment to moral categories is custom.

There is one small problem here. It is precisely the champions of custom and tradition, whose particularist outlook helped foster the climate of relativism, that Berlin so heartily dislikes. Berlin resolves this difficulty by arguing that 'so far as I can see' there is 'no relativism in the best-known attacks on the Enlightenment by reactionary thinkers – Hamann, Justus Moser, Burke, Maistre.'[110] In one sense Berlin is right. None of these reactionary thinkers were self-consciously relativist. But a relativist programme was the logical consequence of their particularist epistemology. And this is precisely the consequence that Berlin seeks to evade.

Berlin, writing during the mid-century, still hesitated to draw out the consequences of his arguments. Only during the past 15 or so years has a full-blown conservative offensive against relativism taken off. To some extent the moral collapse of the Stalinist system makes value-free judgements less necessary. With the decline of the main ideological alternative, capitalist thinkers can set about endorsing a system of values. There are other reasons for this revival of absolute values which will be considered in the next two chapters.

Finally, to anticipate our argument. The debate between absolute and relative values does not correspond to a clearcut political polarisation. Conservatives, who demand moral absolutes today, were the innovators of cultural relativism in the nineteenth century. Many on the left who endorse relativism today are apt to forget that transformative politics developed through Enlightenment thought with a strong commitment to objective truth. From the perspective of historical thinking, the upholding of absolute values requires the *eternalisation* of history and the renunciation of change. Relativism on the other hand robs history of coherence. History becomes arbitrary, random and purposeless. In a sense both positions reflect the present sense of moral impasse. A frantic plea for faith is the flip side of a cynical rejection of truth.

5

Attempts to recover absolutes

As indicated in the previous chapters, there was a close connection between the awareness of a moral impasse, the decline of absolutes and the demand for History. Sensitivity to the scale of these problems was particularly acute at the end of the Second World War, a time when the intellectual crisis of the Western world stood clearly exposed. This chapter is devoted to the examination of that crisis. It traces the themes that were the source of significant anxiety at the time and looks at the attempts to provide a solution. This chapter argues that the intellectual posture of the West remained defensive until the 1960s. The 1960s, not the decade but the *idea* of the 1960s, provided the focus for the counter-attack of the right. This targetting of the 1960s obscured the real source of the problem. The fundamental problems emerged earlier, during the years between the two world wars, when all the themes associated with the 1960s were already in rehearsal. This, 'the other 1960s', is the topic of Chapter 6.

If there is a single experience which dealt a severe body blow to nationalist history, belief in absolute values and identification with society, it is the Second World War. The Great War of 1914–18 had some effect, particularly on intellectuals. But the sense of pessimism it stimulated in intellectual circles between the wars was far less decisive than the more widespread malaise that invaded capitalist societies in the aftermath of the Second World War. Many who lived through the Great War expected that things would soon return to normal. The normal past seemed to be within the reach of society. It was possible to see a future which would be a continuation of the years before 1914.

After the end of the Second World War, it was not possible to think of a return to a normal past. The period pre-1939 was not susceptible to the romanticisation of that before 1914. On the contrary, the past embodied in the interwar years was one to be avoided. After

Hiroshima and Nagasaki, the future did not appear brilliant either. This was a time when pessimism became an overused word – a time when the past was uniquely incapable of inspiring any positive sentiments.

The intellectual crisis of the right

The Second World War forced the right on to the defensive. In particular it experienced a major disaster on the intellectual front. The war had undermined attachments to the past and to tradition and had discredited the concepts of nationalism and national destiny. Precisely these values had been closely identified with the Hitler regime as well and its allies in Italy and Japan. This association of right-wing values with fascism and the perceived causes of war forced explicit conservative ideas to the margins of social thought. As Daniel Bell observed:

> Since World War II had the character of a 'just war' against fascism, right-wing ideologies, and the intellectual and cultural figures associated with those causes, were inevitably discredited. After the preponderant reactionary influence in prewar European culture, no single right-wing figure retained any political creditability or influence.[1]

This was the time when even genuine right-wing thinkers were too embarrassed to present their views in an undiluted form.

The recent past was the first casualty of the intellectual reorientation after 1945. This predicament was most acutely experienced in Germany, followed by Japan and to a lesser extent Italy. A past that is equated with shame is not one that can be used as a source of inspiration or authority. The depth of this dissociation from the past can be seen in the intensity of historical controversies in Germany in the postwar era. The historian Wolfgang Mommsen outlined this predicament which continues to exercise the energy of the German establishment:

> It has become more obvious than ever that the Nazi period stands in the way of reconstructing a notion of German national history which could provide the basis for a decent image of the German past. Is the National Socialist period an aberration from the normal

path of redevelopment which does not really belong to German history, or did it grow out of a trend in German history?[2]

The memory of fascism directly counteracts the project of providing a 'decent image of the German past'.

Indirectly Mommsen touches upon a problem which has implications that are wider than the German past. Whether or not National Socialism was an aberration from the normal path of German history was not the only question asked in the 1940s. Another question sometimes posed was whether the capitalist system had anything to do with the growth of fascism. It was widely held – and not just in Marxist circles – that there was some connection. Consequently fascism tended to discredit traditional right-wing ideas beyond the borders of Germany. Even today there is some sensitivity to the charge that sections of the French or British establishment may have compromised themselves through their association with fascism. It has been suggested that the secrecy that shrouds the Hess affair in Britain and the refusal to open the archives is a symptom of this sensitivity. Richard Norton-Taylor, writing in the *Guardian*, suggests that 'what is clear is that Whitehall, even 50 years on, is determined to cover up the extent of a peace faction which was more worried about Bolshevism than the threat posed by the Nazis.'[3] Whether Norton-Taylor is right about the specifics is unimportant. What matters is the perception that the British establishment remains sensitive on this issue.

The damage that the Nazi experience inflicted on right-wing ideas internationally is illustrated by the sensitivity of Anglo-American liberal and conservative intellectuals to the thesis that fascism was linked to capitalism.[4] Mommsen argues convincingly that the 'relative popularity' of the theory of totalitarianism is 'explained by the need to provide for a liberal alternative to the Comintern's theory of fascism.'[5] Mommsen adds that in Germany themes critical of capitalism in the early totalitarian theories, for example Franz L. Neumann's *Behemoth*, 'completely faded into the background'. Moreover in school texts the 'positing of totalitarian structures and modes of thought has been largely set apart from socioeconomic spheres of interest and concrete social conditions.'[6] The capitalist socioeconomic framework of the Germany of the 1930s became simply a non-issue.

Fascism was not the only blot on the recent past. After 1945 past achievements to do with empire and race had become an embarrassment. The German ruling class did not have a monopoly on racism,

and after Hitler all the Western powers were to some extent forced
on the defensive on this subject. Before the outbreak of the Second
World War the use of the racist concepts which characterised Nazi
ideology were barely questioned in the West. According to Rich, 'the
outbreak of war in 1939 acted as a shock wave on many British
anthropologists, who began to ask why no greater stand had been
made in the 1930s against the use of anthropology in racist and Nazi
ideologies.'[7]

More broadly, Western governments were finding the race issue
difficult to handle. In the past race awareness had been integral to the
elaboration of a sense of national superiority. After the consequences
of Nazi racism became apparent such a standpoint fell into disrepute.
Western racism provoked strong reactions in the Third World and
threatened to undermine the European empires. The British Ministry
of Information was convinced that it possessed no moral authority on
this question, therefore it was best not to say anything. The first plan
for imperial wartime propaganda to the West Indies warned: 'where
possible, we should avoid drawing attention to the existence of a
colour problem.'[8] The American government too was concerned with
the race issue. Reports indicated that many blacks considered the
conflict to be a white men's war.[9]

Imperialism too was becoming something of an embarrassment.
Until the 1930s, the term 'imperialism' tended to have a positive
connotation in the vocabulary of the British establishment. They and
others were taken aback when what hitherto served as a source of
inspiration turned into a term of abuse. 'There are people', wrote Sir
Philip Mitchell, the Governor of Kenya in 1947, 'in our country and
abroad, who call all this "British Imperialism" and mean it as a term
of abuse.' This was a not inconsiderable shock to someone who saw
in the imperial idea an 'expression of faith and purpose'.[10] By 1947 Sir
Philip was very much behind the times, but he was by no means alone
in expressing this view.

Nationalism, race, Western superiority, imperialism; virtually the
entire political vocabulary of the right was put under critical scrutiny.
Clearly it was not only the German ruling class that had something
to live down. A discredited past was also a problem elsewhere. This
point is alluded to by Lord Annan in relation to Britain in his
contribution to a symposium on the German History Debate:

All nations live with guilt of one kind or another. My own
generation in Britain lived with a mild form of guilt. This took the

form of shame about what happened in the nineteenth-century industrial revolution, the poverty, the slums, and unemployment. This mild form of guilt affected our writing of history, and certainly our way of looking at politics. From 1945 until 1979 there was a consensus in British politics that we should try to eliminate this stain in our national life ... There was incidentally another form of guilt which the British lived with – guilt about imperialism and the way they had treated their colonies and India.[11]

By the careful use of the words 'mild' and 'guilt' Annan sought to minimise the problem, which was that the past as it had been traditionally presented had become discredited.

Government propaganda statements during the Second World War consciously reflected these problems and now promised that the 'abuses of the past' would not be allowed to reappear in peacetime.[12] The very fact that the past was now coupled with the word 'abuse' indicated that it had been weakened as a potential source of legitimacy. Previously the past had had an unblemished record and therefore provided instant authority. But once it was conceded that there were abuses, the use of a tarnished past became problematic. Tradition, culture and nationalist history were the other casualties in this setback suffered by the past.

A palpable sense of estrangement from the past counteracted the revival of intellectual optimism in the West in the postwar years. T. S. Eliot, one of the most respected cultural figures of the right, summed up the mood in 1948:

We can assert with some confidence that our own period is one of decline; that the standards of culture are lower than they were fifty years ago; and that the evidences of this decline are visible in every department of human activity.[13]

The sense of regression and failure is evident in the literature of the right in this period. Unable to justify its intellectual tradition, the right opted for a strategic retreat from the intellectual battlefield.

The sense of exhaustion which affected conservatives also inflicted liberal thinkers of the time. Writing in 1949, Daniel Bell drew a picture of cultural impasse and intellectual exhaustion:

For out of the confusions and exhaustions of war, a new non-political attitude is spreading, typified by the French *je m'en fiche*

(I don't give a damn), and the Italian *fanno schiffo tutti* (they all stink), in which the sole desire of the great masses of people is simply to be left alone. Conscripted, regimented, manipulated, disoriented in the swirl of ideological warfare, the basic and growing attitude is one of distrust. And [for] the intellectual, the seed-bearers of culture, the feeling is one of betrayal by power, and the mood is one of impotence.[14]

The sense of distrust and cynicism toward belief conveyed by Bell greatly undermined the appeal of absolute values.

Yet Bell and other liberals understood that the West needed something to believe in. The old absolute values associated with the tradition of conservatism could not be revived. Karl Mannheim argued for a 'new militant democracy' in 1941. This standpoint 'will differ from the relativist *laissez-faire* of the previous age, as it will have the courage to agree on some basic values which are acceptable to everybody who shares the traditions of Western civilization.'[15] Mannheim was less then precise about what would constitute these basic values. Values 'inherited from classical antiquity and even more from Christianity' were mentioned.

Mannheim's project failed because it sought an artificial solution to the crisis of legitimacy. In the absence of plausible absolute values, liberal thinkers in the United States came up with what was to become the main ruling-class response to this problem in the 1940s and 1950s: they attacked all strongly held views as suspect and decreed that moral faith could be sustained through repelling all extremes. The key text to outline this perspective was *The Vital Center*, by Arthur Schlesinger.

Schlesinger, like most Cold War thinkers, linked the problem of social cohesion to the threat posed by communism. His response was to discredit intellectually all forms of extremism, fanaticism or utopianism, terms which often seem to be euphemisms for those who challenge the status quo. Schlesinger preached a hyper-realistic message which verged on the fatalistic. 'We must grow up now and forsake the millennial dreams', he warns. This realism was designed to deflate expectations, which Schlesinger said were artificially pumped up by ideologues. Schlesinger's alternative was the 'spirit of the new radicalism', which was 'the spirit of the center – the spirit of human decency opposing the extremes of tyranny'.[16]

The Vital Center represents what was later to be known as the 'end of ideology' thesis. It represented a concession to the postwar crisis of belief. By renouncing all systems of strongly held beliefs, it sought to make a virtue of the lack of belief in any basic values in the West. At the same time it could also be mobilised in the Cold War against what were characterised as radical extremist ideologies. The ideology of 'end of ideology', that is the ideology of moderation, provided a provisional solution to the decline of absolute values.

Schlesinger's solution exposed the irrelevance of the classical conservative tradition. This tradition had to give way to the pragmatic approach which renounced all strongly held absolutes. Conservatives at the time and to this day have grasped just how much they lost the intellectual and political initiative in the 1940s. In some cases there is still a sense of disbelief about the 'disillusionment with nationalism resulting from the efforts of one nation state, led by a madman, to conquer the world.'[17] But a recognition of the enormity of this intellectual collapse is generally not matched by a comprehension of how it happened. In particular conservatives are not prepared to recall the unpalatable fact that, while in a state of intellectual paralysis, their postwar predecessors willingly allowed liberals to take the initiative and to assume responsibility for tackling the problems.

Those liberal thinkers who attempted to construct a pragmatic alternative were aware that by abandoning the classical traditional values they risked losing altogether the authority of the past. Raymond Aron, French social philosopher and probably the most successful transatlantic representative of the end-of-ideology standpoint, attempted to reformulate the relativist–absolutist couplet. He attacked relativism on the grounds that it robbed history of any meaning and criticised absolutism for claiming to monopolise meaning. In Aron's model, meanings could be drawn but not *the* meaning. He argued that 'history is not absurd, but no living being can grasp its one, final meaning.'[18]

In Aron's schema, meaning now had a more modest status than previously. In practice it was difficult to give meaning new content without falling into the artificiality of Mannheim's renovated values. Aron's resolution of this dilemma was to abandon philosophical speculation and promote American economic prosperity as a meaningful model. He was distinctly upbeat about this model in 1957 when he wrote:

Yet in spite of the deep-rooted American racial prejudice, discrimination is growing less severe and the condition of the negroes has steadily improved. The struggle of the American soul between the principle of human equality and the colour bar deserves to be treated with understanding. The United States remains optimistic after the fashion of the European eighteenth century: it believes in the possibility of improving man's lot; it distrusts the power which corrupts; it is still basically hostile to authority, to the pretensions of the few to know all the answers better than the common man. There is no room there for the Revolution or for the proletariat – only for economic expansion, trade unions and the constitution.[19]

The image of an economically successful United States became the object of confidence. Economic success was its own justification, minimising the problem of values. In the same way the West German establishment hoped that its economic track record would compensate for its lack of legitimacy. The other side of model America was anti-Soviet Cold War propaganda. Aron's denunciation of 'fanaticism' was directed across the Cold War divide.

Even while liberals such as Aron and Schlesinger were evolving a compromise formula, others were trying to revive absolute values. This was to culminate in the conservative offensive of the late 1970s.

Containing the Nazi legacy

The Nazi episode not only limits the viability of the recent German past but also raises questions about the past that preceded it. If this episode can be shown to be the outcome of the previous structures of German society then the past indeed loses its ability to confer legitimacy. This episode also raises wider questions about the past. If the Nazi experience developed in response to the demands of German capitalism then does not this cast doubts on the legitimacy of the capitalist system in other societies? During the 1950s and 1960s these questions dominated the furious controversies over the origins of the Nazi regime.

In this debate Marxist and other left-wing historians attempted to locate the Nazi regime within the framework of the capitalist crisis and the long-term trends of German history. In contrast, conservative and right-wing historians stressed the peculiar and unusual character of Nazism. They associated the singularity of the Nazi experience with the personality of Hitler and treated the period as an abberation from the previous past. As Eley argued:

Identifying Nazism with anti-Semitism, and in some cases with Hitler's personal psychic and ideological obsessions, can obscure its relationship to a larger constellation of right-wing interests and belief. Once the problem of Nazism has been circumscribed in this way, questions of deeper origins and of German society's broader responsibility – that is, the more difficult and disturbing questions of Nazism's structural rootedness in German society at large – are easier to keep from the agenda.[20]

Today attempts to explain the devastating consequences of this era, such as Hitler's Final Solution, on the basis of a structural explanation are invariably attacked as 'trivialising' a peculiar and unique experience. This actually represents an unintended concession to fascist historiography. The Nazi mystification of racial identity is converted into the point of departure for the mystification of fascism. As a result neither the crisis of German capitalism nor the Final Solution yield to rational enquiry.

The thesis that Nazism was the outcome of developmental tendencies immanent to capitalism has been under attack not only in Germany. Peter Novick's excellent treatment of the David Abraham case, which he describes as 'the best-publicized historical controversy of the 1980s' in the United States, serves as a useful example. Abraham's *The Collapse of the Weimar Republic: Political Economy and Crisis*, published in 1981, sought to argue that the authoritarian Nazi regime was the unintended consequence of the breakdown of capitalist society. This book raised a major furore in academic circles. Abraham was accused of fabrication and dishonesty and denounced as a fraud. Abraham conceded there were a number of errors in his book but argued that they were errors in transcription.

Although some reputable historians defended Abraham, he was hounded out of the history profession. The academic who led the witch-hunt, Henry Turner, argued in his book *German Big Business and the Rise of Hitler* that to accord big business a major role in the rise of the Nazi regime was to distort the facts. He argued that such anti-capitalist Marxist interpretations were deployed 'in an effort to discredit and undermine societies with capitalist economies and to legitimize repressive anti-capitalist regimes.'[21] Novick appears to suggest that the attack on Abraham was motivated by political considerations that were internal to the American history profession rather than to the issues raised by the controversy surrounding the roots of the Nazi regime. 'The ideological dimension of the dispute was more salient in Germany than in the United States', writes Novick.[22] No doubt Novick is right to draw attention to the importance of the dispute for German historical discourse, but at the same time it is important not to underestimate the relevance of the dispute for other Western capitalist societies.

The harsh reaction of some historians to the publication of Arno Mayer's *Why did the Heavens not Darken?* in 1989 illustrates the enduring sensitivity of this subject. Mayer's attempt to locate the 'Judeocide' within a wider structural setting stimulated some unusually hostile reviews in Britain and the United States.[23] Hostility towards any social analysis which links the German capitalist class to the Hitler regime has characterised the conservative and liberal literature since the late 1930s. There has been a systematic attempt to discredit this analysis, since any linkage between fascism and capitalism would seriously undermine the usability of the past. It is interesting to note that this wholly ideological campaign has rarely been explicitly recognised and commented on.

Today it may be difficult to recall the intensity of the concern that fascism caused those who argued the legitimacy of the capitalist system. In the late 1930s and 1940s advocates of capitalism were distinctly on the defensive. In 1940 the American Federal Trade Commission warned that 'the capitalist system of free initiative is quite capable of dying and dragging down with it the system of democratic government.' It contended that monopoly 'constitutes the death of capitalism and the genesis of authoritarian government.'[24] Many other analyses of the time perceived a connection between the monopolisation of economic power and the authoritarian political regime in Nazi Germany.

Many of the social theorists that are considered to be the seminal thinkers by contemporary conservative and liberal intellectuals took an active role in the dispute over the origins of the Nazi regime. Their aim was to recover the past and defend the legitimacy of the values of capitalist society. They put forward three propositions: firstly that fascism had little to do with the capitalist system, secondly that the real cause of fascism was not capitalism but Marxism, and thirdly that the fascist state is the mirror image of the Stalinist state. There were a number of variations on these and not all proponents of the argument supported all three propositions, but what characterises all theories of *totalitarianism* is the equation of the Nazi regime with that of the Soviet Union. Theories of totalitarianism sever any connection between fascism and capitalist social relations.

James Burnham, whose book *The Managerial Revolution* is considered one of the earliest systematic expositions of the theory of totalitarianism, was concerned that the belief 'that Nazi Germany is a form of decadent capitalism' was 'by no means confined to Marxists'.[25] His book is designed to show that Germany had become a managerial society with characteristics similar to the Soviet Union.

While Burnham drew a relation of symmetry between the regime of Stalin and that of Hitler, other totalitarian theorists were more concerned to show that fascism was *caused* by Marxism or socialism. In this way totalitarian thinkers not merely defended capitalism from the charge of compromising with fascism but went on the offensive, to charge socialists with the responsibility for causing this evil. Karl Popper, in his *Open Society and its Enemies*, sets the scene by holding the spiritual breakdown of Marxism responsible for the growth of fascism.[26]

Hayek, writing in 1941, links fascism to socialism through the device of linking Lasalle to Bismarck's social policy. Authoritarian Prussian socialism then provides the language for 'German theoreticians who laid the intellectual foundation of the doctrines of the Third Reich'.[27] This tortuous argument is elaborated further three years later in Hayek's major work, *The Road to Serfdom*. This is probably the key text in the campaign to contain the damage that fascism inflicts on the legitimacy of capitalism.

In a retrospective preface to *The Road to Serfdom*, Hayek explains that writing the book was motivated by annoyance at the misinterpretation of the Nazi movement in English 'progressive' circles. Hayek is particularly distressed that in Britain all shades of political opinion seem to accept the view that the Nazis were close allies of German capitalism. 'Have not the parties of the Left as well as those of the Right been deceived by believing that the National-Socialist Party was in the service of the capitalists and opposed to all forms of socialism?' he asked in frustration.[28] Hayek dismisses such views by provocatively elaborating the totalitarian thesis. Accordingly, rather than capitalism, it is socialism that causes fascism; Chapter 12 of *The Road to Serfdom* is titled 'The Socialist Roots of Nazism'. Hayek's central argument is simple and to the point: 'Few are ready to recognise that the rise of Fascism and Nazism was not a reaction against the socialist trends at the preceding period, but a necessary outcome of those tendencies.'[29] He presents the struggle between the German left and right in the thirties as between 'rival socialist factions'.

The main appeal of Hayek's argument for the right is that he not only blames socialism for the Nazi regime but also counterposes to both a robust defence of individualism. Hayek argues from an elitist standpoint. He observes that the problem in Weimar Germany was that the power of the masses was excessive and that of the bourgeoisie was too weak. The main culprit in this scenario is the collectivism of the masses. His particular version of the totalitarian thesis is self-consciously anti-mass and supportive of a German bourgeoisie that has been unfairly accused of complicity with Nazi crimes. He writes: 'it was from the masses and not from the classes steeped in the Prussian tradition and favoured by it that National-Socialism arose', and 'It was certainly not through the bourgeoisie, but rather the absence of a strong bourgeoisie, by which they [the Nazis] were helped to power.'[30] The absence of a strong capitalist class created a climate where anti-competition and collectivist views could gain influence. Thus fascism thrived through the growing influence of anti-capitalist forces.

Hayek's explanation of fascism not only turns the tables on anti-capitalist critics, it also provides a coherent attack on collectivism. Fascism as the negation of individualism is Hayek's main contribution to the ideological armoury of the right. Although Hayek's strong endorsement of individualism is not always to the liking of conservatives, his coherent attack on the collectivism of the left has earned him widespread respect among the intellectuals of the right. By blaming collectivism for the development of totalitarianism, Hayek puts forward a usable line of defence against the left-wing coupling of fascism and the capitalist system.

Hayek's standpoint is by no means original. The approach has become well-rehearsed by other thinkers on the rightward end of the political spectrum. Ludwig von Mises follows a similar line of attack on 'the collective creed' which he describes as 'by necessity exclusive and totalitarian'. But with von Mises there is a perceptible shift in emphasis from the early theories of totalitarianism, whose main focus of concern was still that of Nazi atrocities. These theories sought somewhat defensively to characterise the content of the Hitler regime alongside that of Stalin. By the 1950s, the locus of concern had changed. Instead of Nazi atrocities, the spotlight was on the anti-individualist orientation of totalitarian systems. Von Mises directed his fire at the 'system of all-round planning and totalitarian regimentation'.[31] The shift in focus towards the problem of the individual helped convert the theory of totalitarianism from a defensive reaction to the Nazi experience to an offensive resource in the Cold War.

In a seminal article published in 1951, the American historian of ideas H. Stuart Hughes points towards the new attitude towards fascism that was developing in Western Europe. The article, based on a journey to Europe during the summer of 1950, reports on his discussions with intellectuals and politicians. The dominant influence is of course the Cold War. This is the period of the Korean War, when for many Westerners the prospect of another global military conflict seemed imminent. According to Hughes, the danger of a Soviet occupation of Western Europe seemed to many Westerners far worse than what actually happened in the Nazi era.

> A Westerner, even a left-wing intellectual, as he thinks back on the fascist experience, recalls a certain air of familiarity, of remaining within the European tradition. At the thought of Soviet occupation, whatever may be his conscious political affiliation, he instinctively shudders as at something barbarous and alien.[32]

Hughes noted that the escalation of anti-Soviet panic had led to a revision of attitudes towards Franco's Spain. He observed that 'moderate leftists, who once could scarcely bear the mention of Franco's name, now point to the virtual cessation of resistance activities within Spain itself and grant that there is some merit in Franco's contention that his only sin was to recognize the communist menace somewhat earlier than the rest.'[33]

No doubt there is an element of exaggeration in Hughes' account of the decline of anti-fascist sentiment, but that is always a penalty to be paid for isolating new trends. Hughes has clearly captured an important watershed in the sanitisation of the fascist experience. He writes of a 'process of reclassification' where 'the word "fascism" has lost most of its terrors', and notes that 'in conservative circles many people avoid the term entirely.'[34] This is where the term 'totalitarian' proved to be invaluable. It assisted in redirecting all the anti-Nazi fears in a different direction. Writing retrospectively, Hughes argues:

> In the late 1940s and early 1950s, the term served to ease the shock of emotional readjustment for Americans or Englishmen – or *émigrés* – who had just defeated one enemy and were now called upon by their governments to confront another. If it could be proved that Nazism and Communism were very much the same

thing, then the cold war against the late ally could be justified by
the rhetoric that had proved so effective against the late enemy.[35]

By the early 1950s the emotional readjustment to which Hughes refers
was almost complete. There was an almost instinctive transference of
anti-fascist energies towards the conduct of the Cold War among
liberal and conservative intellectuals. Thus most of the books on the
history of German fascism written at the time are really warnings
about another kind of 'totalitarianism'.

Increasingly with the passing of time the core of the problem of
totalitarianism was redefined towards the Soviet Union. According
to Schlesinger this reorientation towards the Soviet Union was
motivated by the sentiment that whereas fascism was intellectually
discredited, Marxism continued to exercise considerable appeal:

> While fascism is a fairly candid expression of nihilism,
> Communism retains an appearance of existing within a framework
> of intelligible values. What argument survives in fascism is ...
> argument in terms of myth, psychosis and blood. But Marxism has
> endowed Communism with a respectable intellectual lineage
> saturated in nineteenth-century values of optimism, rationalism
> and detailed historical enquiry.[36]

What Schlesinger did not go on to spell out was that increasingly
studies of 'German fascism' were turning into veiled polemics against
the 'totalitarianism' of Marxism.

During the past two decades the only purpose of the theory of
totalitarianism seems to have been to criminalise the Soviet Union. A
series of essays on the Third Reich published in 1985 exemplifies this
trend. Their editor, H. W. Koch, introduced the text with the remark
that ' the schemes of the early propagators of mass murder remained
on paper; it was left to Lenin and Stalin on the one hand, to Hitler on
the other, to transform theory into practice.'[37] The inference is clear.
Not only was the practice of the Hitler regime not unusual, it was also
an imitation of earlier pioneers in mass murder. There is an explicit
agenda here which ranks the Soviet regime as the worst offender.
Koch assures the reader that 'the murder of millions of Jews ranks
second only to the murders carried out by Stalin's regime.'[38] Another
essay in this collection, by Ernst Nolte, suggests that Auschwitz 'was
above all a reaction born out of the anxiety of the annihilating
occurrences of the Russian Revolution.' While Nolte writes of

annihilation in relation to the Russian Revolution, he can only bring himself to write of the 'so-called annihilation of the Jews during the Third Reich.'[39] Here the Holocaust becomes a justifiable response to the threat posed to Germany by the red menace.

Increasingly the tendency has been to remove the question of the origins of the Hitler regime from a consideration of the German social structure – and from reality for that matter. According to David Horowitz, in what is a typical conservative contribution of the 1990s on this subject, the fault lies with Marx:

> If no one had believed Marx's idea, there would have been no Bolshevik Revolution ... Hitler would not have come to power. There would have been no cold war. It is hard not to conclude that most of the bloodshed of the 20th century might not have taken place.[40]

Some are not happy to blame Marx alone for the evils of the Nazi regime. Writing in *Encounter*, formerly the leading periodical of the Anglo-American Cold War intelligentsia, a leading French historian traces the roots of fascism and communism to the ideas of the revolution of 1789.[41]

During the 1980s, the French right developed the argument that it was itself anti-fascist, since socialism, its opponent, is the source of fascism. The ability of the far right in France to argue that its left wing opponents are the true fascists shows the plasticity of the theory of totalitarianism.

The apologetic character of totalitarian theory is seldom considered. Sometimes, when it is used by Germans to absolve their past from the consequences of the Nazi legacy, the apologetic character of the theory is criticised.[42] But as a theory used for the legitimation of non-totalitarian market economies it has a privileged position of being above criticism. Finally, it is worth noting that the term 'totalitarian' has been recruited to characterise authoritarian Third World regimes. It has become a descriptive concept that connotes the imposition of a political objective by force.[43]

Whitewashing imperialism

It is easy to forget that until the 1930s the moral claims of imperialism were seldom questioned in the West. Imperialism and the expansion of the West were represented in unambiguously positive terms as a major contribution to human civilisation. Until the late 1920s individual representatives of the Anglo-American ruling class would often positively define themselves as imperialist. The term 'imperialist' was used in a manner similar to characterising one's belief as conservative, liberal or socialist. Imperialism and its tradition provided inspiration and confidence to the ruling elites. Even British socialists and liberals were selective in their criticism of imperialism. Taylor is to the point when he states that 'liberals and socialists did not object to British imperialism *per se*, but to the particular aggressive form which it was perceived to take after the Jameson raid of 1895.'[44]

As late as 1949 the future British Labour prime minister Harold Wilson argued that 'no party can or should claim for itself the exclusive use of the title Imperialist, in the best sense of the word.'[45] For Wilson imperialism was a national tradition; 'in the best sense of the word' it was above question and above party politics. However by the 1940s this type of reaction was out of time and exceptional. As a result of the experience of the Second World War imperialism had become widely discredited. Instead of basking in the glory associated with high morality, imperialism had become in many quarters a term of abuse.

The shift in emphasis in the use of the term 'imperialism' is particularly striking in relation to school textbooks. According to one account of education in the United States a shift is perceptible in the 1940s:

> The word 'imperialism', which was once freely used to describe United States adventures in Asia and the Caribbean at the end of the nineteenth century, no longer applies to the United States. According to these books, imperialism is a European affair.[46]

This was not an option for a European power like Britain, where treatment of the subject was fraught with more difficulties than in America.

The imperial ideal first came under serious questioning in the aftermath of the First World War. Lenin's association of imperialism with the drive to war found a widespread public resonance in Europe. At the same time the escalation of anti-colonial revolts in Asia and the Middle East put to question the moral claims of imperialism. Left-wing opinion in Europe and liberal opinion in the United States was gradually turning against imperialism.

Already on the defensive, imperialists particularly in Britain were thrown into disarray by the experience of the Second World War. The war appeared to confirm Lenin's linkage of imperialism and military conflict. From the point of view of the British establishment there was a danger that the war would be seen as merely a squabble between rival imperialist powers. German imperialism under Hitler actively discredited all forms of imperialism. British imperialism, with all of its assumptions of racial and cultural superiority, faced the problem of guilt by association. These were issues which preoccupied the British establishment from the mid-1930s onwards. Although most of the deliberation on this subject was pursued consciously in private, on occasion it would enter the public domain.[47]

Just a few months after the outbreak of the Second World War, an editorial in the *Economist* observed with a sigh of relief that 'the colonial question did not, after all, play as large a part in the outbreak of the war as had at one time appeared possible.' The article defended Britain from the charge of imperialist exploitation. Arguing the thesis that the colonies on balance benefited from Britain's attention, the editor put forward a robust case for imperialism:

> The only real question is not whether there should be an end to 'Imperialism', but whether our brand of Imperialism is the best. It has an immense amount to be said for it. Indeed, the criticisms that can justly be made are the exact opposite of those that are made by those who attack 'capitalist exploitation'. There is far more evidence in the British colonies of under-development than of over-exploitation.[48]

The approach of the *Economist* was representative of the arguments of the time. Imperialism would be defended by drawing a sharp distinction between a benevolent British variety and other more squalid types.

However this defence of imperialism was vulnerable to the growing disenchantment with all the values associated with it. Imperialism was not only becoming a term of abuse, it also tended to undermine Britain's claim of moral superiority against Hitler's Germany. Nothing less than Britain's imperial past and History was at stake in this discussion, according to John Murray, a correspondent to *The Times* in April 1940. 'Is it not time that some protest should be made against the misuse of the word imperialism?' he wrote. Murray objected that 'it is used only as synonym for ruthless aggression' and demanded to know 'what is the position of an Imperialist, a name

honourably linked with some of the most famous and beneficent men
and women of our history?' Murray's solution was to devise a
different word when the German variety was under discussion:

> If it were not such a horrible hybrid Reichism would do, as it would
> finally link the worst 'spirit of Empire' with the worst transgressor.
> The spirit of the British Empire, which has meant and continues
> now more than ever to mean so much to us, is too fine a thing to
> have any term that can be used to define it degraded.[49]

Others were also concerned that the association of British with
German imperialism would discredit the imperial tradition. Major-
General Sir Frederick Sykes, chairman of the council of the Royal
Empire Society, pursued Murray's line of argument. He too objected
to 'the perverted meaning that has been fastened upon' the term
'imperialism'. He denounced those who argued that as imperialists
'we have no moral right to condemn and resist others who are
possessing themselves of *Lebensraum*.'[50]

In the subsequent debate Norman Angell argued that Hitler's
depiction of the British empire as decadent is 'accepted by nearly all
neutrals, including the majority of Americans'. Anthony Eden,
Secretary of State for the Dominions and future prime minister,
replied by attempting to draw a sharp contrast between British and
German imperialism:

> The German conception of dominion and the modern British
> conception of Imperialism present as sharp an antithesis as
> mankind has ever known. The German conceptions is based upon
> subjection and repression, ours upon equality and development.[51]

Eden was backed by the editor of *The Times* himself, who attacked the
'propaganda that represents the present war to neutral audiences as
a struggle between rival imperialisms'.[52] The editor probably had the
American public in mind. By the early 1940s the British government
was so concerned with its image in the United States as an imperialist
power that it set up a special committee to counteract its effect.[53]

Although the British establishment succeeded in winning the
propaganda battle against Germany it could not save the reputation
of imperialism. Imperialism and colonialism were no longer accepted
as positive or even as neutral terms. After the Nazi experience they
acquired an essentially negative connotation in most parts of the

world, though from time to time British propagandists attempted to retrieve the situation by attempting an intellectual distinction between good and bad forms of imperialism and colonialism.

It took some time for the British establishment to comprehend the depth and the breath of the reaction to imperialism. In June 1948 one propagandist in the Foreign Office informed his counterpart in the Colonial Office that the 'feeling that to possess colonies is *per se* immoral or, at the very least, incompatible with twentieth century ideas' is a point 'so important as to overshadow the rest.'[54] The discovery that imperialism was immoral took some time to sink in. Almost a decade later a former colonial governor noted in quiet disbelief that 'there are those who believe that any form "colonialism" is inherently evil.'[55]

The discrediting of imperialism disoriented the British ruling class. The imperial ideal, with its sense of moral purpose, played a critical role in providing the establishment with confidence and coherence. The imperial past had an important legitimising function. The new negative sentiments associated with imperialism strongly undermined the use of the British past as a source of inspiration and authority.

The retrospective defence of empire

As in the case of German reinterpretations of the Nazi past, there has been a systematic attempt to reinterpret the history of British imperialism. Traditional and conservative historians have been in the forefront of this project. Their main argument is that the poverty of the post-independence Third World suggests that they were better off under the empire. The other common argument is to offer a balance sheet, where the benefits of imperialism always outweigh the disadvantages.

As in Germany, British conservatives exhort the public not to feel guilty about the past. Simon Pearce criticises school textbooks because of an 'emphasis on British guilt' and because 'there is no balanced discussion of colonial achievements.'[56] Paul Johnson writes of 'periodic orgies of self-abasement' and that 'loaded with quite unnecessary guilt, we have given aid and comfort, and received nothing but abuse and violence.' Ray Honeyford concurs and asks: 'is it not time to challenge the supposed necessity for men of liberal sympathies to feel guilt ridden about our imperial past?'[57] From this standpoint, the problem is that of guilt rather than the record of imperialism. Guilt creates – in Honeyford's words – a 'disabling tradition', the imperial past as such is otherwise unproblematic.

The reinterpretation of imperialism is not the monopoly of conservative thinkers. Just as there is a consistent tendency to separate fascism from any association with capitalism so too there is a wide body of literature which seeks to decouple imperialism from any economic motive. So for example a liberal text directed against bias in history criticises post Second World War German school books for drawing attention to the economic aspects of the British empire:

> Too much is said about the economic and military side of British imperialism, too little about the role of religion in the foundation of the early colonies. Similarly, the abolition of slavery in the British Empire in 1833 is sometimes attributed solely to economic motives, whereas every Englishman knows that pure philanthropy played a prominent part indeed.[58]

This whitewashing of imperialism, the good bits always outweighing the bad, is a consistent theme in Western literature. It is no less evident in American than in British contributions.[59]

A close inspection of the literature of the 1940s, 1950s and 1960s reveals that most of the conservative and liberal thinkers of the time actively participated in the retrospective defence of Western imperial expansion and colonialism. Many of the key figures who popularised the theories of totalitarianism and the end of ideology were also committed to the rehabilitation of the imperial past. One reason why this tendency has not been widely discussed was perhaps the manner in which the arguments were conducted. Comments on imperialism were usually made in casual asides and throwaway remarks in texts about other subjects. The anti-imperialist climate of the time must have made a more explicit defence of the Western imperial past more difficult to pursue.

To give a flavour of this literature, here is Hans Kohn, who was a bitter critic of German historicism and the whole tradition of nationalist historiography, writing a celebration of the British empire:

> The liberal imperialism of the nineteenth century was not only controlled by the recognized plurality of empires and by the restraining force of the acknowledged validity of universal ethical standards above class or race, but its inner logic led to its own withering away. The process of decolonization, of increasing

concessions to the independence of colonial peoples, had begun on
the part of Britain, the leader in liberty well before the outbreak of
the First World War.[60]

Kohn's arguments very much reflected the outlook of the postwar
totalitarian theorists. Hannah Arendt, who wrote the major work on
totalitarianism in the postwar era, devoted a significant part to a
discussion of imperialism. Arendt shows considerable sensitivity to
the development of racist and authoritarian sentiments through
British imperialism, yet she draws back from following through the
logic of her analysis. She writes how the 'conscience of the nation' in
Britain, called the 'imperial factor', created an 'imperialism with the
merits and remnants of justice it so eagerly tried to eliminate'.
According to Arendt 'the natives were not only protected but in a way
represented' by the British Parliament.[61] This statement is all the more
astounding in that it follows a vivid depiction of the growth of
imperialist racism in the nineteenth century.

The end-of-ideology theorists also shared Arendt's approach.
Raymond Aron's lecture on 'Imperialism and colonialism' suggests
that France acquired her African empire by accident and that no
economic causation was involved.[62] For Aron the very idea of a
structured causal link between capitalism and imperialism was
anathema, no more acceptable than that between big business and
fascism would be to German conservatives. Aron declared: 'how can
we accept the proposition that colonial conquest is the extreme form,
the inevitable expression, of an expansion inherent in capitalist
economies?'[63]

'The chief ideological passion in the world today is anti-
imperialism', wrote Daniel Bell as a prelude to rubbishing this
'common rhetorical cry for Arab feudal sheikhs, African nationalist
leaders, and Latin American military dictators, as well as for left-wing
revolutionaries.'[64] Bell's line of argument was standard in the
campaign to whitewash imperialism. It did not so much defend
imperialism as attack the moral authority of anti-imperialism. By
emphasising the cynical manipulation of anti-colonial sentiments by
'feudal sheikhs' and 'military dictators', the legitimacy of anti-
imperialism itself is put to question.

The consistent concern of theorists of totalitarianism and the end
of ideology with the problem of imperialism exposes some of the
underlying anxieties of Western intellectuals. They felt intensely
vulnerable on the question of imperialism. It appeared that at least on

this question, Soviet Marxists had the edge. The sheer scale of reaction to the West by the Third World was a source of anxiety. Often the ascendancy of the Third World was emotionally and intellectually experienced as the decline of the West. 'The West no longer believes in itself', wrote Aron in 1950. Hannah Arendt was even more pessimistic when she wrote of an 'ill-defined, general agreement that the essential structure of all civilizations is at the breaking point'. Some, like Hans Kohn, put on a brave face and declared their faith in 'the modern West's strength and glory'.[65]

Even a fanatical supporter of Western civilisation found it difficult explicitly to condone imperialism, but the same time the moral authority of the West could not be sustained without rescuing at least the fundamentals of the imperialist past. The intellectual resolution to this problem was to re-pose the issues. The record of post-colonial Third World regimes became the focus of discussion. A consistent denigration of their record ensured that the spotlight swiftly shifted from the West to the Third World.

Anti-Third World ideology

The implicit defence of imperialism was executed through an explicit attack on the legitimacy of Third World societies. The substance of the argument was that the Third World was congenitally incapable of looking after its own affairs. Chaos, decay and corruption were the characteristics associated with independent Third World States. Typically, the colonial era was presented as something of a golden age. Problems were always portrayed as the fault of Third World societies. The implication that imperialism had left behind a legacy of difficulties was invariably rejected.

An article on 'Britain's Imperial Legacy', published in the 1950s in the American international relations periodical *Foreign Affairs*, expressed the classic Anglo-American wisdom on the subject:

> Should the British be blamed for the persistence and sometimes the aggravation of these internal divisions after independence? Many Asian and African nationalists have talked of a sinister policy of 'divide and rule' whereby the British stirred up local hostilities in order to delay the transfer of power. But since self-government has, in virtually all cases, been granted, the accusation of conspiracy can hardly be sustained. The critics forget two factors – the degree to which the institutions introduced by contact with Britain require a

certain measure of communal unity and the time it takes to over-come religious, linguistic and racial diversity by broader loyalties.[66]

This was the standard response to the argument that the problems of the Third World were a legacy of imperialism. Gradually, decade by decade, the arguments against the Third World became stronger and more extravagant.

By the mid-1970s, periodicals such as *Foreign Affairs* and even more liberal journals were depicting the Third World as a frightening threat to global peace. The West was now the victim and the Third World guerrilla was the aggressor. An article in *Foreign Affairs* in July 1975 is typical of the more aggressive style of anti-Third World propaganda:

> The generations that have come to maturity in Europe and America since the end of the Second World War have asked only to bask in the sunshine of a summertime world; but they have been forced instead to live in the fearful shadow of other people's deadly quarrels. Gangs of politically motivated gunmen have disrupted everyday life, intruding and forcing their parochial feuds upon the unwilling attention of everybody else.[67]

The idyllic image of a peaceful West is in sharp contrast to the evil that emanates from the Third World. Certainly by the 1980s the terms most associated with the Third World were those of brutality, corruption, senseless violence and above all *terror*. By this time Third World terrorism had emerged as an international issue in its own right. In terms of media attention, it was hyped up to be the greatest danger to world peace. Even before *glasnost*, Third World terror appeared on the verge of overtaking the Evil Empire as the number-one problem for the West.

Anti-Third World ideology did not acquire a coherent analytical form. It was a makeshift, reactive set of ideas motivated by the need to discredit. Nevertheless its role in helping to recover the past is comparable to that played by the theory of totalitarianism. In some right-wing literature, particularly in France, anti-Third Worldism and totalitarianism are synthesised into one package. Third World regimes become not only illegitimate but are also totalitarian.[68] The French New Right has developed a stridently anti-Third World political vocabulary. The *Club de l'Horloge*, a network of right-wing intellectuals, has developed a clear line of attack whereby anti-racist leftists are denounced as 'anti-French, anti-European, anti-Western, or anti-White'.[69] One of the central themes of a collection of papers published by this group in 1987 'was the "expurgation of guilt" of the West in general, and of the Right in particular, by eliminating the "toxins" of "communist and pro-Third World ideologies".'[70]

The whitewashing of imperialism remains essential for the rehabilitation of the Western past. As a footnote to this chapter, it is worth noting that during the past few years this rehabilitation has been completed. The disintegration of the Third World has been effectively used retrospectively to justify imperialism. By the time of the Gulf War of 1991 imperialism was morally rearming. For the first time in half a century the term 'imperialism' could be used without the previous negative connotations.[71] An editorial in the *Wall Street Journal* in February 1991 said it had been wrong for the United States to stop Britain from invading Egypt in 1956. 'Perhaps the biggest strategic mistake in the postwar era' was 'shrinking from the British and French use of military force against Nasser', it noted.[72] This imperial mood was contingent on the perception of military and moral glory that followed the defeat of Iraq. Just how long this mood will last depends to some extent on whether the moral rearmament of imperialism is a success. 'It is my hope that when this is over, we will have kicked once and for all the so-called Vietnam syndrome', said President Bush in the final stages of the Gulf War.[73] The realisation of this hope at least in part depends on the success of the ideological offensive against the Third World.

There is now an entire genre of anti-Third World journalism and literature throughout the West. The conservative offensive has pushed this theme in Britain, France, Germany and the United States with great success. Of all the intellectual experiments of the conservative reaction, the promotion of prejudices against the Third World has been probably the most effective. It is in this area that the tentative steps in the recovery of the past have been most successful.

The theme of betrayal

The only phenomenon that compares with the Third World as a source of obsession for the post-Second World War right is the 1960s. The 1960s have become a code word that expresses everything that the right-wing intelligentsia finds repulsive. All the frustration and anxiety connected with society's moral impasse were displaced and concentrated around the 1960s. The 1960s have become a contemporary mythical equivalent of the fall from grace.

As an aside it is useful to recall that Third Worldism and the 1960s are closely linked. During this period the experience of Vietnam led to a major re-examination of the Western way of life. This point has not escaped Karl Bracher, a German proponent of totalitarian theory.[74] Others too have drawn attention to the fact that in the 1960s the moral balance between the West and the Third World appeared to favour the latter. According to the 'end-of-ideology' political sociologist Lipset, this was a 'serious source of American weakness'. He had in mind 'the extent to which major segments of the intellectual and bureaucratic elites have lost faith in the moral superiority of Western democracy generally and of the United States in particular in the contest with the communist world.'[75] It appeared that the loss of moral credibility combined with opposition to the war against Vietnam was actually leading many anti-war Americans to favour the 'victory of a communist state'.

But there are other more compelling reasons that explain the special place that the 1960s have in the conservative imagination. At the beginning of this chapter the intellectual crisis of the right was shown to coincide with the erosion of credible absolute values. The postwar attempts to solve this crisis had the character of a compromise. The responses discussed in this chapter were more an exercise in damage limitation than solutions to the intellectual crisis. Until the late 1970s the right-wing intelligentsia lacked conviction and exercised little influence on public life. This is where the 1960s become crucial. One of the key points of this book is the proposition that it was through a *reaction* to the 1960s that the right attempted to overcome the intellectual paralysis from which it had suffered since the Second World War. Moreover it is through interaction with the 1960s that a new system of conservative ideas was elaborated. It matters not that the 1960s of the conservative imagination bear little relationship to much that happened in that decade. What is important is that the 'violence' and 'intolerance' of the 1960s is accepted as a historical fact. Along with totalitarianism and the Third World terrorist, the 1960s constitute the final component of the evil trinity of the right.

That the 1960s acted as a catalyst for the subsequent conservative reaction is widely known. Kusmer writes that it is 'one of the ironies of recent American history that the most significant consequence of the "radical" 1960s was the emergence of a conservative backlash against the social and political concerns of that tumultuous decade.'[76]

According to Robert Nisbet, one of the leading American neo-conservative thinkers:

> Neoconservatism was born in the mid-1960s. It is almost inseparable from the 'Student Revolution' which played something of the role in the conservative renaissance that the French Revolution had played in the rise of the philosophy at the end of the eighteenth century.[77]

Nisbet's rather exaggerated comparison notwithstanding, the conservative reaction to the 1960s provided the dynamic for its subsequent intellectual development.

This was by no means merely an American reaction. According to one account of the German history debate, 'like its counterparts in the United States and other Western nations, West German neo-conservatism developed largely in reaction to the perceived excesses of the New Left of the 1960s.'[78] According to Kurt Sontheimer, a social democratic professor, the rightward shift in the German political spectrum means that '1968 and its consequences are now history.'[79]

1960s: reality and myth

During the 1960s, establishment values were ridiculed and rejected by an active minority of young people. This was the period when nothing appeared sacred. National traditions were mocked and authority became more and more questioned. In retrospect the period appears as a dramatic phase in the breakdown of bourgeois thought. For the first time there were no popular optimistic visions of the future. Science and modernity had lost its mystique. However this breakdown was experienced as the consequence of a challenge from radical quarters. Radicalisation, which was a consequence of the fragmentation of old ideas, was perceived as its cause.

Unable to come to terms with the decline of traditional ideas, conservative intellectuals blamed 'insidious' influences for seducing the youth. Other thinkers blamed the new prosperity for helping to undermine old values. 'Life has ceased to be as difficult as it used to be but it has become pointless', wrote the author of a study on *Permissive Britain*.[80] What many supporters of the status quo could not face was the manifest irrelevance of traditional conventions and values. For the historian J. H. Plumb the public rejection of 'hollow' values was proof of *The Death of the Past*. In a lecture given in 1968 he observed that 'wherever we look, in all areas of social and personal life, the hold of the past is weakening.'[81]

The 'weakening of the past' felt by Plumb was made possible by the cumulative effects of the intellectual crisis of the right and the erosion of the traditions associated with them. In the 1960s what had hitherto been mainly the malaise of a narrow stratum of the Western intelligentsia exploded into the public domain. In virtually all the industrial capitalist societies accepted values and traditions were now widely questioned. This precipitated a major crisis of confidence in the ruling class. It seemed almost incomprehensible that at a time of relative prosperity the legitimacy of society could face such a barrage of criticism. From the vantage point of the conservative imagination something insidious seemed to be at work.

That something gradually turned into the betrayal of social values by the 1960s intellectual. It took some time for the theme to emerge. The initial emphasis was on 'ingratitude', 'spoiled children' and 'infantile regression'. Gradually darker forces were discovered to be at work. It was suggested that 1960s radicals were systematically destroying the Western way of life by infiltrating the media and institutions of culture and education. In some cases the forces of subversion were noted but left unspecified, in others specific groups were identified as the enemy. So for Norman Podhoretz the problem was the 'culture of appeasement' associated with homosexual literary culture. According to Podhoretz, the homosexual intellectual was anti-American.[82] The 'immorality' of the individual was held responsible for encouraging the 'permissive society'.

The view that a 'New Class' or the 'Liberal Establishment', or some variation thereof systematically subverted Western societies during the 1960s continues to this day. Roger Kimball's *Tenured Radicals: How politics has corrupted our higher education* provides an up-to-date version of the stab-in-the-back theory. According to Kimball, the radicals of the 1960s are now tenured professors who dominate American universities. They are now in a position to carry out what they set out to do three decades previously.[83] The same point is expressed in Britain by Michael Jones, political editor of the *Sunday Times*, in relation to the school system. He seems pleased that 'teaching morale has fallen' and that 'teachers are leaving the profession in droves' since many of them are the 'undesirables in the 1960–1970s intake'. 'The bad news is that thousands of such teachers are still in mid-career.'[84]

Rather than gradually dying off, the legend of the 1960s seems to gain force with the passing of time. The 1960s are routinely blamed for all manner of social problems. It appears that the most improbable linkages can be made through incantation of the 1960s. Listen to David Owen, president of the Association of the Chief Police Officers in Britain, holding forth on the problem of crime in January 1991. Owen blamed the growth of crime on a:

> decline in standards, and it is a very serious one. It began, I think, with the 'anything goes' ideas of the sixties. You cannot pretend that it doesn't matter that there has been such a decline in private and public morality, in family discipline and the education system.[85]

In one short statement the idea of 'anything goes' 30 years ago becomes the cause of the growth of crime in 1991. Other casualties of the 1960s listed by Owen are morality, discipline and education.

The durability of the 1960s legend is fuelled by the traumatic memories of a period when the empty and meaningless character of ruling-class values stood exposed. This unprecedented lack of confidence accounts for the hysterical reaction to the period. The youth movement of the 1960s is a conservative nightmare which has veritable demons. According to the chair of the Adenauer Foundation 'the revolt of 1968 destroyed more values than did the Third Reich'.[86] The 1960s were also represented as the seedbed of terrorism. According to one version of this argument it was the expansion of the university system in the West during the 1960s which provided the impetus for the 'intellectual and moral assault on free enterprise'. For Paul Johnson the scope of this 1960s conspiracy is truly awesome:

> The 1960s, during which most Western nations doubled, and in some cases trebled, their university places ... produced the students' revolts, beginning in Paris 1968; they detonated the Northern Ireland Conflict, which is still harassing Britain. They produced the Bader-Meinhof gang in West Germany, the Red Brigades in Italy, the Left Fascist terrorism of Japan. They produced an enormous explosion of Marxist studies, centred around the social sciences, and especially sociology, and a new generation of university teachers and school teachers dedicated by faith and by a sort of perverted religious piety, to the spread of Marxist ideas.[87]

This demonisation of the 1960s is actually backed up by a substantial literature. Much of this is deliberately tendentious and simply exaggerates the threat of student terrorism, but a lot is written with a conviction inspired by a uniquely unrestrained hatred.

The demonic literature on the 1960s adopts the procedure of the totalitarian theorists that were discussed earlier. Emotive terms such as 'fascist', 'terrorist', 'violence' are linked to the 1960s counterculture and radical movements. There is a particular emphasis on violence in the university. The Nazi suppression of free speech is often evoked as a comparable event. Such condemnation of violence and intolerance in the university is never backed up by facts and figures. Certainly, someone growing up today who reads this literature could be excused for believing that hundreds, maybe thousands, had died as a result of this violence. Such a reader would not guess that most of this 'violence' consisted of the forcing open of doors in the course of student occupations and shoving-matches with the police on demonstrations. Even a superficial acquaintance with the statistics demonstrates that the violence of the 1960s was of the imaginary kind. What was sociologically interesting was the scale of the state response in Germany and Italy to crackpot terrorist groups such as the Red Brigades.

Let's look at some typical arguments. According to the German social scientist Karl Bracher the 1960s counterculture represented the movement which, 'ever since the German Youth Movement of the turn of the century, has been charged as an ideally and morally justified counter-position to western civilization and politics'.[88] For Bracher the fact that the Nazis also constituted a 'movement' is highly significant. The 1960s are thus discredited because of an ostensible association with the Nazis.

In the Anglo-American literature the linkage of the 1960s with German and Nazi metaphors is particularly evident. Sidney Hooks' paranoid recollection of student unrest in American universities is appropriately titled 'The academic ethic in abeyance: recollections of *Walpurgisnacht* at New York University'. It appears that Hook used to believe that the 'German professoriat had been guilty of a fundamental betrayal of the mission of the university during the regime of Hitler and his National Socialist Party.' However after students disrupted a faculty meeting at New York University, an event which Hook calls 'the most shocking experience of my life', his view of German academics mellowed. Why? Because his comparable experience in New York led him to 'modify' the severity of his judgement of 'the German professors under Hitler'.[89] The real message of course is that American student protestors are as bad as the Nazis.

Hook's observations are further embellished by Bloom, who states that the 'American university in the 1960s was experiencing the same dismantling of the structure of rational inquiry as had the German university in the 1930s.'[90] In Bloom's imagination the tradition of the infamous Nuremberg rallies is carried forward at events such as the Woodstock pop music festival. 'Whether it be Nuremberg or Woodstock, the principle is the same', states Bloom as if the argument was entirely self-evident.[91]

This linkage with Nazi Germany is generally subservient to the wider emphasis on violence. Even a sensible academic such as Ernest Gellner, in his article on student unrest at the London School of Economics, wrote that 'keeping violence out of the university must of course be our first priority.'[92] As usual the violence is not quantified. The reader does not know how many people died or were injured at the London School of Economics. But clearly there must have been considerable casualties, otherwise why prioritise the problem of violence. That there is probably more violence at an average London pub on any weekend than there was during the entire student unrest at the LSE would probably come as a surprise to many readers.

Daniel Bell is also concerned with campus violence. But for Bell violence tends to evoke a sexuality that defies all logic. He describes the 'sensibility' of the 1960s as 'a concern with violence and cruelty; a preoccupation with the sexually perverse; a desire to make noise'.[93] Something clearly depraved was born in this permissive decade and Bell, like many of his colleagues, was determined to discredit it.

This irrational reaction to the 1960s represented a semi-conscious awareness that the culture of 'anything goes' was the inevitable consequence of the breakdown of absolute values. Once moral absolutes gave way to scepticism, it was only a matter of time before all values would be questioned. This is what happened *en masse* in the 1960s. The erosion of tradition and authority were often experienced as the violent displacement of accepted roles. For many who were used to the exercise of unquestioned authority the world appeared to have turned upside-down. It was difficult to face the bitter truth that the breakdown of bourgeois values and conventions was responsible for the 1960s. It seemed far more plausible to seek out those who had betrayed the cause of Western capitalism: a new class of university lecturers, state bureaucrats, social workers and assorted do-gooders seemed to fit the bill. Through a confrontation with the ideas of this new class the conservative reaction was to acquire intellectual coherence.

Reaction to the 1960s

In an interesting study of the conservative offensive in American education, Ira Shor argues that it could not defeat the legacy of the 1960s. He recognises that conservatism has grown in influence but suggests that the opposition culture of the 1960s still survives. He writes:

> As long as opposition culture did not cohere into a single party or gather around one ideology, it could not be decisively smashed by a conservative counter-attack. Egalitarian resistance was simply everywhere and nowhere at the same time. This created mutual incoherence on both the left and the right. The conservative forces had far more organized power but they were unable to focus it terminally on the diffuse protest culture.[94]

Shor's account misses some of the key developments in this battle for ideas. Certainly the conservative campaign has not been an unambigious triumph, but that is not the issue. What is significant is that there was a conservative counter-attack in the first place.

What Shor ignores is that the ideas and values associated with conservatism were marginalised for the three decades that followed the Second World War. Yet ideas that were marginal in 1945 were able to make a comeback through the crusade against the 1960s. It is the revival of the intellectual credibility of the right that is particularly significant.

Conservative defenders of capitalism were never entirely reconciled to defeat. Friedrich Hayek clearly personifies this trend. Back in the 1940s Hayek bitterly attacked the intellectual trends of the time. He was particularly concerned not to abandon the battle for ideas. He was concerned about the influence of the left over the Western intelligentsia. He was active in the Mont Pelerin Society, which he described as a 'gathering of an international group of economists, historians and social philosophers' who regularly met to 'discuss the problems of preservation of a free society against the totalitarian threat'.[95] Hayek was concerned to correct what he saw as an intellectual 'anti-capitalist bias'. In particular he was anxious about the impact of critical historians: 'The influence which the writers of history thus exercise on public opinion is probably more immediate and extensive than that of the political theorists', he wrote.[96]

Whereas in the early 1950s Hayek's views exercised only a marginal influence on the intelligentsia, by the late 1970s the situation had dramatically turned in favour of conservatism. This shift occurred through a reaction against the 1960s, which were a perfect foil for the conservative reaction. This was a decade when supposedly everything went wrong. This image of the 1960s now tended to obscure the more embarassing episode of the 1940s. The relatively incoherent and inward-looking nature of the 1960s counterculture ensured that the right had a target that was susceptible to caricature.

Other factors assisted the conservative reaction. In the postwar decades the conservatives often had to play second fiddle to the liberals in America and the social democrats in Europe. The 1960s exposed the dangers inherent in the relativism of liberalism. Pluralism carried too far tended to weaken the claims of any *single* source of authority. Relativism led to uncertainties. Many liberals realised that their position was untenable and reacted by becoming bitter foes of the 1960s. Indeed the so-called neo-conservatives of the late 1970s were the Cold War liberals and social democrats of an earlier era. These new converts to the conservative cause provided the intellectual leadership to the reaction against the 1960s in Britain, France, Germany and the United States. The collapse of liberalism and the conversion of many of its prominent thinkers to conservatism helped the revival of the right.

The 1960s also helped focus the establishment mind towards conservatism. The more liberal and libertarian trends were compromised by the events of the 1960s. More important, it became clear to many liberals that relativism had got out of hand and Western capitalist society needed the certainty of moral absolutes. This has led to a palpable sense of defensiveness on the part of liberal upholders of the capitalist system. Thus for example a recently published reader on liberalism written by one of its proponents assures the reader on the first page that the 'relativist defence of liberalism is no defence at all'.[97] The flight from relativism is particularly striking in the case of the libertarian wing of the right. In his last major work Hayek adopted a consistently conservative tone. Almost the entire work is devoted to the defence of tradition and religion. Hayek even has a good word for superstition.[98] It is one of the contentions of this book that most pro-establishment thinkers have adopted conservative intellectual concerns regardless of their political affiliations.

Finally, the conservative revival has been assisted by the apparent incoherence of traditional left-wing alternatives. The apparent failures of Stalinism in Eastern Europe and of the social-democratic welfare state in the West have dealt a severe blow to the ideas traditionally associated with these alternatives. In a sense the failure of these alternatives has allowed conservatives to turn the tables on their opponents. In the past the experience of 'totalitarianism' worked to the disadvantage of the right. In the late 1970s the Gulag emerged retrospectively to haunt the left. The rediscovery of the Gulag was the consequence of the intellectual collapse of the traditional Western left. The invasion of Afghanistan and the declaration of martial law in Poland helped to give the Gulag a sense of contemporaneity. It was the convergence of this reaction to Stalinism and to the 1960s which gave the conservative crusade a measure of intellectual credibility, particularly in Western Europe. Curiously, the Gulag made less of a contribution to the intellectual crusade of the right while it existed than after it was dismantled.

The conservative revival, however, has been boosted by the decline of its opponents rather than through any major breakthrough on its own account. The right has not been able to produce a vision of the future or a usable sense of the past. There is an obvious search going on for the big idea that will allow for the reintroduction of credible absolute values. John Gray has stressed the importance of history in this respect. Conservatives, he says, 'must return their theorising to history' if they are to win intellectual hegemony.[99] The problem facing conservatives is that History cannot just be invented, it needs to be based on experience.

The artifical character of the conservative vision is highlighted by its incessant call for the revival of religion. This is not driven by religious passion but by intellectual calculation. Thus Hayek is not concerned about the details of religion, though he warns that '*the only religions that have survived are those which support property and the family*'.[100] This taste for religion is entirely motivated by ideological concerns and is a testimony to the limits of the conservative imagination. Often the plea for religion manifests the intellectual impasse of conservatism. Lord Thomas spends more than seven hundred pages arguing for the need to re-establish Western confidence through history. He shows only his own lack of conviction when in passing he notes that the solution to the problem of humanity is 'the absolute value which Christianity gives to the soul'.[101]

Discussions of religion in conservative circles these days invariably have an academic character. Contributors have a shopping-list approach to what they consider an adequate religion or code of morality. An illustration of this scholastic approach is provided by Rolf Gruner:

> Obviously any ethics which conservatives could embrace have to meet certain conditions. The emphasis must be on personal conduct and responsibility, morality must have its basis in individuals rather than collectives. It must be definitive and spare, neither sicklied over with relativism nor of the insistent preaching kind.[102]

Such list of platitudes simply confirm the absence of a viable religion or ethics. Effective morals cannot be made to order, either they emerge out of human experience or they have an entirely formal character. An artificially constructed religion based on sound logic still lacks the central dynamic of successful religions, the ability to harness the act of faith.

A recent contribution, 'A Conservative Research Agenda for the 90s' by Adam Meyerson, editor of the American publication *Policy Review*, illustrates the conservative reaction's lack of intellectual content. Like many similar contributions, it expresses a sense of unease at the ending of the Cold War, since it is now necessary to demonstrate the virtues of capitalism on its own account. Meyerson is bereft of any specific intellectual objectives. His only big idea is the preservation of the family. He writes:

> as Communism collapses, the greatest ideological threat to western civilization now comes from within the West's own cultural institutions – the universities, the churches, the professions such as law and medicine, and above all the disintegrating family.[103]

This concern with universities and comparable institutions indicates that the campaign against the 1960s is far from over. Unable to rework a relevant past or project a vision of the future, the right needs something like the 1960s to blame for the 'disintegrating family' and other problems. That is about as far as the right has been able to go in its tentative attempts to recover the past. It can set the terms of intellectual debate and that is its main achievement. But it has made no significant advance on the intellectual front. The poverty of contemporary right-wing thought is illustrated by the fact that most conservatives almost always rely on the same handful of thinkers to argue their case. It is always Koestler, Hayek, Popper, von Mises and a few others who provide the substantial arguments – arguments, by the way, that were developed as far back as the 1930s. That no single figure of intellectual substance has been produced by the right during the past two decades illustrates the limits of this movement. As the next chapter argues, the lack of progress made by the conservative reaction against the 1960s is due to its inherently *evasive* character.

To summarise the argument of the chapter. The experience of fascism accelerated the erosion of the intellectual certainties of the West. Besieged by profound doubts, the Western idea readjusted by assimilating highly sceptical, relativist and pluralist strands. As a reflex reaction to the damage caused by fascism, it was disposed to get stuck into the Cold War. It sought to contain the damage on three broad fronts: it sought to discredit ideology, extremism and fanaticism, and embraced the middle road. It reoriented the discussion of fascism towards totalitarianism and specifically the threat of Stalinism. It built a line of defence around imperialism by evolving the the concept of 'the West' and a successful anti-Third World ideology. These arguments were gradually systematised and made plausible by concentrating on the emotional theme of betrayal during the terrible 1960s.

6

The other 1960s and the fatal compromise

The reaction of establishment intellectuals against the 1960s represents an act of self-deception. The ideas thrown up in the 1960s were far from original. Many have their roots in the nineteenth century and most were widely discussed in the years between the two world wars. Most of the ideas which the right finds objectionable today they accepted as part of a compromise solution to prevent more extreme ones from gaining influence. Certainly at the level of ideas, the real 1960s took place between the wars. This was when the legitimacy of bourgeois thought was put on trial. Then, the conservative and liberal intelligentsia were too much on the defensive to push for a verdict. Instead of fighting their critics, they compromised. Half a century later, the conservative campaign against the 1960s signified a belated attempt to limit the ideological damage caused by this compromise. The 1960s provided the pretext for settling old scores – and this enterprise masked an attempt to confront problems that remained unsolved from an earlier era.

The abandonment of progress

During the 1960s the ideas hitherto held by relatively small but influential groups of artists and intellectuals began to influence the wider public mood in the West. A lack of belief in society and a fear of the future began to find general expression. This is what made the 1960s appear to be an era so different from what went on before.

But the ideas of the 1960s were hardly original. As one would expect, the ideas and sentiments had first been expressed by artists and imaginative writers. The period between the wars had seen the rise of a 'lost generation' of writers and artists. Artistic pessimism was the order of the day, characterised by the rejection of prevailing values. Artists such as Paul Valery, D. H. Lawrence, Ernest Hemingway, Franz Kafka, James Joyce, T. S. Eliot and Ezra Pound expressed in different ways a rejection of modern civilisation. An artistic and intellectual climate of hopelessness conveyed a sense of detachment from society. The retreat from society into introspection was overwhelming. Virginia Woolf, sensitive as ever to the fluctuation of artistic sensibilities, personified the trend. Writing in the early 1920s, she dismissed writers such as H. G. Wells, Arnold Bennett and John Galsworthy as 'materialists'; they were, she said, 'concerned not with the spirit but the body'. In contrast 'Mr Joyce is spiritual.' She concluded that future concerns lay 'very likely in the dark places of psychology'.[1]

The shift towards introspection also implied a rejection of or at least a reaction against material reality. It represented a questioning of reason and a concern with the inward, instinctive and irrational. In this sense it expressed some of the sentiments of the nineteeth-century conservative reaction. But it did so from an extremely sceptical point of view. It could not even bring itself to romanticise the past. The past seemed lost. And with regression rather than progress the order of the day, the future too looked disturbing. Writing in 1922, Paul Valery epitomised this sensibility:

> We think of what has disappeared, we are almost destroyed by what has been destroyed; we do not know what will be born, and we fear the future, not without reason. We hope vaguely, we dread precisely; our fears are infinitely more precise than our hopes; we confess that the charm of life is behind us, abundance is behind us, but doubt and disorder are in front of us and with us...
>
> The Mind has indeed been cruelly wounded: its complaint is heard in the hearts of intellectual men: it passes a mournful judgment on itself. It doubts itself profoundly.[2]

Valery's depiction of the human condition is not quite that of the 1960s 'anything goes' rhetoric. It is more a contemplation of a state where anything can happen.

In a situation where anything can happen, values and beliefs lose their meaning. It is never clear whether a lack of belief precedes something becoming unbelievable or if something ceases to be relevant and therefore causes a lack of belief. What is clear is that in the years between the wars, the mood at least among the intelligentsia fluctuated between deep pessimism and the conviction that everything was absurd. 'People are coming to believe that everything is breaking down: there is nothing that can't be questioned: nothing that is real stands the test', wrote Karl Jaspers in 1931.[3] Jaspers may have expressed a pessimism more thoroughgoing than most, but his sentiments very much reflected the times. According to Sontag, the panic which gripped Western Europe in 1931 was not merely a financial one. It was a 'crisis of confidence', where the 'accepted precepts for directing the life of man in society seemed suddenly not to work'.[4] Artists and philosophers like Jaspers were merely giving coherence to fragmented reactions in society.

The sense of doubt also prevailed in the Anglo-American context, in Britain in particular. The dimensions of the crisis of confidence which Britain experienced between the wars are comparable to America's disorientation in the 1960s. Britain's 'Vietnam Syndrome' was its heightened sense of imperial self-doubt. Nothing expresses this sentiment more poignantly than George Orwell's description of his disturbing thoughts when called on to kill a rampaging elephant in Burma. A former colonial policeman, then a novelist, Orwell wrote:

> And it was at this moment, as I stood there with the rifle in my hands, that I first grasped the hollowness, the futility of the white man's domination in the east. Here was I, the white man with his gun, standing in front of the unarmed crowd – seemingly the leading actor of the piece; but in reality I was only an absurd puppet punched to and fro by the will of those yellow faces behind. I perceived in this moment that when the white man turns tyrant, it is his own freedom that he destroys.[5]

Orwell's doubts about the empire expressed a wider sense of questioning about his way of life. A loss of another faith.

Artistic introspection and intellectual disenchantment were among the dominant expressions of this loss of belief in progress. This was the decisive development that shaped the growth of ideas in the period between the wars. In this respect the main legacy of the First World War was to undermine confidence in the possibility of positive purposeful change. This question mark regarding the meaning of the future was often understood by intellectuals as a loss of faith in history. The catastrophe of a world war was interpreted as the negation of the view which linked history with progress. According to Paul Fussell, the First World War was the last time when the future could be imagined as the continuation of the past:

the Great War was perhaps the last to be conceived as taking place within a seamless, purposeful 'history' involving a coherent stream of time running from past through present to future. The shrewd recruiting poster depicting a worried father of the future being asked by his children, 'Daddy, what did *you* do in the Great War?' assumes a future whose moral and social pressures are identical with those of the past.[6]

This sense of continuity was another casualty of the war.

The war and the social upheaval that followed had a devastating impact on the European ruling class and the intelligentsia. Virtually an entire era, from 1914 to 1945, could be summed up by the expression 'wasted years'. The barbarism of war, followed by a protracted period of economic depression and class conflict, then a further barbaric war, shattered belief in progress. This produced above all a crisis of confidence in the ruling class itself. As the American historian William McNeill argued:

> Meanwhile in Europe, the shock of World War I had called earlier generations' faith in progress into question. Especially from the point of view of the educated upper classes, it often seemed that instead of progress of civilisation, its decline was taking place around them – what with the 'revolt of the masses' at home and the natives' growing restlessness in empires overseas.[7]

From the point of view of the European bourgeoisie, the revolt of the working class and of colonial peoples was bad enough. Far more embarrassing was what it considered to be the betrayal of the 'educated upper classes' or the intelligentsia. A clear anticipation of the 1960s? Far worse, for the crisis of ruling ideas coincided with the emergence of a challenge far more radical than experienced either before or since.

In the early 1920s there was a sense of faith in progress sustained by the belief that science and technology would eventually guarantee the advance and well being of society. But such optimism tended to elude most of the intelligentsia. Scientific development could not restore the credibility of the idea of progress. This remains the case to this day. Although it is possible to identify periods of relative optimism here and there – particularly in the United States – in the post-1945 years, the idea of progress never came back into intellectual fashion. As McNeill notes, after the Second World War:

The idea of progress, discredited since 1914, was not revived by the technological marvels that continued to pour forth from research laboratories. Political anguish was too widespread, social strains too acute for such an optimistic vision of mankind's career on earth to have much appeal.[8]

Popular belief in the benefits of technology coincided with a sense of malaise among the intelligentsia regarding its consequences.

Instead of progress, a sense of crisis and decline saturated Western thought.[9] Most histories of ideas of the period tend to draw attention to Oswald Spengler's *Decline of the West* as symptomatic of the spirit of the time. Although Spengler's actual influence during the years between the years is difficult to discern, he certainly expressed a mood of despair that characterised the ideas of the time. Not everyone followed or emulated Spengler's preoccupation with racial and cultural decline. The more common response was a revitalised Nietzschean view which correlated technological advance with spiritual impoverishment. Aldous Huxley, grandson of the progressive scientist Thomas Huxley, clearly illustrates the scepticism of the intellectual towards the contribution of technology. His anti-utopian fiction *Brave New World* (1932) projects a future where the world is technically perfect but empty of humanity.

Instead of progress, new theories and concepts were based on the idea of crisis. Crisis in one form or another is the central motif in the discussion.[10] The loss of confidence had the character of a moral collapse. For many members of the establishment, the experience was far more painful than that of their inheritors in the 1960s. Their reaction to the Great War anticipated the Vietnam syndrome. For the English intellectual the war undermined all the ideals of the past. It represented the 'moral enfeeblement' of England.[11]

Although far more private than the great public manifestations of the 1960s, the social malaise of the British ruling class in the 1920s and the 1930s was just as profound. Between the wars Britain's consciousness of itself as a highly moral imperial power suffered a major setback. Britain's own decline accelerated, and the imperial project became discredited. Significant sections of the middle class and the intelligentsia ceased to believe in Britain. Lord Eustace Perry wrote in 1934 that there was 'no natural idea in which we any longer believe. We have lost the easy self-confidence which distinguished our Victorian grandfathers, and still distinguishes our American contemporaries.'[12]

Increasingly the British establishment experienced the humiliation of becoming an object of ridicule for its own intellectuals. The image of Colonel Blimp would not be easy to shake off. Across the channel in France the situation was no better. There too the ruling class had lost touch with the intelligentsia and large sections of the middle class. 'The 1930s have conventionally been depicted as an era of almost unparalleled squalor in modern French history', writes Hughes.[13] The unsavoury features of the period are usually 'grouped under the heading of "moral decay".'

The term 'generation gap', invented in response to the exigencies of the 1960s, would have been no less appropriate for use in the 1930s. Another description might be 'lost generation'. The rulers of capitalist Europe had lost a generation. Very few were prepared to admit that this was the case at the time. Instead the problem was dismissed as minor, affecting only small *côteries* of decadent intellectuals. E. H. Carr was one of the few who believed something could be gained from this lost generation. He wrote in 1944:

> The most encouraging feature of the present situation is the prevalence, especially among the younger generation, of a deep-seated conviction that the world of the past decade has been a bad and mad world, and that almost everything in it needs to be uprooted and replaced.[14]

But most of Carr's colleagues did not share his optimism. On the contrary it appeared that optimism had become a characteristic associated with evil forces in the East. This was the most bitter irony of all. If Western capitalism could not inspire hope and confidence in itself, then the optimism of others was experienced as a condemnation. Many Western thinkers were horrified that other alternatives seemed to inspire a belief in progress. Many drew the conclusion that if progress could be so easily associated with totalitarianism then such convictions were dangerous altogether.

The big compromise

The European establishment, convinced that it had lost the intellectual battle for progress, reacted by abandoning it altogether in case it became a weapon in the hands of its opponents. If the establishment could not be seen as the representative of progress, then it was far better no one else should be able to make that claim either. Competing alternatives still seemed to motivate commitment to a belief in progress. This was true of Stalin's Soviet Union and to a lesser extent of fascism. To a considerable extent the attraction of these alternatives was that they were not yet compromised and discredited like classical bourgeois ideas. In retrospect it is clear that it was the weakness of the capitalist intellectual legacy rather than the strengths of its competitor that accounted for the appeal of Stalinism at the time. E. H. Carr, who was concerned to reform Britain in order to pre-empt a totalitarian detour, explained the lack of enthusiasm for prevailing values and solutions thus:

> The attraction of Bolshevism, Fascism and National Socialism lay not in their obscure, elastic and sometimes incoherent doctrines, but in the fact that they professedly had something new to offer and did not invite their followers to worship a political ideal enshrined in the past.[15]

Many Western intellectuals combined a private despair with a strident dislike of those who believed in progress through political involvement. The term *ideology* was applied particularly to communism, but generally to any political project involving social transformation. It seemed that the very ability of the communist movement to convey a sense of progress provoked even greater denunciation of the concept. Karl Jaspers expressed this view when he argued that 'cheating others and oneself by means of ideologies' seemed to be the way that people managed to retain beliefs.[16] In other words ideology persuades people to believe in unrealistic and simplistic solutions.

Jaspers' argument was elaborated further by a number of writers who implied that in a condition of social malaise and uncertainty, there is among the masses a yearning for answers. Ideologies – communist or fascist – feed off these anxieties and this explains their success. This view characteristically expresses an elitist disdain for the gullible masses. The American theologian and philosopher Reinhold Niebuhr argued that Western society 'created atomic individuals who, freed from the disciplines of the older organic communities, were lost in the mass and became the prey of demagogues and charlatans who transmuted their individual anxieties and resentments into collective political power of demonic fury.'[17] To cast doubt on the proposals of these ideological charlatans,

Niebuhr was forced to question *any* political vision of progress.

In effect Jaspers and Niebuhr sought to preserve the status quo by calling into question the legitimacy of any project committed to progressive change. Western thinkers ended up rejecting what they have already lost in case the cause of progress becomes a powerful weapon in the hands of others. Thus as a result of the experience of the 1930s, progress became too dangerous a concept to leave intact.[18] The intellectual abandonment of the idea of historical progress was symptomatic of the upheaval of the Western world view. Today it is difficult to comprehend its extreme defensiveness. It seems almost incomprehensible that at the time Stalinism actually appeared to be winning the battle for ideas. All the key Western thinkers of this period seemed preoccupied and at times overwhelmed by this phenomenon.

The renunciation of history

An intellectual defence of the West could not be conducted by explicit negation of the idea of progress and purposeful change. Yet in the context of the Cold War, these ideas had to be contested as long as they were associated with the Soviet model. To negotiate this problem, pro-Western intellectuals began to adopt a new political vocabulary, one which expressed a deep suspicion of ideas of radical change. Unable to attack the concept of progress without inflicting damage on their own intellectual tradition, they renamed it. Terms such as 'historical inevitability', 'historical determinism', 'the philosophy of history', 'historicism' and 'ideological politics' were used as euphemisms for progress.

It would be inaccurate to depict the creation of this new vocabulary as a conscious act of deception. Rather it expressed disappointment and fear. Disappointment that the experience of the 1930s and 1940s had invalidated all hope of progress and a profound fear that continued belief in progress could only lead the masses astray and benefit the enemies of Western capitalism. It was suggested that such passions would fan the flames of fanaticism and ultimately destroy Western civilisation. Fear of ideology and a deep dislike of history became the characteristic sentiments of Western political theorists during the 1950s and 1960s.

This reaction to history and ideology is well described in Hall's sympathetic account of these anti-historical theorists:

A set of passionate authors deeply marked by personal experience, most notably Raymond Aron, Isaiah Berlin and Sir Karl Popper, argued the simple and clear case that the practice of the philosophy of history is *dangerous*. Such authors were hugely successful in establishing in the public mind a close link between the search for historical laws and the practice of bloody, totalitarian politics.[19]

This drawing of a close relation between 'believing' in history and destructive upheavals was designed to neutralise Marxism. Hall is right to conclude that this anti-historical project was successful, at least in providing a coherent alternative. However there was a high price to be paid. The attack on purposeful history threatened to call into question purposeful action as such. It did not require a great leap of imagination to draw the conclusion that if history had no purpose then life itself was without meaning. From this perspective it was difficult to avoid a pessimistic accommodation to a life without meaning. In historiography this meant the replacement of a vision of history with the presentiment that what happened in history was more or less arbitrary.

The critics of history were conscious of the pessimistic consequences of their standpoint. Their solution was to work out limited areas where meaning, purpose and change could have some positive application. Karl Popper's *Open Society and Its Enemies* typifies this tendency. Popper says he wrote the book 'to show that the prophetic wisdom is harmful and the metaphysics of history impede the application of the piecemeal methods of science to the problems of social reform.'[20] Popper's procedure is paradigmatic. By coupling metaphysics with history and by characterising historical thinking as prophetic wisdom the problem is disposed of. The advocacy of history is akin to a religious faith. To this metaphysics Popper counterposes 'piecemeal' reform. Within narrow confines piecemeal change can be pursued purposefully, and the consequences of complete intellectual pessimism can be avoided.

One obvious consequence of the renunciation of history is the flight towards relativism. If history has no overriding meaning than it is open to a variety of equally valid interpretations. The problem was that this deprived the tradition of the authors under discussion of moral certitude. As a result there was a continous attempt to combine the renunciation of history with arguments that could limit the damage that relativism could cause to the defence of the West.

Of all the major end-of-ideology theorists, Raymond Aron seems peculiarly sensitive to the dilemma posed by the renunciation of history. His reaction is to make a virtue out of necessity. In his article on the 'Philosophy of History', written in 1950, he accepts the triumph of relativism in history. However he argues that this is a positive development, a 'sign not of scepticism but of philosophical progress'.[21] The recognition that history cannot supply a 'final, universally valid account of societies' is itself a firm and common belief which belies the charge of scepticism, says Aron. There is no cause for concern, because all that has happened is that the 'ascendancy of pluralist philosophies' has led to the 'decline of unitary philosophies'.[22] This implies progress, since closed dogmas have given way to open-ended free-thought.

Aron is continually sensitive to the twin dangers of abandoning the concept of history and of progress altogether. His solution to the problem is to map out areas where these concepts can be used legitimately. Like Popper's piecemeal reforms, Aron seeks to establish piecemeal truths and absolutes within a pluralist framework. He emphasises that he is not against history as such, only against Marxist history:

> The idolisation of history of which Marxism represents the extreme form teaches violence and fanaticism. History correctly inter-preted, teaches tolerance and wisdom.[23]

Aron understands that to reject history altogether would encourage intellectual nihilism. He proposes a history that is unfinished and can therefore only explain a limited range of relationships. This 'better than nothing' view of history reflects the intellectual heritage of the postwar ideological compromise in the field of social philosophy.

Unable to uphold the traditional moral absolutes, the pro-West intellectuals were also repelled by the nihilism of extreme relativism. The sense of despair and loss of direction was all too painfully evident in the milieu of the postwar European artist and intellectual. Hughes' account of intellectual trends reminds us that in the late 1940s 'the existential philosophy of Jean-Paul Sartre figured as the most discussed intellectual movement in the Western world.'[24] Aron's intellectual confrontation with Sartre revealed a profound anxiety at the difficulty of finding a clearcut meaning to history. Aron sought to overcome the problem by rejecting both absolutism and relativism in history. He argued that meanings could be drawn but not *the* meaning.

Aron's attempt at a resolution of the dilemma posed by the renunciation of history is to find piecemeal, or little, meanings in the social process. He argues that 'history is not absurd, but no living being can grasp its one, final meaning.'[25] This model still leaves the problem unresolved but at least it establishes limited areas that can be meaningfully understood. The unsatisfactory resolution of this problem is shown by the continued demand of end-of-ideology theorists for absolute moral values. They are thus inconsistent. Having renounced meaning in history, they have to go outside their own theoretical system to seek these values.[26]

The question of values was reintegrated into the end-of-ideology perspective as a matter of arbitrary subjective choice. Judith Shklar complained that there could not be a concept of political justice without a 'moral imperative'. She promptly accepted that 'at least an ounce of utopianism' was preferable to not have anything to believe.[27] Her ounce of utopianism, like Popper's piecemeal reforms or Aron's little truths, represented an instinctive reaction to the consequences of their renunciation of history. They sought to retrieve some lost values by the back door without taking responsibility for their relativist intellectual posture.

The new consensus

By the late 1930s there was an intellectual consensus, which had the support of virtually the entire ideological spectrum, that the notion of a free-market capitalism was not sustainable. The manifest problems of capitalism were fully exposed by the Great Depression. While the capitalist world suffered the effects of economic stagnation, it appeared that Stalin's centrally planned Soviet Union was going from strength to strength. Virtually every economic comparison between the two systems appeared to favour the Soviet Union. In retrospect it is clear that it was the absence of confidence caused by perceptions of the weakness of the capitalist system that permitted many Western thinkers to have such exaggerated views about the Soviet Union. In other words a heightened sense of fragility disposed many to believe their competitors' extravagant claims.

One consequence of this crisis of confidence was the widely held view that some kind of socialism or some form of planned society would eventually prevail over free-market capitalism. Carr for one was certain that the free market was an outdated nineteenth-century idea. 'The moral crisis of the contemporary world is the breakdown of the system of ethics which lay at the root of liberal democracy, of national self-determination, and of *laissez-faire* economics', wrote Carr. As a result, the 'foundations of liberal democracy's *laissez-faire* had crumbled away.'[28] As an illustration of the exhaustion of free-market liberalism, Carr cited the United States government's imposition of controls on the entry of immigrants. Here was a nation with a reputation for providing refuge to all, which had closed its doors to immigrants in 1923. Carr reflected that 'this act more than any other was the symbol of a world grown static and stereotyped.'[29]

Even the most ardent defenders of capitalism and the most bitter opponents of the Soviet Union found it difficult to put up an enthusiastic case on behalf of the free market and all the values associated with it. Koestler, who will eventually emerge as one of the most often cited anti-communist thinkers, was distinctly guarded in his observations regarding the Soviet economy during the Second World War. In line with most anti-communist intellectuals of the 1940s, his indictment of the Soviet Union was not backed by a stand on behalf of free enterprise. Koestler was very much a man of his time when he wrote in 1943 that 'the economic structure of Russia is historically progressive compared with private capitalist economics.'[30]

Koestler's standpoint would have been entirely uncontroversial at the time. Planning was an intellectually acceptable concept while free-market economics had a tired and stale image. Intellectual trends of the time were directly opposed to the later economic liberalism of the 1980s. Hayek, probably the most renowed ideologue of the free market and widely celebrated in the 1980s, sounded much more tentative four decades earlier. Anyone rereading *The Road to Serfdom* will be struck by its defensive tone. 'Scarcely anybody doubts that we must continue to move towards socialism', Hayek informs the reader. Despite such doubts, Hayek's views are very much against the stream. His arguments against planning are hesitant. Planning is not inevitable, he says. He concedes that monopolies have increased but says that their economic weight has been exaggerated. He is prepared to accept that some rational planning is unavoidable and insists that he is not a supporter of dogmatic *laissez-faire*, but pleads:

The fact that we have to resort to the substitution of direct regulation by authority where the conditions for the proper working of competition cannot be created, does not prove that we should suppress competition where it can be made to function.[31]

This is from the most articulate and vociferous opponent of planning in the 1940s! One friendly critic argues that Hayek and Mises, like everyone else, also had an exaggerated view of Soviet success. In the past they had both argued that socialist planning was an impossibility. With *The Road to Serfdom*, published in 1944, the argument changed. They 'began to warn that the great choice was between socialism and the market economy – as if the former, far from being an impossibility, now existed in Russia.'[32]

One by-product of the general loss of faith in capitalism was the creation of a new consensus, around the acceptance of planning and the creation of a mixed economy that was also committed to welfare provision. This was a response to the perception of capitalist weakness and the ideological alternative posed by the Soviet Union. Its most articulate advocates were New Deal liberals in the United States and social democrats in Europe. However this consensus drew a far wider constituency; it included many conservative thinkers in Britain and individuals who would be associated with Christian Democracy after the war.

One of the key texts to articulate this consensus was Karl Mannheim's *Diagnosis of our Time*. Written in 1943, this attempts to provide a cure to what could become a terminal malady of the system. A Hungarian *émigré*, Mannheim is often described as a man of the left and even a Marxist. Although he had past links with the European left, by the outbreak of the Second World War his intellectual and political contacts straddled the party divide. He had close contacts with Conservative Party reformers in Britain as well as with Labour intellectuals.

Mannheim was deeply concerned about the future. He summarised the situation in 1943 in the following terms:

> We are living in an age of transition from *laissez-faire* to a planned society. The planned society that will come may take one or two shapes: it will be ruled either by a minority in terms of a dictatorship or by a new form of government which, in spite of its increased power, will be democratically controlled.[33]

So for Mannheim there was no question of whether society in the future would be planned or not. The only issue was planning under what kind of political regime.

Like Burnham and other early totalitarian theorists, Mannheim believed that these societies were more efficent than those that were less planned. Moreover he argued that free-market methods were 'destructive' in the economic field, because of the devastation they had brought in the 1930s, and that they were 'partly responsible for the lack of preparedness in the liberal and democratic states' for the war.[34] Mannheim warned that free societies would perish unless they intellectually and morally rearmed themselves against their totalitarian competitors. He argued that 'our democracy has to become militant if it is to survive.' What this implied was not spelled out very clearly. Reading between the lines, it seemed to consist of a conscious campaign to renew democratic values along with the establishment of a society that would be a 'third way' between totalitarianism and free-market capitalism.[35]

Although the 'third way' embodied a conscious strategy of preserving Western capitalist society, it also represented a compromise. By its own admission, the criticisms of free-market capitalism were legitimate. Through its acceptance of the need for a system of welfare it conceded some of the moral criticisms made of capitalism. At the time the 'third way' compromise was self-consciously seen as taking on board some of the traditions associated with socialism. According to the proponents of the 'third way', this was acceptable so long as it was driven not by dogma but by pragmatism. Niebuhr, whose bitter hostility to Marxism was almost matched by his lack of confidence about capitalism argued that 'the programme of the socialization of property is a proximate answer to the immediate problem of achieving justice in a technical age'. He added, that 'European civilization will undoubtedly resort to increasing socialization of property on pragmatic and experimental terms.'[36]

Probably the most systematic exposition of the 'third way' compromise is to be found in Arthur Schlesinger's *The Vital Center*. The role of this book in contesting extremism was discussed in the previous chapter. Published in 1949, it combines an explicit rejection of faith in capitalism and progress with a commitment to a mixed economy. Although this is an early Cold War text, it is also a summary of all the arguments that constitute the 'third way' compromise.

Schlesinger declares progress to be an illusion and calls upon the reader to 'foresake the millenial dreams'. He is clear that such beliefs must favour the opposition and therefore counsels resignation to the human condition. 'Important problems are insoluble', he concludes.[37] The need to lower expectations becomes a strategic principal in the struggle against the totalitarian menace. 'We are confronted with the spread of a ruthless totalitarianism abroad', he warns. The propaganda of this enemy 'may well undermine our own faith' and 'sap our capacity to resist foreign tyranny'.[38] It is very much a sign of the time that Schlesinger can explicitly admit that his reservation about the belief in progress is motivated by the fear that such views lead to the Soviet experiment. 'The degeneration of the Soviet Union taught us a useful lesson, however, it broke the bubble of the false optimism of the nineteenth century.'[39]

Schlesinger identifies extremism as the enemy and offers the middle way of the third road as the alternative; 'the spirit of the center – the spirit of human decency, opposing the extremes of tyranny'.[40] The models are postwar Britain, Denmark, Norway, Sweden, Belgium, Holland and Austria. The compromise 'third road' is clearly embodied in the postwar social-democratic consensus around the mixed economy. The main political emphasis of this perspective was not the promotion of any specific party. It was the project of establishing the *centre* as the only legitimate *locus* for political action.

As Schlesinger indicated, the compromise united politicans of the left and of the right. He held up Britain as the ideal model for his American audience:

The British tradition of responsible conservatism has prevented the possessing classes from seeing a national disaster in every trifling social reform; while British labor has itself developed a profound sense of national responsibility ... We desperately need in this country the revival of responsibility on the right – the development of a non-fascist right to work with the non-Communist left in the expansion of free society.[41]

Here was the foundation for what would soon be known as the politics of consensus. During the 1940s, there were very few either on the non-Communist left or on the non-fascist right who would disagree with this standpoint.

Today it is fashionable to attack the politics of the 'third way' compromise. Many right-wing writers blame this compromise, or specific policies associated with it, for the problems of late twentieth-century capitalism. One widely discussed study of wartime Britain blames the extension of welfare policies for the country's subsequent decline.[42] Similarly it is customary to blame liberal values for what is termed a moral malaise. These retrospective criticisms tend to be thoroughly anachronistic. They ignore the fact that the standpoint of economic liberalism was discredited during the 1930s. So too were traditional conservative values. In the circumstances, fundamental readjustments had to be made if the challenge posed from radical quarters was to be contained. The 'third way' was more than a compromise, it was a strategy for survival. And to some extent it worked. It helped neutralise the effects of the previous crisis of confidence. To blame that which assisted the reproduction of Western capitalism for the subsequent problems of the system is to lose sight of the grim realities of the years between the wars.

But however necessary, the 'third way' compromise could not resolve the ideological problems facing Western societies. Having abandoned the dreams of progress, capitalism now lacked a vision of the future. Western societies could engage neither the intellect nor the spirit. To some extent the Cold War served to motivate belief in the system. But Cold War sentiments were no substitute for a positive identification with a system of values. This was the problem that exercised the energies of social thinkers like Daniel Bell. Bell was deeply concerned with the inability of the capitalist system intellectually to enthuse. He wryly observed that the 'welfare state and the mixed economy were not the sort of goals that could capture the passions of the intelligentsia.'[43]

Bell wrote consistently of a disjuncture between what he saw as bourgeois economics and culture. He was concerned that capitalism could never recover from its intellectual defeats in the interwar period and that it would lose the battle for culture. He warned:

> The traditional bourgeois organization of life – its rationalism and sobriety – has few defenders in the serious culture; nor does it have a coherent system of cultural meanings or stylistic forms with any intellectual or cultural respectability. What we have today is a radical disjunction of culture and social-structure, and it is such disjunctions which historically have paved the way for the erosion of authority, if not for social revolution.[44]

Capitalism's failure to generate any cultural or intellectual system of support exercised the thought of Bell as much as it had his predecessors during the years between the wars.

Even some of those actively engaged in the construction of the 'third way' compromise were conscious of the issues raised subsequently by Bell. Karl Mannheim for one was convinced that the absence of intellectual support for capitalism was closely related to the erosion of the system of values associated with it. Mannheim recognised that there could be no return to the past but insisted that there needed to be values in which society could believe. This was the nub of Mannheim's dilemma. As a sociologist he was convinced that the days of the absolute values of the nineteenth century had passed. At the same time he was concerned with what he saw as the 'chaos and the crisis in our system of valuations'.[45]

Mannheim attempted to resolve his dilemma by adopting what he termed a 'new attitude to values'. This would renounce value neutrality but not adopt a too moralistic posture. Mannheim sought a third way 'between totalitarian regimentation on the one hand and the complete disintegration of the value system at the stage of *laissez-faire* on the other.'[46] This third way was an attempt to synthesise elements of the conservative stress on tradition with the classical liberal suspicion of moral regulation.

According to Mannheim, this approach 'will differ from the relativist *laissez-faire* of the previous age, as it will have the courage to agree on some basic values which are acceptable to everybody who shares the traditions of the Western civilization.'[47] In other words, value relativism uncontained was too destructive. Society required agreement on basic values. These values would stand on the traditions of Western civilisation. Mannheim did not spell out this tradition, except to imply that the 'set of basic values' was inherited from classical antiquity and even more from Christianity. This was the traditionalist Mannheim speaking – although a traditionalist with a difference. Acceptance of basic values implied *agreement* rather than acceptance of the authority of the past, of God or whatever.

Mannheim also understood that in the conditions of the 1940s, he could not push the terrain to be covered by the basic values too far. Accordingly tradition had to make its peace with liberalism. He wrote: .

But militant democracy will accept from Liberalism the belief that in a highly differentiated modern society – apart from those basic values on which democratic agreement will be necessary – it is better to leave the more complicated values open to creed, individual choice or free experimentation.[48]

This looked, at least on paper, like a harmonious compromise between relative and absolute values. Absolutes would be restricted to 'basic values on which democratic agreement will be necessary'. Relativism would be allowed to prevail in relation to more 'complicated values'. This was then a dual system of values, where absolute and relative considerations would operate at different levels. Tradition could thrive but only within restricted parameters.

In fact Mannheim's model would come to prevail in postwar Western capitalism. The main virtue of this arrangement was that it was sufficently pluralistic formally to include everyone in society. The main limitation of this compromise was that although it did not repel, nor could it enthuse. The agreed basic values represented a formality which possessed a mainly ceremonial function. Such values could not counter the effects of the growing trend towards relativisation. Indeed, inadvertantly, Mannheim conceded the crucial point when he accepted that society was highly differentiated and that many values were too complicated for tradition to handle. Mannheim's synthesis could not resolve the dilemma. His defence of basic values proved to be formal, clearly unable to contain the growing influence of relativism.

Mannheim's pluralistic orientation, his advocacy of individual choice and free experimentation, is not inconsistent with the rhetoric of the 1960s. This was a pluralism that sought to *regulate* the disenchantment that emerged *en masse* during the interwar years. It could not provide a solution to the intellectual malaise and crisis of confidence of those years but it could provide a framework which could assist damage limitation. This attempt to regulate what Mannheim called the crisis in the system of valuations worked reasonably effectively until the 1960s. Then this system of regulation proved ineffective and the sense of alienation that had hitherto influenced the intelligentsia temporarily acquired a wider public. The 1960s temporarily reminded the world that all the problems raised during the years between the wars still remained unresolved.

From our perspective, the widespread lashing out at the 1960s represents an evasion of the problem. The reaction to the 1960s is really a retrospective attempt to address the problems raised during the interwar period. The subsequent compromise is now called into question by those who fear the consequences of the growth of value relativism. It appears to many conservatives that a stalemate between basic values and complicated values works in the long run to the disadvantage of tradition. In any case the times have changed. When Mannheim was working through his ideas, the stock of conservative and right-wing ideas seemed at an all-time low. Many conservatives explicitly accepted the compromise in order to pre-empt an even worse arrangement. By the late 1970s, it was the ideas of the left that stood discredited. The reversal of fortune in the image of Stalinism between those two epochs is truly breathtaking. In these circumstances conservatives felt more at ease about changing the terms of the compromise or trying to get rid of it altogether. By focusing on the 1960s, they sought to close their eyes to that nightmare of 'the other 1960s'. Through the process of selective historical amnesia, right-wing thinkers could forget that what they now attacked as a problem was in the 1940s experienced as an acceptable compromise solution.

The betrayal of the intellectual

The denunciations of long-haired students and their indulgent professors, common among today's new right, has a long and honourable tradition. The reaction to the 1960s liberal or Marxist intellectual has also been well rehearsed. It is a theme that reoccurs throughout this century. This concern with the intellectual contains an important ambigiuity. In one sense it expresses an epistemology which blames the intellectual for the prevailing climate of opinion, but this is not an all-embracing strategy. The establishment in fact wants to win the intelligentsia to its side. So it adopts a typical carrot-and-stick approach. This strategy is often too subtle for some, or does not appear to work. The reaction is then to let rip. Usually it is suggested that the intellectual is too out of touch with real people, the 'silent majority' to use former US President Richard Nixon's term. Frustration in the battle for ideas leads to outbursts of anti-intellectual sentiment.

As in the 1960s, the ideological malaise in the West has frequently been blamed on the intellectual. Many a right-wing critic in France blamed Marcel Proust for single-handedly causing the moral decay of the Third Republic. In Britain the Bloomsbury set represented the villains in the conservative imagination; they were blamed for sowing the seeds of doubt about Britain's imperial mission. They were portrayed as the decadent beneficiaries of Britain's greatness, who took a delight in systematically destroying all the values that made up the identity of the nation.

Orwell was particularly scathing about the British intellectual, especially the left-wing variety. In his writings the decline of Britain and the corrosion of its moral order is directly blamed on its intellect-uals. Even the Colonel Blimps are discussed in more favourable terms than the 'Bloomsbury highbrow, with his mechanical snigger'. Orwell accuses the intellectual of being anti-English: 'England is perhaps the only great country whose intellectuals are ashamed of their nationality.' Using language that will find an echo in the accusation of anti-Americanism levelled against the 1960s intellectual, Orwell argues:

> All through the critical years many left-wingers were chipping away at English morale, trying to spread an outlook that was sometimes squashily pacifist, sometimes violently pro-Russian, but always anti-British.[49]

From this perspective the intellectual becomes the enemy of the nation. Some are accused of hoping to see England become 'Russianized or Germanized' after the war.[50]

In the 1940s continuing concern with the exhaustion of ideas led to a new preoccupation with the intellectual and his or her role. Many supporters of the establishment perceived the crisis of intellectual confidence as the product of the action of the intellectual. There seemed to be a suggestion that the intellectual through his or her ideas was responsible for the demoralisation of society. The other suggestion was that the intellectuals had become a special group with interests that contradicted those of society. In embryonic form this was the 'new class' thesis of the years that followed the 1960s.

Dangerous clerks

The exaggerated importance attached to the role of the intellectual was based on the peculiarly aristocratic epistemology of most of the thinkers under discussion. In line with traditional elite theories it was suggested that the masses acted only in response to the ideas fed to them by demagogues.[51] In the twentieth century these classical demagogues tended to be seen as the intellectuals. Hayek for one was convinced that many of the anti-capitalist ideas current in the 1950s were myths consciously or unconsciously circulated by well-meaning intellectuals.[52] Other interpretations of the intellectuals' motives were less charitable.

The most systematic exposition of the theory of the politically motivated intellectual influencing public opinion to the detriment of society is to be found in Julien Benda's *The Betrayal of the Intellectual*. This work published in the 1920s is, curiously, not well known, even though all the main thinkers so far discussed are influenced by it and often refer to it.

Benda's thesis is straightforward. He argues, that intellectuals – or 'the clerks' as he calls them (after the medieval clerics) – were traditionally involved in the disinterested search for the truth. Until the middle of the nineteenth century clerks sought 'their joy in the practice of an art or a science or metaphysical speculation, in short in the possession of non-material advantages.'[53] These were independent individuals, disinterested in worldly goods, who pursued ideas for their own sake. Their lives were in 'direct opposition to the realism of the multitudes'. They were prepared to take an independent stand and preached against the dominant passions.[54]

This rather romaticised portrait of the traditional intellectual is directly contrasted to its venal counterpart in the twentieth century. In the past the clerks acted as the guardians of truth, ready to steer society away from disaster. According to Benda, the modern clerk is no longer detached from the multitude. The 'great betrayal' of the clerks is that they now seek to adopt political passions. He accuses the clerks of 'divinizing' politics and of being responsible for the unleashing of political passions.[55]

Benda in particular blames the intelligentsia for the growth of xenophobia. 'This adhesion of the "clerks" to national passions is particularly remarkable', he notes.[56] Much of the book is devoted to detailing the betrayal of the cause of intellectual detachment and the disinterested search for the truth.

As a description of the involvement of the intellectual in partisan politics, Benda's work is not particularly significant and is unlikely to have merited much interest in subsequent years. But it contains a couple of ideas which Benda elaborates at great length and which became the central motifs in the subsequent discussion.

The first argument which will be taken up by others is the connection between extreme political passions and the involvement of the intellectual. Benda doesen't just accuse intellectuals of abandoning their cherished traditional role. He suggests that the involvement of the clerk in politics actually gives greater focus to political hatreds and makes them far worse. In other words by giving coherence to political passions, the clerks ideologise them. These are no longer intermittent outbursts but a system of hatred. Through ideology, passions acquire shape and uniformity, they become a permanent problem. 'Our age is indeed the age of the *intellectual organization of political hatreds*', writes Benda.[57]

It is Benda's coupling of the clerk and ideology with the explosive mass movements of the twentieth century that makes his work so interesting to those concerned with stability and order. It will provide the raw material for the theories of betrayal in the interwar years as well as the 1960s. Intellectuals and their ideologies will reappear in the theories of totalitarianism and the end of ideology. For some defenders of the social order the intellectual will emerge as the main threat facing an otherwise well balanced society.

Benda's other influential theme is slightly more complicated. This is his romantic counterposition of the detached and truth-seeking 'clerk' of the past to the partisan and materially oriented intellectual of the present. This counterposition appears in much of the anti-1960s literature, especially in the United States. The theme is central to the work of Bloom, Rieff and others, mainly in the form of upholding the concept of a non-political and autonomous university.[58] At first sight it is far from clear why this point is so strongly insisted on. Even a cursory acquaintance with history shows that the detached clerk is a figment of the imagination. Intellectuals were no more and no less part of society than today.

It is evident that the main purpose of the romaticisation of the traditional clerk is to discredit the involvement of the modern one. It is almost as if fearing that intellectual involvement will be oppositional to the system, Benda and others denounce involvement as illegitimate. The celebration of the detachment of the clerk from society becomes an argument for curbing and ultimately controlling the activities of the intellectual. More to the point, it offers a flattering role to the clerk – a disinterested explorer of the truth – in exchange for renouncing social involvement. With Benda there is a way back for the lost intellectual. This is a far superior way of handling intellectual dissent then the populist denunciations of demagogues.

Explaining treason

There are many subsequent variations of Benda's argument. What all have in common is the supposition that *the intellectual crisis experienced by Western capitalism is in fact the crisis of the intellectual*. The literature of the high Cold War period was particularly pessimistic on this point. It contained the often unstated assumption that the intellectual could not be counted on in the contest against the totalitarian menace. This sense of pessimism pervades Koestler's 1944 article 'The Intelligentsia':

> If, in the long run, Burnham's diagnosis comes to be true (as I believe it well may), and if, after some intermediary oscillations, we are in for an era of managerial super-states, the intelligentsia is bound to become a special sector in the Civil Service.[59]

Koestler's doubts about the direction of the intellectual was widely shared by the establishment in all Western societies. These doubts soon led to a questioning why such a pampered section of society had proved so fickle in its loyalty.

Schumpeter saw the intellectual as a threat to the survival of capitalism. In his major work of the 1940s, *Capitalism, Socialism and Democracy*, he argued that the intellectual was responsible for establishing 'the atmosphere of hostility to capitalism'. He advanced a rather journalistic history of the rise of the intellectual to explain this hostility to capitalism.

According to Schumpeter, the intellectual was born in the monastery of the medieval world. But it was the technology of capitalism, particularly the printing press, which allowed this group to extend its impact over society. The growth of this technology allowed the intellectual a greater access to public opinion and incidentally a degree of independence from his capitalist patron. Schumpeter particularly emphasises the 'power of a free-lance intellectual' to manipulate public opinion. He suggests that in the absence of any other institutional role, the freelance intellectual establishes himself by manipulating the views of the masses.

Since the intellectual lives on criticism, his impact on the masses tends to question the status quo. At this point Schumpeter introduces an argument which recurs time and again and with great force in the 1960s. This refers to the overproduction of intellectuals whose wants cannot be satisfied and who therefore become opponents of the system. Schumpeter suggests that 'discontent breeds resentment', which the intellectual rationalises into 'social criticism'. From this perspective he suggests that the intellectual gives coherence to all the anti-capitalist passions that already exist. So 'the role of the intellectual group consists primarily in stimulating, energizing, verbalizing and organizing' this anti-capitalist raw material.[60]

But the intellectual's greatest betrayal, according to Schumpeter, is his base manipulation of the irrationality of the masses. According to this model the intellectuals 'invade' labour politics in order to establish a position of influence for themselves. To establish their credibility, the intellectuals are prepared to do anything to build up their authority over the masses. Schumpeter's description of this process is revealing:

> Having no genuine authority and feeling always in danger of being unceremoniously told to mind his own business, he must flatter, promise and incite, nurse left wings and scowling minorities, sponsor doubtful or submarginal cases, appeal to fringe ends, profess himself ready to obey.[61]

This then is Schumpeter's case for indicting the clerks. In their obsessive search for status, they provoke the grievances of the masses and encourage hostility towards the system. The alienated intellectual thus becomes the most formidable threat to society.

Another way of explaining the betrayal of the clerks is provided by Bertrand de Jouvenel. De Jouvenel seems to see the entire Western intelligentsia as a problem. He writes:

> An enormous majority of Western intellectuals display and affirm hostility to the economic and social institutions of their society, institutions to which they give the blanket name of capitalism. Questioned as to the grounds of their hostility, they will give *affective* reasons: concern for 'the worker' and antipathy for 'the capitalist', and *ethical* reasons: 'the ruthlessness and injustice of the system'.[62]

As the inverted commas suggest, de Jouvenel does not believe intellectuals are concerned about anyone other than themselves. They lack the impulse of altruism. According to de Jouvenel, intellectuals have an ambivalent attitude towards the legacy of capitalism and the industrial revolution. What they like about this development they attribute to the 'force' of progress and what they dislike to the 'force' of capitalism.

The main explanation put forward by de Jouvenel appears to suggest that the intellectual envies the success of business. In particular there is resentment that the intellectual's worth is considered to be less than that of the capitalist. Consequently, it is difficult to get the intellectual to accept the prevailing values and structures of society. The intellectual's bitter criticism 'may be to some degree explained by the inferiority complex he has acquired.'[63]

The conclusion which de Jouvenel draws from his analysis is that it is the intelligentsia which represents the greatest threat to society:

> It has for long been assumed that the great problem of the twentieth century is that of the industrial wage-earner's place in society; insuffcient notice has been taken of the rise of a vast intellectual class, whose place in society may prove the greater problem.[64]

Within a decade this argument had acquired the status of a conventional wisdom. Certainly by the 1960s no one would pause to remark that not enough attention had been paid to the role of the intelligentsia. Interminable discussion about how the intelligentsia had replaced the proletariat as the truly revolutionary class soon followed. Out of a concern to substitute the crisis of the intellectual for the intellectual crisis of Western societies a 'new class' was born.

The main point of the plot in this betrayal of the clerks is to exonerate the prevailing system of values from any failings. The fault lies with the sectional interest of the 'new class'. Benda's argument and all the others that are its derivatives counterpose the legitimate to the illegitimate intellectual. In the 1960s the betrayal was accounted for sociologically by the mass expansion of the institutions of higher education. In a sense the 1960s type theories are even cruder than those of Benda and others. Benda and Schumpeter actually conceded that cricial ideas and radical political passions emerged independently of the intelligentsia. Their indictment of the clerks was that they gave coherence to these passions and thus helped establish a climate of opinion hostile to the capitalist system. The anti-1960s literature saw them far less as mediators. In many cases it suggested that the radical criticisms of the time were invented entirely on the campuses by miscreants who were marginal to society. As proof, it was held that the sensible silent majority accepted the values of the system. The long-haired radicals had no purchase on society.

The anti-1960s literature contains a curious contradiction. Its elitist perspective of blaming malevolent intellectuals for the misguided ideas of the gullible masses coexists with a populist assertion that ordinary people were never fooled by the antics of the 1960s generation. The good sense of ordinary folk is sharply at odds with the mischief of the intellectual. So John Carroll was pleased to report that 'popular culture in the West has retained its moral sense ... common consciousness has not followed high culture and the elite intelligentsia in their nihilistic attacks on tradition.'[65] A triumph no doubt for instinct and good sense.

There is an element of the crude witch-hunt about the anti-1960s literature. To take one example:

> There can be no doubt that the intellectual and moral assault on free enterprise, and the exaltation of marxist collectivism, which is such a striking feature of the 1970s, is directly related to the huge expansion of higher education, put through at such cost to the capitalist economies in the 1960s.[66]

The link drawn between the expansion of higher education and radicalism was of course tenuous. The intellectual climate of the time was influenced by a number of different determinants, the size of higher education being at best one of a number of contingent elements. On its own, the expansion of education may result in the growth of radical ideas or it may not.

The various attempts to explain the ideas of the intelligentsia as the result of something internal to its social position are essentially tautological. The so-called new class is explained by its radical ideas and the ideas are radical because they are those of the new class. Lipset observes that what he calls the 'new intelligentsia' are 'highly critical of the values and institutions of existing Western societies'.[67] Fair enough, but are they so critical because those ideas are part of the general intellectual climate or because they possess a special quality or interest which disposes them in such a direction? What happened if those designated to constitute the new intelligentsia become less critical and come to reconcile their views with the traditional values of their society? Are they then no longer part of the new intelligentsia or does it mean that this stratum has ceased to exist? As a description of reality, back in 1978, Lipset's comments were possibly accurate. A decade later even at the level of description they would not do justice to reality. So have the intellectuals ruptured their affiliation with the new intelligentsia, or has this group ceased to exist?

The betrayal of the intellectual is ultimately an unsuccessful thesis because it reduces the causes of the intellectual climate of society to the acts of those agents who express the unpalatable views. As with the conservative view of education, the messenger is blamed for the bad news.

Yet the betrayal of the intellectual remains the key construction of the conservative reaction to the 1960s. Based on the arguments forged in reaction to the problems of the 'Other 1960s', it is no more and no less effective than most conspiracy theories. Mere denunciation is not a suffient basis for winning the battle for ideas. In the end it was the ability of the right to *influence* sections of the intelligentsia that boosted its capacity to wage an ideological crusade in the late 1970s. The next three chapters will examine the theoretical issues raised by this crusade, by focusing on the contending views of 'history'.

Prolonging the pain

If all the elements of the contemporary conservative reaction were evident in the response to the 'other' 1960s, why was it necessary to wait so long before the launching of an intellectual counter-offensive?

With the advantage of hindsight it becomes evident that there was considerable reluctance to abandon the ideological compromise forged in the 1940s. The more ideological right was actively discouraged from pursuing its project. Daniel Bell argued that unadulterated liberalism and conservatism had 'lost their intellectual force'. With a dig at Hayek, Bell remarked that few liberals 'insist that the State should play no role in the economy, and few serious conservatives, at least in England and on the Continent, believe that the Welfare State is "the road to serfdom".' A no-nonsense pragmatic moderation was the consensus. This provided an inhospitable climate for a right-wing ideological offensive. Bell concluded with an air of certainty:

> there is today a rough consensus among intellectuals on political issues: the acceptance of a Welfare State; the desirability of decentralized power; a system of mixed economy and of political pluralism ... the ideological age has ended.[68]

This statement implied a warning not just to the left but to any attempt to introduce ideology into political affairs. It seems that among many end-of-ideology thinkers there was a concern that a too explicit restoration of the traditional values of Western capitalism would unnecessarily ideologise political affairs and even galvanise radicalism into action.

By the late 1970s, however, the political climate had changed. In many Western societies changes had to be made to the mode of economic and political regulation. These changes were inconsistent with the terms of the big compromise. The global shift from Keynesianism to monetarism reflected this. By the early 1980s, the West was also less defensive then at any time since the years between the wars. The left appeared politically weak and intellectually confused. The Soviet Union had changed from a pole of intellectual attraction to one of repulsion. As a corollary, the confidence of right-wing intellectuals was boosted. Finally, the time had come for intellectually confronting the legacy of the other 1960s.

That it took so long to confront this legacy exposes the exhaustion of the Western capitalist intellectual tradition. The clearest evidence of this exhaustion was its inability decisively to defeat Stalinism until very recently. This failure was in no way due to the depth and eloquence of Stalinist ideas, rather it was due to the state of the capitalist intellectual armoury. To return to H. Stuart Hughes' trip to Europe in the summer of 1950. Hughes' account provides an invaluable insight into the ideological climate of the time. He writes of the 'new conservatism of 1950', the successful Western unity forged against perceptions of the Soviet threat. Reading the article it becomes clear that Marxism and other associated trends were to some extent discredited and on the defensive. Yet they were not decisively routed.

The weakness of the Western capitalist tradition is shown by its inability to make significant gains after the exposure of Stalinist terror and the show-trials in the 1930s. According to Brick many of the individuals who were repelled by these events and broke with Stalinism found the Western mainstream traditions less then attractive. He writes that three works of the early 1940s, 'well-known for their reconsideration and repudiation of Marxian socialism, *presumed* the obsolescence of bourgeois society and bourgeois thought.'[69] These were Edmund Wilson's *To the Finland Station: A study in the writing and acting of history*, James Burnham's *The Managerial Revolution* and Reinhold Niebuhr's *The Children of Light and the Children of Darkness: A vindication of democracy and a critique of its traditional defence*. Wilson himself summed up the mood of the authors when he characterised the period as 'a time when the systems of thought of the West were already in an advanced state of decadence'.[70] While all three books were bitterly critical of Stalinism, they all self-consciously refused to endorse the capitalist alternative.

The 'third way' intellectual compromise was too defensive to inspire enthusiasm and a strong sense of direction. This led to a sort of ideological stalemate. Radical ideas were contained and the political movements associated with Marxism lost their capacity to enthuse people in the West – and to a considerable extent it was the growing perception of the internal incoherence of Stalinism that was responsible for this freezing of the left – but at the same time a compromise Western political tradition gave the system a measure of coherence without resolving the intellectual crisis of the interwar years.

By the early 1950s, it was clear that the real problem for the upholders of the Western capitalist tradition was not the dynamism of its ideological opponents but its own deficiencies. This was particularly the case in Western Europe, where the abandonment of traditional political values left a major gap. Unable to resolve this, the ruling class in Europe opted for the old-fashioned answers of tradition. As Bracher argues, the most successful political innovation in Europe in these years was the rise of Christian Democracy: 'It was Catholicism above all that proved able to counterpose a value-oriented doctrine of society and state to the political vacuum.'[71] This reappropriation of traditional religious doctrine for the purpose of confronting a modern moral vacuum indicated that the 'third way' compromise could not generate a positive vision of society.

If anything, this actually strengthened the pessimism of the Western intellectual. One symptom of this intellectual exhaustion was the defensive tone of the Western discussion of the Soviet Union. Today it seems astounding that Western anti-communist intellectuals could have such high respect for the capacities of the Soviet social system. Instead of going on the offensive many Western intellectuals were more interested in arguing that the Soviet Union was not superior to their own societies.

At a conference of the leading pro-Western intellectuals in Milan in the 1950s, organised under the auspices of a leading Cold War publication, *Encounter*, there was general agreement that the Soviet Union and capitalist societies were converging.[72] The theory of convergence suggested that there was a similar logic at work in all industrial societies: as these societies developed and became more affluent they would become less ideological and move closer together.[73] Convergence theory embodied the pessimism and low expectations of the Western intellectual. By emphasising the similarities of the two systems, this theory abandoned the attempt to construct a positive vision based on the unique tradition of Western capitalism. Instead of stating that 'we are morally superior', convergence theory suggested that 'you are no better than us'.

Convergence theory provided a consistent perspective based on intellectual compromise and the piecemeal approach to values discussed previously. Raymond Aron put the argument clearly when he stated that 'all regimes are imperfect' and that the issue was not one of doctrine but of the technical requirements of growth.[74] Aron and other convergence theorists were quite happy to abandon the battle of doctrines, a battle with which they felt all too uncomfortable.

Another source of the defensiveness of the Western intellectual was the growing challenge of the Third World. The Milan conference felt relaxed about containing the Soviet challenge but extremely concerned about the prevalence of anti-Western sentiment in the Third World. There was a widespread suspicion that just when the battle was won in Europe, the war could be lost in Asia and Africa.

Daniel Bell, whose name was most prominently associated with the end-of-ideology thesis, had no illusions that the intellectual battle had been won in the Third World. According to his account, there was no end of ideology in the Third World. Worse still, it appeared that in this part of the globe the moral authority of Stalinism remained intact. 'Russia and China have become models' for Third World societies concerned with economic development, remarked Bell.[75]

Bell argued that the political and intellectual compromise that was forged in the 1940s worked adequately in the West, but in the Third World ideology had come into its own:

And yet, the extraordinary fact is that while the old nineteenth-century ideologies and intellectual debates have become exhausted, the rising states of Asia and Africa are fashioning new ideologies with a different appeal for their own people.[76]

He saw this as an outstanding problem. The decline of the moral standing of the Western world weakened its intellectual legacy.

From today's standpoint, the conclusion to be drawn is that the 'third way' compromise was effective as a strategy for survival. It was ineffective as a solution to the intellectual crisis that had emerged during the interwar years. Back in the late 1950s Daniel Bell sensed this limited effectiveness. His best-known work, *The End of Ideology*, was as much a mourning of the passing of political passion as a celebration of the defeat of ideology. Almost instinctively Bell grasped the crucial point that without a positive view of the future the battle for ideas could not be won. There was always the danger of losing the soul of the intellectual. He warned that the young generation of intellectuals were searching for a 'cause': 'The young intellectual is unhappy because the "middle way" is for the middle-aged, not for him; it is without passion and is deadening.[77] This was an accurate assessment of the situation. Something like the 1960s was waiting to happen all along. Bell and his co-thinkers certainly could not take the new generation of intellectuals for granted.

It is ironic that many of of the leading pro-Western thinkers, especially in the United States, were concerned to activate the new generation of intellectuals. There was concern that the postwar compromise would turn the younger generations into cynics. Pells writes:

> Throughout the 1950s, magazines and newspapers berated the young as members of a 'silent generation' – politically apathetic, intellectually passive, caring less for social causes than for economic security, preoccupied with their private lives.[78]

There was even concern about about the lack of political engagement on the campuses. Clearly the postwar Western intellectual was out of touch with the new generation. Intellectually there was no point of contact. This represented the fatal weakness of the 'big compromise'. The compromise that involved the renunciation of history and progress and could accept only 'little meanings' lacked the power to enthuse. This was its weakness, indeed its flaw.

In such circumstances great care had to be exercised in the management of intellectual life. The middle way may not represent the high point of human achievement but at least it was safe. This was the dominant reaction of the Western intellectual until the late 1970s.

7

Dreading change:
The closure of the historical mind

It is time to pull together the strands of the reaction to historical consciousness. This chapter aims to provide a historical-logical reconstruction of the closure of the historical mind. It suggests that the expulsion of the historical subject, of men and women, from the process of change is the recurring theme in the story.

History and the codification of the past developed as reaction to the sense of historical change that emerged with the Enlightenment. This development of History did not merely represent a reaction to the *idea* of change. The eighteenth and early nineteenth centuries were indeed periods which experienced massive change. For those allied to the existing order, the process of change that followed the French revolution and the subsequent Europe-wide military conflict appeared ominous and threatening. In this context, History provided a sense of stability by recreating a consciousness of continuity with the past.

The same forces that led to the emergence of History also contributed to the rise of historical thinking. This was stimulated by the perception of cumulative change. Experience appeared to validate the conviction that history was an endless progress marking humanity's path to reason, unceasing change where the present was transient. The new consciousness of history led to the conceptualisation of new social structures and societies. This consciousness implied a critical attitude towards the present state and a commitment to direct, purposeful change towards some objective in the future. The experience of the French Revolution was taken as confirmation of the possibility of *making history* through the conscious negation of the existing state.

Historical thinking, with its emphasis on the transience of all social arrangements, is inherently revolutionary and critical of what exists. It is a form of thinking that arose with the ascendency of the bourgeoisie, but one that was difficult to sustain. As the new order of industrial capitalism emerged, criticism and the idea of change was gradually interpreted more ambiguously by the bourgeoisie. As the preservation of the status quo became the predominant intellectual problem of the day, historical thinking became increasingly hesitant and more and more drawn towards accommodation.

Change that imprints itself on the human consciousness is rare. But when it occurs, the force it lends to the sense of transience overwhelms society for a long time afterwards. Thus the French Revolution became the main point of reference in the nineteenth century as arguably the Russian Revolution did for the twentieth. It is astonishing how rare historical thinking is as a dominant intellectual influence. Historical thinking flourished for a very brief period of time and under very special circumstances. Many of the theoreticians who initially exhibited an acute sense of historical consciousness modified their views in their later years. Thus Hegel was prepared to accept 'the end of history' and argued that the Prussian state was the realisation of reason. Here was a social system that no longer needed to be transcended.

Auguste Comte, like Hegel, could recognise that a sense of historical change was relevant for the past, but went on to question its relevance for his own time. He wrote in this vein that 'the fact that Reason in modern times has become habituated to revolt, is no reason to suppose that it will always retain its revolutionary character.'[1] Comte clearly differentiates his positivism from its early 'negative' phase, that is the phase of revolution. The 'positive phase' concerns the consolidation of the new society. That is why Comte self-consciously sided with the forces of law and order against those of radical republicanism and the urban masses, writing that 'the right view is well expressed in the motto, Liberty and Public Order, which was adopted spontaneously by the middle classes.'[2] Thus for Comte history ends with the consolidation of middle-class society. The insights and consciousness of the preceding negative phase are now no longer appropriate. The consciousness of history is relegated to the past.

The inability consistently to theorise the sense of historical temporality should not lead to the conclusion that this form of consciousness was insignificant. Historical consciousness had a dominant impact on nineteenth-century thought. Even the more conservative thinkers could not avoid confronting intellectually the experience of change. As Hobsbawn points out many conservatives appropriated change into their system by transforming the sense of the past. Change in this conservative form became the past evolving into the present or, as Hobsbawn puts it, the 'past as a process of becoming the present'. This teleological view of history, where the past is realised in the present, recreates change in the form of continuity. The fact that change had to be incorporated into the system of thought of the conservatives was a sign of the time. As Hobsbawn states, 'faced with the overriding reality of change, even conservative thought becomes historicist.'[3]

Despite the overwhelming experience of change it is clear that even at its late eighteenth and early nineteenth-century high point, historical thinking never existed in a pure form. There were always certain customs, traditions or religions which were retained as constants, not susceptible to change. There was also a tendency, even within Enlightenment thought, to emphasise progress as inevitable rather than as the possible outcome of human history-making action. By treating progress as a natural working-out of history it was possible to conceive of it as a *religion*. In this way history becomes objectified; it becomes a transcendental force beyond human intervention. Non-humanist versions of progress treat it as an unproblematic process of human advance. In this form progress is reconciled with a metaphysical interpretation whereby it represents the working out of the Divine Will. This is precisely what happens in the case of Saint-Simon and Comte when their philosophic treatment of progress collapses into a secular religion. Once progress assumes a religious form it directly modified the consciousness of transience, which was part of its initial premise.

Enlightenment rationality had a one-sided limited character. It posed reason as a transcendental force which was destined to be realised through history. This abstraction of reason into a transcendental idea minimised the significance of reasoning human beings. Reason was there to be worshipped but not applied to the making of history. In this form, reason itself became a constant, violating the fundamentals of historical thinking.

The modification of the consciousness of transience allows progress to be robbed of its critical content. If progress is merely the realisation of a pre-given idea of human development, it is possible to argue that the idea has been achieved. By suggesting that society expresses the ideals of progress, the end of history can be declared . A sense of terminus develops as a direct antithesis to historical thinking.

Historical thinking is undermined by the fear of change. Historical change disrupts and destabilises society. In such circumstances even those who possess a consciousness of history can become perturbed and disoriented. Anxieties towards change often lead to the suspension of critical thought, which can make individuals more disposed towards accepting historical constants. Since the early nineteenth century the area covered by these constants has extended and by implication the terrain open to change has narrowed.

The most effective argument against change is the contention that history has no purpose. If that is so, then banking on change becomes a risky business since without purpose or direction everything is a matter of luck and accident. As Sir Lewis Namier argued, 'there is no more sense in human history than in the changes of the season.'[4] The corollary of this argument is that to seek change is senseless.

The depiction of the senselessness of history is designed to call into question the purpose of change. This mystification of history is helped by the absence of any obvious connection between individual human action and its unintended consequence. Since humans rarely achieve *directly* what they set out to do, the charge of senselessness is a plausible one. The absence of a direct connection between self-awareness and the consequences of individual action leads Hayek to celebrate the mysteries of the market. He even calls on intellectuals not to attempt to understand that which is not knowable. Indeed for Hayek the very attempt to understand is counterproductive.[5] Hayek has far more confidence in the spontaneous and anarchic forces of the market than in the power of human potential. In the reaction to historical consciousness there is a close connection between the philosophical devaluing of history and scornful dismissal of purposeful human action.[6]

In the past the mystification of history and the belittling of the relevance of knowing was a direct expression of the fear of change, particularly of the consequences of the French revolution. These fears, for example, inspired Edmund Burke to uphold the validity of prejudice. He wrote in his *Reflections on the Revolution in France*:

> I am bold enough to confess that in this enlightened age we are generally men of untaught feelings; that instead of casting away all our old prejudices we cherish them to a very considerable degree ... and the more generally they have prevailed, the more we cherish them.[7]

This defence of prejudice is clearly counterposed to the application of reason for the solution of human problems. The main virtue of prejudice, it seems, is that it is 'old'. It is its survival through the years that suggests it is worthy of respect. Prejudice, then, is the underside of tradition – and the defence of tradition, allied with a challenge to the claims of reason and of purposeful human action, constituted the main argument against historical thinking. In plain English, survival was itself a virtue to be preferred to the untested promise of the new.

Fear of change

Historical thinking, and the tendency towards the social experimentation that it inspired, gradually gave way to a more conservative outlook. By the late nineteenth century the qualities of change were discussed in terms which were strikingly pessimistic. Krishan Kumar writes of a 'sense of ending', which accompanied this dramatic transformation of the intellectual climate. To illustrate this Kumar cites H. G. Wells' prophetic novel of 1907, *The War in the Air*, where Wells writes of the suddenness of the coming of the end:

> Up to the very eve of the War in the Air one sees a spacious spectacle of incessant advance, a worldwide security, enormous areas with highly organized industry and settled populations, gigantic cities spreading gigantically, the seas and oceans dotted with shipping, the land netted with rails and open ways. Then suddenly the German airfleets sweep across the scene, and we are in the beginning of the end.[8]

The sense of terminus, so clearly captured by imaginative writers like Wells, had also permeated the outlook of the turn of the century Western intellectual.

The sense of terminus, which will be explored later in this chapter, represented above all a statement about the experience of change. Nietzsche expressed an abhorrence towards change, when he warned that 'European culture' was 'moving towards a catastrophe, with a tortured tension that is growing from decade to decade: restlessly, violently, like a river that wants to reach the end.'[9] In the case of Nietzsche, anxiety regarding change was mainly focused on the consequences of widening access to culture. From his elitist standpoint the 'total secularisation of culture' turned it into a common means of gain. His hatred for the 'socialist rabble' stemmed from his fear of what the consequences of change represented for the 'genuine culture' of the elite.[10]

Conservatives had always opposed the ideas of the Enlightenment. Liberals, on the other hand, advocated many of these ideas in their challenge to outdated institutions. John Stuart Mill had consistently criticised those who sought to explain social phenomenon through non-rational means such as intuition, tradition or prejudice. He described *intuitionism* as the 'intellectual support of false doctrines and bad institutions'.[11] These doctrines defended religion and tradition. According to Greta Jones, Mill opposed them because they 'suggested that certain institutions – religious and political – were not the result of historical or social development but the outcome of ideas planted in the mind by God and, for this reason, largely unchangeable.'[12] In the debate about the origins of society and its institutions, nineteenth-century liberals and conservatives expressed fundamentally different opinions, at least until the middle of the century.

The liberal advocacy of rationality was never maintained consistently. Liberal thinkers, even one as wholeheartedly egalitarian as John Stuart Mill, were seriously concerned about the disruptive effects of social change. In particular they had serious reservations about applying the criterion of rationality when the *masses* were under consideration. In this respect Mill shared Nietzsche's elitist stance. Mill saw the influence of the masses on society as less than welcome. He wrote:

> At present individuals are lost in the crowd. In politics it is almost a triviality to say that public opinion now rules the world. The only power deserving the name is that of masses and of governments while they make themselves the organs of the tendencies and instincts of the masses. Those whose opinions go by the name of public opinion are not always the same sort of public: in America they are the whole white population; in England, chiefly the middle class. But they are always a mass, that is to say, a collective mediocrity.[13]

Mill feared the levelling-down effects of mass society and the consequent loss of individuality that such a process implied.

The reaction of many liberals to the social consequences of change was far more profound than that of Mill. There was a widely held concern that with the decline of traditional institutions, the stability of society would be undermined. Looking towards the 'darkness of the future', de Tocqueville warned of 'men, not being attached to each other any longer by the ties of caste, class, association, and family' who are 'always thinking solely of themselves and shutting themselves up in a narrow individualism where all public virtue is suffocated.'[14] According to Giner there developed for the first time the concept of the atomised mass. Giner argues that:

> For the first time in its long evolution within the framework of Western social thought, the notion of the mass ... does not bear a relation to riotous or unruly crowds, but is linked rather to a holistic vision of society, which is now conceived as a vast, dispersed collectivity of frightened and isolated individuals.[15]

This perception of the masses as of isolated individuals has as its counterpoint the image of past stable organic communities. The idea of mass society is thus haunted by the sensibility of lost traditions.

Concern with the problem of social order inevitably led liberals to reconsider their attitude to change and tradition. The reaction of Walter Bagehot to the events that occurred in France during the years 1848 to 1851 is instructive in this respect. 'The first duty of society is the preservation of society', he wrote. His apprehension of social instability led Bagehot to promote the centrality of sentiment within society, such as the sentiment which bound the masses to the symbols of the monarchy.[16] Bagehot's support of sentiment was part and parcel of the wide-ranging reappraisal of tradition that was taking place in liberal circles at the time.

This reappraisal was motivated by the sense of disappointment with what change bought about. Society did not appear to be following a rational course; in many ways the situation seemed threatening. The rational optimism of liberalism did not survive beyond the nineteenth century. As Jones remarks:

> Politics had by the turn of the century developed in ways unacceptable to those who would, by inclination, have belonged to the tradition of liberal rationalism. The aim of integrating the working class into a moral consensus and liberal political tradition had not been achieved to the extent that many liberals had hoped ... in concert with these developments occurred an increasing resort to an explanation of political behaviour in terms of irrationality.[17]

During the last three decades of the nineteenth century classical liberalism broke down. Its standpoint regarding the nature of change had moved close to that of conservatism and its commitment to rationalism underwent a significant revision. It still declared itself a supporter of reason, but suggested that the area within which the irrational prevailed was growing all the time. Fifty years later Shklar could write without any fear of being contradicted that 'liberalism has become unsure of its moral basis, as well as increasingly defensive and conservative.'[18]

The breakdown of liberalism was symptomatic of the difficulty of reconciling a rationalist belief in progress with a commitment to maintain the existing social order. The exigencies of conserving society drove liberalism towards conservative conclusions. A recent study by an author sympathetic to the liberal philosophy concludes that by the First World War 'liberalism had lost its former sway, even to the extent that liberal ideas had been wholly abandoned by the Liberal Party.'[19] In practice this meant that former liberal views, for example on the free market, were synthesised with conservative sentiments regarding the past and its tradition.

Friedrich Hayek personifies this liberal/conservative synthesis. A recent attempt to defend Hayek from the charge of conservatism does not stand up to the force of the evidence. Green argues that what characterises conservatives is the 'fear of change', a point of view that is alien to Hayek.[20] In reality Hayek, like all conservatives, is deeply suspicious of change. Where he differs from classical conservatives is that he recognises that tradition must evolve if it is to be effective in countering the claims of change. 'We must build on tradition', writes Hayek.[21]

The fear of change has filtered into every aspect of twentieth-century social thought. The pervasive existence of this sentiment has been underwritten by the overwhelming image of failure associated with the main attempts at social transformation. This experience has directly contributed to the gradual displacement of historical thinking. The conclusion drawn by most commentators is that the attempt to change society leads to a situation which is actually worse than what existed previously. Hence it is common to blame the attempt to change society for a variety of problems. One British political columnist has argued: 'Transformational ideologies have inflicted vast harm upon our century and a death toll numbering many millions.'[22] The inference of this statement is all too clear.

Whatever the problems of society as it is, the attempt to change it can only make the situation far worse. In recent times even modest initiatives to ameliorate life through a system of welfare have been renounced on the grounds that they make the situation worse.

The hostility towards change has fostered a mood where events of the past are continually reinterpreted as warning signs to those who would dare to undertake any social experiment that is remotely ambitious. Back in 1988, the bicentary of the French Revolution saw an outburst of retrospective rancour against those who supported the celebrations. Douglas Johnson, a professor of history at University College, London, wrote:

> But the word revolution today conjures up visions of the Soviet Gulag or of Iranian intolerance. It could be said that only the terrorist will now take moments of the French Revolution as a point of reference. No wonder that lots of its history is depicted as murderous and conspiratorial.[23]

This reappraisal of the French revolution was itself an eloquent comment on the conservatism of the times. Back in time, William Wordsworth wrote in celebration of the French Revolution:

> *Bliss was it in that dawn to be alive*
> *to be young was very heaven.*

Only a terrorist could harbour such sentiments in the 1980s, according to one distinguished professor.

The primacy of tradition

The fear of change corrodes a history that is oriented towards the future. Instead of looking to the future for solution, the trend throughout this century has been to investigate the past for answers. Anti-historical theory has emphasised the survivals of the past and underlined the elements of continuity rather than change. This was the dominant theme at a symposium on culture held in Poland in May 1991. In the opening statement Jan Bielecki, the Polish Prime Minister, stated that 'Poland's communist past is but a 40-year aberration in a history that stretches over a thousand years ... a short-lived, insane experiment.'[24] Here the immutability of a tradition stretching over a millennium demonstrates its strength by despatching into oblivion a 'short-lived insane experiment'.

Tradition is worshipped not merely on the ground that it has been around for a long time but because it provides a better insight into the secrets of life than does historical thinking. Karl Mannheim contrasted the approach of traditionalism to futurism in the following terms:

> For progressive thought everything derives its meaning in the last analysis from something either above or beyond itself, from a future utopia or from its relation to a transcendent norm. The conservative, however, sees all the significance of a thing in what lies *behind* it, either its temporal past or its evolutionary germ. Where the progressive uses the future to interpret things, the conservative uses the past.[25]

Conservatives argue that the past and the customs and conventions that have gradually emerged contain more wisdom than the intelligence of a single generation. The wisdom of the past surely outweighs the pretensions of a single individual, argues the traditionalist. In any case, conservative thinkers can always count on the emotional appeal of the past. As one of their numbers argues: 'conservatives, knowing well the appeal of tradition, the depth in the human mind of nostalgia, and the universal human dread of the ordeal of change, the challenge of the new, have rested their indictment of the present frankly and unabashedly on models supplied directly by the past.'[26]

It is not only conservatives who have integrated tradition into their epistemology. Hayek, his libertarian reputation notwithstanding, adopts a consistent intellectual defence of tradition. Hayek argues that tradition and morality are both logically and chronologically prior to the ability to reason. He uses the following circular argument to substantiate the importance of morality and tradition. These institutions developed spontaneously through human interaction. Following the perspective of the free market, the very survival of tradition and morality is proof of their superiority over the others that have fallen by the wayside. These 'spontaneously generated moral traditions' by their very existence, that is because they have survived, demonstrate their relevance for humanity. They exist because they work and precisely because they work they cannot be dispensed with. Hayek contends that 'if humankind owes its very existence to one particular rule-guided form of conduct of proven effectiveness, it

simply does not have the option of choosing another merely for the
sake of the apparent pleasantness of its immediately visible effects.'[27]
Unlike conservatives who defend tradition on the grounds of religion
or some other essentialist criteria, Hayek argues for its inviolability
because it provides an efficient system of rules.

For Hayek, tradition provides the foundation for human development. It is only through the acceptance of tradition that the capacity
to learn develops. So 'human interactions governed by our morals
make possible the growth of reason and those capabilities associated
with it.' The primacy of tradition in this schema is self-evident: 'Man
became intelligent because there was *tradition* – that which lies
between instinct and reason – for him to learn.'[28]

Furthermore, argues Hayek, tradition is the most powerful guide
available for human understanding. It outweighs the power of
reasoning: 'Moral traditions outstrip the capacities of reason.'[29]

In a sense Hayek's own intellectual development indicates not
merely the collapse of liberal ideas but also how the reaction to change
leads inherently towards traditionalism. A shift in emphasis in
Hayek's work is discernable. His early polemical attacks on economic
planning and his defence of free-market capitalism gradually give
way to the exploration of human nature and of tradition. His last
major work, *The Fatal Conceit: The Errors of Socialism*, reads almost like
a religious text. Both God and the Market work in strange and
mysterious ways and for Hayek both helped to evolve effective
traditions.

For Hayek, the 'truth' of religion is irrelevant. He fears the
'premature loss of what we regard as nonfactual beliefs' because it
would deprive humanity of a 'powerful support'. He argues that
'even now the loss of these beliefs, whether true or false, creates great
difficulties.'[30] Hayek is coy about spelling out what these difficulties
are about. Reading between the lines it is clear that the loss of this
'powerful support' hurts, above all, the powerful who run society.
That the author of *The Road to Serfdom* crowns his career with a
celebration of the worship of the 'nonfactual' is symptomatic of the
extremes to which anti-historical writing is pushed. Hayek's
obscurantist posture combines a naive faith in the power of the Word
with a species of Social Darwinism.

We owe it partly to mystical and religious beliefs, and, I believe,
particularly to the main monotheistic ones, that beneficial
traditions have been preserved and transmitted at least long

enough to enable those groups following them to grow, and to have the opportunity to spread by natural or cultural selection.[31]

Truth becomes a revelation of a tradition born out of the survival of the fittest.

In Hayek's defence of tradition the manipulation of the past is taken to an extreme. The tradition and morality of today are to be celebrated because they prevailed in the struggle for survival. To prove this assertion, Hayek simply reads history backwards. The proof of the superiority of Western traditions is that only they survived the test of time. Hayek reminds his reader that *'the only religions that have survived are those which support property and the family'*.[32] Past survivals are the only relevant guide for humanity, according to this perspective. Hayek's mind is closed to any vision which is oriented to the future.

Restraining reason

Once the primacy of tradition is established, the field for rational action necessarily becomes qualified. Even when there is no conscious attempt to counterpose the two, the claims of reason are subverted by something which is recognised as sacred in its own right. For those who are repelled by historical thinking, tradition serves as a veritable monument to the past, as a warning to the pretensions of reason. In the years between the Enlightenment and today, the direction of intellectual development is towards restraining the claims of reason.

In many cases the initial doubts about reason are a reaction to the social upheavals that follow the development of capitalism. From this point there is a clearly defined elitist perspective which interprets the actions of the recently urbanised mass of workers as those of an *irrational* mob. Once this conclusion is drawn, it follows that reason does not provide a sufficient bases for understanding the 'rabble'. This was for example the reaction of J. A. Hobson, the liberal reformer, to the outburst of popular chauvinism in England during the Boer War. For Hobson, this was 'an instinctive display of some common factors of national character which is outside reason and belongs in ordinary times to the province of the subconscious.'[33]

The studies of the psychology of crowds and mobs which were fashionable in the late nineteenth century tended to emphasise the irrational instincts of the herd. Gustave Le Bon argued that the non-rational actions of the masses would force out of social life the conscious behaviour of the individual. Although Le Bon was not prepared to support the prescription of religion to cool down these irrational urges, he argued the need for a 'single unifying myth' to bind society. This myth, with its armoury of simple symbols and repetitive images, was in fact a secular religion – a religion whose explicit objective was to curb the unpredictable and therefore uncontrollable passions of the mob. This emphasis on myth rather than the power of reason illustrates just how far the balance had shifted towards a respect for the irrational by the late nineteenth century.[34]

The tendency to emphasise the non-conscious in crowd action had an explicit apologetic connotation. This was the prelude to the standpoint that equates social protest with irrational action. During the first half of this century many writers even suggested that the rationalist culture of capitalism was responsible for the periodic social explosions. Rationalist culture had weakened the institutions of tradition which restrained the forces of irrationalism. The weakening of tradition means the erosion of control, and chaos follows.

Joseph Schumpeter argues that rationality is no 'match' for the non-rationality that explodes in after the erosion of tradition. Indirectly, Schumpeter expresses a reverence for the traditions of the past, which have at least kept dangerous passions in check:

> Capitalist rationality does not do away with sub- or super-rational impulses. It merely makes them get out of hand by removing the restraint of sacred or semi-sacred tradition. In a civilization that lacks the means and even the will to discipline and to guide them, they will revolt.[35]

In this scenario, tradition is an effective countervailing influence to the 'extra-rational driving power that always lurks behind' mass action. Clearly reason has no role in all this. Schumpeter is convinced that 'political criticism cannot be met effectively by rational argument.'[36]

The consequence of Schumpeter's thesis is not explicitly elaborated. Presumably it is not a thousand miles away from that of Le Bon. Implicit to this standpoint, however, is the stress on restraining the non-rational sentiment of the masses by insulating the political system from them. Schumpeter admits his pessimism and alludes to the need to limit access to public affairs.[37] Despite a reluctance to spell out the logic of the argument, Schumpeter's thesis serves to invalidate social protest, which can be dismissed on the ground that it is driven by non-rational forces. Moreover, a reasoned response is declared to be inappropriate since 'utilitarian reason is ... no match for the extra-rational determinants of conduct'.[38]

The restraint of reason through the affirmation of tradition is one response of a society that is increasingly preoccupied with the problem of order. However it would be wrong to suggest that all attempts to restrain reason are directly or indirectly motivated by anxieties concerning order.[39] The disappointments with capitalism experienced by individuals often seem to lead to the questioning of the relevance of reason. For many artists and intellectuals intuition rather than rational thought seems to provide a superior form of knowing. Alongside the traditionalist reaction to historical thinking in the early years of this century there developed a romantic reaction against the intellect. In this case it was not so much tradition but instinct that acted as the conveyor of truth. D. H. Lawrence expressed this sentiment with great clarity in a letter to Ernest Collinge in 1913:

> My great religion is a belief in the blood, the flesh as being wiser than the intellect. We can go wrong in our minds. But what our blood feels and believes is always true. The intellect is only a bit and bridle. What do I care about knowledge? All I want is to answer to my blood direct without fribbling intervention of mind, or moral or what not.[40]

Not everyone adopted Lawrence's extreme stress on instinctual drive. Nevertheless there was a large body of opinion that accepted the insight of the artist as superior to the rationality of science.

The famous fact–value distinction made by Max Weber provided a closely argued case for restraining reason. Reason had little relevance for understanding values. Weber himself was ambivalent, to say the least, about the relationship of art and science. A semi-conscious fear of transience directed Weber towards an admiration of the permanence of objects of great art. As against this, the achievements of science seemed pedestrian. 'In science, each of us knows that what he has accomplished will be antiquated in ten, twenty, fifty years', wrote Weber.[41]

Weber's approach was but one strategy for restricting the application of knowledge. The analytical philosophy that became so fashionable in the interwar years had an extremely sceptical stance towards what constituted objective knowledge. This position was summed up by Ludwig Wittgenstein's statement that the 'correct method in philosophy would really be the following: to say nothing except what can be said.'[43] After this extreme delineation of the scope for reasoning, very little can be said about anything.

The tendency to limit the application of reason has become more and more a dominant feature of Western intellectual life. In a recent survey of this subject, the sociologist Jeffrey Alexander writes of the 'omnipresence of irrationality'. According to Alexander, reason 'has been experienced as a hollow shell, progress as inconceivable, and often actually undesirable.'[44] The reaction against reason today is far stronger than at any time since the development of capitalism. In the nineteenth century the romantic revolt against reason did not question the possibility of knowing, it merely challenged one possible -- that is, the rational – form of knowing. During the past sixty years even the very possibility of knowing has been called into question.

Consequently, contemporary reactions against reason and historical thinking are far more pessimistic than in the early nineteenth century. This point was clearly stated by Judith Shklar in 1957:

> While the early romantics showed considerable combative vigour and really believed that the spirit of poetry might yet conquer the world of prose, the contemporary romantic cherishes no such hope – indeed, no hope of any sort. Instead of dramatic energy there is now only a feeling of futility. Romanticism now expresses itself in a denial of the very possibility of our knowing – much less controlling – history, nature, or society.[45]

This rolling-back of the frontiers of knowing seems to be the dominant achievement of Western thought this century.

Of course a modern industrial society cannot reproduce itself entirely by relying on a diet of irrationalism. Many establishment thinkers are deeply disturbed by the entrenched position of the irrational. They are particularly worried about the sceptical and relativist consequences that flow from the breakdown of reason and objective knowledge. As discussed in previous chapters, the conservative reaction is itself an attempt to reassert absolute values. So the attempt to uphold a semblance of rationality is directed above all at the nihilistic logic of irrationalism. Because it seeks to conserve rather than criticise, the traditionalist critique of society does not stimulate much response from establishment rationalists. Indeed many of the right-wing critics of relativism attempt to uphold the claim of reason while celebrating some eternal truths.

The attempt to synthesise reason and tradition can never resolve the tension between the two. Bloom's work provides an eloquent testimony to the failure to defend rationalism from the standpoint of conservatism. Here and there in his lengthy book, *The Closing of the American Mind*, Bloom alludes to his attachment to the principle of reason. He confesses that his youthful ideal was the pursuit of disinterested truth:

> In a nation founded on reason, the university was the temple of the regime, dedicated to the purest use of reason and evoking the kind of reverence appropriate to an association of free and equal human beings.[46]

It is immediately evident, however, that Bloom perceives reason in a non-rational religious sense, for in the next paragraph he denounces the 'facile economic and psychological debunking' of theoretical life, and warns that such criticism 'cannot do away with its irreducible beauties'. Pure reason becomes a kind of secular divine revelation which can only be contaminated by earthly criticism. Reason is a museum exhibit and not a tool to be used. Throughout the book the reader can virtually see Bloom sneer whenever the word debunking is used. In Bloom's cosmology criticism implies destruction

Bloom's mourning of tradition saturates the book. He writes of the disappearance of religion and of moral learning. Predictably he bemoans 'the unhappy, broken homes' which are symptomatic of the 'decay of the family's traditional role as the transmitter of tradition'. He is worried about the 'corrupting effect on Americans' of Nietzsche and Freud. But what concerns Bloom is that the rejection of tradition threatens to demystify social life: 'Thus we demystify economy and sexuality, satisfying their primary demands, taking away what our philosophy tells us is their creative impulse, and then we complain we have no culture.'[47] The problem of knowing too much is obviously inconsistent with the rationalist outlook. They can only be reconciled by taking reason out of history. Thus reason becomes what exists. As for Hegel it was realised in the Prussian State, with Bloom it is the American Way. In effect reason has been transformed into a tradition.

Bloom's contemptuous references to 'openness' and 'debunking' converges with the general tendency to narrow the range of knowable subjects. In fact throughout this century, *the delimitation of reason has been the central theme in the intellectual defence of the status quo*. The argument that human knowledge is limited is consistently used to discredit attempts to reform or transform society. The superiority of the past or of tradition is ultimately justified on the grounds of human ignorance. The depreciation of reason and understanding justifies the dismissal of social and political action as absurd. That is why the disparagement of knowing has become central to the intellectual defence of the status quo.

During the past two decades Hayek has developed a veritable system of arguments against the claims of reason. The title of his recently published book, *The Fatal Conceit*, expresses an indictment of the arrogance of rationalism. Hayek argues that the central defect of socialism is that it does not recognise the limits of human understanding. In effect, Hayek argues that humanity lacks the knowledge for the pursuit of social transformation. In Hayek's world view it is ignorance rather than knowledge that characterises the human condition. 'Though governed in our conduct by what we have learnt, we often do not know why we do what we do,' he writes.[48]

Hayek's veneration of 'not knowing' is not simply a result of an oversensitive appreciation of a complex reality. This liberal defender of the free market possesses a profoundly irrational view of history. His is a history where chaos and chance are far more significant than meaning. His rejection of the 'Age of Reason' is based on the premise that there is no knowable pattern to the development of humanity. He writes:

> What the age of rationalism – and modern positivism – has taught us to regard as senseless and meaningless formations due to accident or human caprice, turn out to be in many instances the foundations on which our capacity for rational thought rest.[49]

The acclamation of accident completes Hayek's dismissal of the role of man and woman in history. Against the sheer weight of tradition and the force of accidents, it does indeed require conceit to believe that purposeful human action can make any difference. What we have is a concept of history which consists of a series of accidents, which develops on its own accord, and where humanity is assigned the role of a spectator in an otherwise meaningless drama.

Consciousness devalued

With the emergence of historical thinking, the sense of change became theorised for the first time. Change itself became an issue, the premier intellectual problem of the time. This sense of change was closely linked to the recognition that subjectivity was not external but part of history. As Brook Thomas argues, the 'modern concept of reality, in which the *mundas novas* becomes possible, is related to the rise of historicism because it depends upon a changed notion of temporality.'[50] Key to this new notion of temporality was the affirmation of men and women acting as the agents of history. This perspective actually expected change; it was open to the 'new' and believed that the future was to some extent the product of human action. Thomas is right to suggest that from this perspective events 'take place not only in history but through history, and temporality has become a component part of reality.'[51] It is only necessary to add that this sense of temporality allowed the consciousness of making history to flourish. It is therefore not surprising that the reaction against historical thinking must contest every claim made on behalf the role of consciousness in the making of history.

It is precisely on this point, on the role of consciousness, that anti-historical thought is most vitriolic. The attempt to act in accordance with a system of ideas is invariably denounced as ideological, fanatical, utopian or millenarian. All these arguments share the premise that human beings have little control over their action and still less over its outcome. The ridiculing of reason leads directly to the dismissal of the concept of humanity controlling its destiny.

Hayek takes a special delight in continually stressing the weakness of the human being. The corollary of his view of history as a series of accidents is that man and woman are always the objects but never the subjects of history. He concludes his discussion of human values on the following note:

Man is not and never will be the master of his fate: his very reason always progresses by leading him into the unknown and unforeseen where he learns new things.[52]

Fate, like history, is entirely external to human intentions. From this thesis it follows that the attempt to shape the future is necessarily doomed. The sense of fatalism in Hayek's writings virtually overwhelms the reader. Hayek dislikes Freud, no less then Marx, for acting as a catalyst for the idea of 'freeing ourselves from repressions and conventional morals'.[53]

Hayek takes as the counterpoint to his views the title of the book

Man Makes Himself, by Gordon Childe. For Hayek the very idea of 'man making himself' is preposterous. As an alternative Hayek offers a spontaneous theory of human evolution. He offers a vulgarised version of Social Darwinism as an antidote to historical thinking. By the time he is through there is hardly a trace of subjectivity left in this interpretation of history. Hayek, anticipating the obvious criticism, distances himself rhetorically from Social Darwinism. He writes that 'Social Darwinism is wrong in many respects', but the 'intense dislike of it shown today is also partly due to its conflicting with the fatal conceit that man is able to shape the world around him according to his wishes.'[54] As far as Hayek is concerned, anything that discredits the ability of human consciousness to shape the world has got to be good.

Hayek's proximity to Social Darwinism is quite understandable. Of all the irrationalist trends that emerged in the nineteenth century, the most anti-historical was that of Social Darwinism. Evolution, natural selection and the struggle for survival were projected as natural processes independent of society. Thus history became naturalised and the role of the historical subject was totally annulled.

The disparaging of consciousness is ultimately reduced to the banal proposition that unless the limitation to purposeful human action is recognised, ideas get out of hand. It is the fear of change that motivates the charge of fanaticism or utopianism towards any serious social experiment. Such experiments are at first dismissed as unrealistic, then denounced as a religion unconnected to reality. Ideologies are routinely described as serving the function of religion. Because these dreams are not restrained by any consideration of reality they are potentially dangerous. 'Our dream of heaven cannot be realized on earth', warns Popper.[55] The coupling of ideology with religion is crucial to this argument. Ideas gain force not because they make sense but because they unleash hidden passions. According to Bell, 'what gives ideology its force is its passion'. Apart from religion, ideology is one of the few forces that 'can tap emotion', he suggests[56] Ideology takes on almost magical properties in this scenario, where the human agent is reduced to a bundle of irrational emotions.

Ideas stir passions and soon the fanatic is born. The construction of the fanatic is one of the main achievements of the reaction to historical thinking. This genesis is not unlike that of the possessed in the modern Hollywood horror film. Herman Kantorowitz, historian and Jewish refugee from Hitler's Germany, expressed this process most succinctly when he told his audience that 'men possessed thoughts, but ideas possessed men.'[57] The fanatic, possessed by ideas which ignore the evident limits of human action, personifies the danger represented by change.

Such fanaticism invariably invites the label utopianism. This used to have a neutral if not positive connotation, but has recently acquired a menacing image. The non-acceptance of the fatalism counselled by Hayek becomes proof of the fanatic's inability to accept reality. This 'conceit' in the history-making potential of humanity demonstrates yet again the problem of emotional immaturity. The British right-wing historian Lord Elton can always be relied on to articulate every dimension of anti-historical thinking. Not for the first time we hear:

> Being adult means being able to accept people and things as they really are, whereas the young idealist can see only the call for changes prescribed by radical faiths and can ignore the blood spilt.[58]

This hostility towards 'idealism' in an indirect sense represents a reaction against belief in the power of ideas. The mechanical counterposition of 'things as they really are' to the 'call for changes' rules out the possibility of any mediated relation between the two.

The 'big compromise', discussed in the last chapter, represented an attempt to separate ideas from history. It was based on the premise that the application of consciousness to history-making does not work. This standpoint is neatly summarised by the phrase 'End of Ideology'. In Daniel Bell's treatment of this subject, ideology was examined as the carrier of displaced religious or chiliastic passions. The end of ideology was meant to signify the exhaustion of these passions. Ideology has lost its 'power to persuade', argued Bell. 'Few serious minds believe any longer that one can set down "blueprints" and through "social engineering" bring about a new utopia of social harmony.'[59]

Scepticism regarding blueprints and the human potential was only one aspect of the belittling of consciousness. Arguments regarding the irrationality of the masses were elaborated to suggest that if anything the attempt to influence the direction of history invariably led to disasters. It was precisely the irrationality of the masses which made history-making activity so dangerous. The irrational masses provided the raw material for the fanatic with his or her ideology to work on. This was the scenario that lingered in the conservative imagination.

At its worst, the disparaging of consciousness could actually blame social struggles for virtually every evil experienced by humanity. A recent book on the conservative imagination by Robert Nisbet held the masses responsible for the 'new and terrible society', totalitarianism.[60] Nisbet and others suggest that democracy may be the source of the problem. Why? Elitist theory argues that it is because people do not know how to act rationally. Consequently they can be swayed by Benda's self-serving clerks and an assortment of other demagogues. As Mommsen reminds us, this argument is used by German conservatives to strengthen the self-serving claim that Nazism was the consequence of 'voting-booth democracy'. That is to say, the responsibility for the rise of Hitler lies with unrestricted mass democracy.[61]

The blaming of mass democracy for the Nazi era shows just how far the attack on the role of consciousness can be pushed. The argument used by German conservatives is by no means atypical. Insofar as democracy is seen to allow for the involvement of the masses in the making of history, it becomes a subject of criticism. Roger Scruton, the leading philosopher of British conservatism, expressed the anti-democratic implications of the argument with admirable clarity when he warned about the dangers of public hysteria, when 'fanned by the democratic arrogance which thrives in the modern world'.[62] Allan Bloom's defence of the university is motivated by the aristocratic fear of mass society. Following Alexis de Tocqueville, nineteenth-century author of *Democracy in America*, Bloom argues that an intellectual elite is essential to contain the volatility of the masses. Bloom is repelled by majority opinion and dismisses it as the 'great democratic danger'. He warns of the 'tyranny of the majority' and calls for some authority that transcends contemporary society.

In Bloom's system, the fear of change and of the majority is represented as the argument for the perpetuation of tradition. The call to revive the past is explicitly linked to the need to curb the sentiments of the present:

> Without being seduced by its undemocratic and antirational mystique, tradition does provide a counterpoise to and repair from the merely current, and contains the petrified remains of old wisdom (although with much that is not wisdom). The active presence of a tradition in a man's soul gives him a resource against the ephemeral, the kind of resource that only the wise can find simply within themselves.[63]

Since wise people like Bloom are in short supply, tradition becomes the desirable alternative to people attempting to control their destiny. This aristocratic devaluing of the role of the human agent in history invariably precipitates the closure of the historical mind. The 'petrified remains of old wisdom' is all there is to the reaction to historical thinking.

The sense of terminus

The publication during the summer of 1989 of the article 'The End of History', by Francis Fukuyama, set off a heated controversy, especially in the Anglo-American world. Superficially, at least, it seemed to represent an obituary for the Soviet challenge to the West. The failure of this challenge allowed Fukuyama and others an opportunity to revel in a bit of intellectual triumphalism. But ironically, the very terms in which the discussions were couched tended to minimise the celebration. The idea of the end inevitably raised the existential question 'so this is it?'

The sense of terminus which Fukuyama's contribution exudes is in every sense representative of the dominant themes of Western culture.

This culture of increasingly low expectations continually warns off utopian dreams. In the past the insignificance of human beings tended to be posed by anti-historical thought primarily in relation to tradition. During the present era the insignificance of human beings is counterposed to the overwhelming power of nature. In the shadow of ecological catastrophe, human action seems to have less meaning then before. Whereas in the past men and women were warned to conform to tradition, today they are told also to adapt to nature. Popular natural histories stress with great exaggeration the insignificance of the human species.[64] By underlining human insignificance, they thus stress our weakness to evade the end.

In one sense it is surprising that Fukuyama's article caused such a stir. The view that history is coming to an end has been consistently reproduced in Western thought for the past century. It is one of the most consistent intellectual responses to the fear of change. Since it directly negates historical thinking, the argument is often expressed as a call to defend the status quo. The intellectual representation of the sense of terminus is governed by a variety of distinct motives. In general it is an expression of anxiety regarding change. From the late nineteenth century onwards, it also increasingly expresses a sense of decline, experienced in a number of different forms: spiritual, cultural, racial or natural. Such a reaction to change always sees progress as problematic, since the process leads to the loss of spirituality, humanity and so on. The loss far outweighs the gains of progress, goes the argument.

By the interwar years, the end-of-history contributions were two-a-penny. Oswald Spengler's *Decline of the West* was a fashionable talking point in European *salons*. In those days Fukuyama's contribution would have gone unnoticed. This intellectual climate was well summed up in 1936 by the sociologist Louis Wirth, who pointed to the 'extensive literature which speaks of the "end", the "decline", the "crisis", the "decay", or the "death" of Western civilization.'[65] Wirth explained this state of affairs in relation to the prevailing fashion for questioning the 'norms and truths which were once believed to be absolute'. Ironically, Wirth himself gets carried away by the influence of 'endism'. In his case it is precisely the explosion of the sense of terminus that constitutes the potential catastrophe. For Wirth the problem is the 'depreciation of the value of thought'. This 'threat to exterminate what rationality and object-ivity' has achieved represents the 'deepening twilight of modern culture'. 'Such a catastrophe can be averted only by the most intelligent and resolute measures', concludes Wirth.[66] For Wirth the very questioning of reason, which the sense of terminus implied, threatened not only to bring reason to an end but to destroy its achievements.

Spengler forcefully captured the sense of terminus through a historiography which represented history as a series of cycles, in which every culture reaches its limit and decays. He wrote:

The future of the West is not a limitless tending upwards and onwards for all time towards our present ideals, but a single phenomenon of history, strictly limited and defined as to form and duration, which covers a few centuries and can be viewed and, in essentials, calculated from available precedents.[67]

The inexorable decline of the West is blamed specifically on the rise of the masses. Spengler has no inhibitions about expressing his venomous hatred for the masses. The mass 'recognises no past and possesses no future'. It hates 'every sort of form, every distinction of rank, the orderliness of property, the orderliness of knowledge'. This rabble, without the restraint of the past, is itself the embodiment of the end; it is the living negation of class society. 'The mass is the end, the radical nullity.'[68] Clearly, in this interpretation the end really means the end of a particular social arrangement. The threat of the masses to a particular way of life is systematically re-presented by Spengler as the end in general.

It is interesting to note that the sense of terminus is often expressed as the threat to Western civilisation. The explanation for this is the aristocratic emphasis on the achievements of a select group of superior personalities. Mass society is experienced as the negation of this culture. It imperils a way of life. T. S. Eliot expressed the fear that this culture might perish when he concluded his wartime broadcast to Germany:

> My last appeal is to the men of letters of Europe, who have a special responsibility for the preservation and transmission of our common culture ... we can at least try to save something of those goods of which we are the common trustees: the legacy of Greece, Rome and Israel, and the legacy of Europe throughout the last 2,000 years. In a world which has seen such material devastation as ours, these spiritual possessions are also in imminent peril.[69]

Not everyone was as pessimistic about the imminent danger to Western culture. However even those of a more optimistic disposition were convinced that the old order had come to an end. This was the viewpoint of E. H. Carr, who in 1944 noted casually that the 'old world is dead'. In his case this was not a problem, since he concluded that the 'future lies with those who can resolutely turn their back on it and face the new world with understanding, courage and imagination.'[70]

However Carr was very much the exception. The sense of terminus tended to be expressed in pessimistic terms. Writing in 1943 Koestler suggested that the period which saw the 'ascendancy of reason over spirit' had come to an end. He predicted that a 'new global ferment will arise' that will 'probably mark the end of our historical era'.[71] Others projected an end in quasi-religious terms. The theologian Niebuhr stated that the New Testament 'envisages a culmination of history'. He explained that it 'looks forward to a final judgement and a general resurrection which are at once both the fulfilment and the end of history.'[72]

Although there is a world of difference between the concentrated despair of Spengler and the liberal optimism of Carr, all these reactions were symptoms of the awareness that history had reached an impasse. After the Second World War the extremes of pessimism and optimism were overwhelmed by a middle-of-the-road sentiment. The sense of terminus was now conveyed in the pragmatic form of the end-of-ideology thesis. This would be the first of a succession of terms which implied that what existed had ended. The prefix 'post' would be used to suggest that society was now beyond what had happened. The diversity of names given to this new state is illustrated by Kumar:

> Thus Amitai Etzioni speaks of the 'post-modern era', George Lichtheim of 'the post-bourgeois society', Herman Kahn of 'post-economic society', Murray Bookchin of the 'post-scarcity society', Kenneth Boulding of 'post-civilized society', Daniel Bell simply of 'the post-industrial society'.[73]

To this one could add 'post-imperialist', 'post-fordist' and a number other terms.

The 'post' terms are, in different ways, symptoms of the sense of ending. They share a common approach towards change as they seek theoretically to suppress the sense of temporality. As Brook Thomas argues, the label 'post' 'announces that we are past the new'. He argues that 'post' implies a 'belatedness, an age in which everything has always already occurred'.[74] By means of this rhetorical device, 'post' theories revoke history. Appropriately Fukuyama affirms this revocation by declaring the Western world to be 'post-historical'.[75] If change is now excluded, than what exists must be the end result of human development. By projecting an immutable present into the infinite stretch ahead, the revocation of history exposes its own fundamentally apologetic intent. For these theories do not merely imply that history has ended but that this also means the fulfilment of the human ideal.

So for Fukuyama the end of history is the realisation of the principles of liberal democracy and of the free market. The same apologetic intent was also evident with the earlier end-of-ideology theories. The ending of history helps eternalise the past and retrospectively legitimises tradition. Because the ideals of tradition have been realised, they must have been sound in the first place. That is why 'endism' is wholeheartedly traditionalist. Edward Shils, one of the early proponents of the end-of-ideology thesis, argued back in 1955:

The belief that our traditional ideals have now been exhausted because of their complete fulfilment must be avoided as much as the conviction that our virtue consists in our rejection of whatever exists. We must rediscover the permanently valid element in our historical ideals – elements which must be recurrently realised without ever being definitively realisable, once and for all.[76]

The recurrent celebration of traditional ideals becomes the intellectual challenge for a society living through post-historical times.

The Fukuyama thesis explored

Much of the reaction that greeted Fukuyama's original article tended to miss the point of the argument. Fukuyama did not seek to imply that history had literally ended and that nothing new would ever happen again. He was using the term 'history' in the special Hegelian sense. As he outlined:

'History', for Hegel, can be understood in the narrower sense of the 'history of ideology', or the history of thought about first principles, including those governing political and social organization. The end of history then means not the end of worldly events but the end of the evolution of human thought about such first principles.[77]

In fact this version of history is close to the concept of historical thinking developed in this book, for the emphasis is on the active, on the role of the subjective force in history.[78]

So when Fukuyama declares the end of history, it is the demise of historical thinking that he has in mind. What he sees as ending is the further evolution of human consciousness in ways offering new and superior social arrangements. This represents the 'end of ideology'; there are no credible ideas that seek to take humanity beyond the status quo. The proof of this thesis for Fukuyama lies in the fact that liberal democracy enjoys a greater legitimacy then at any time previously. 'This ideological consensus is neither fully universal nor automatic, but exists to an arguably higher degree than at any time in the past century', he writes.[79] The establishment of liberal democracy as the *final* form of government represents the closure of history. It excludes the subjective factor from history. It excludes the possibility that humanity can attain any higher level of self-knowledge.

Fukuyama's thesis contains one important insight, which is the evident weakness of historical thinking. But his fatalistic conclusion that the limit to human consciousness has been reached is not based on logic. It is simply an extension of the empirical recognition that at present there is no ideological alternative to liberal capitalism. But then this is in substance the argument at the core of all 'endist' theories. The crisis of ideas is invariably presented as conclusive evidence of the non-availability of new ideas. Spengler's decline thesis is paradigmatic in this respect. He wrote that the 'age of theory is drawing to its end ... That of Marx is already half a century old, and it has had no successor.'[80] Following the same method, Fukuyama argues that liberal democracy has been around for a long time yet it has no successor. Fukuyama's one rational insight, that ideas of change are exhausted, is presented in an irrational form: as the freezing of history.

The end-of-history thesis would be more appropriately called the 'triumph of the past'. All the 'endist' arguments are self-consciously committed to establishing a framework where the continuity of the past is insisted on with the same vigour as the termination of history. Bell's main objection to ideologies, particularly that of Marx, is that they wanted to 'rid the present of the past'.[81] His argument regarding the exhaustion of ideology served as proof that a complex society could not be ideologically changed.

Compared to virtually all theories of historical closure, that of Fukuyama comes across as unusually optimistic. The self-conscious triumphalism of Fukuyama is one of the most distinct features of his contribution. From the point of view of emotional and mental outlook, it seems almost foolhardy to discuss Spengler and Fukuyama in the same breath. Bell too cannot be accused of mindless optimism. His recollection of the period when the end-of-ideology thesis developed exudes a sense of intellectual impasse. Bell recalls that the 1950s were 'essentially a decade of political conservatism and cultural bewilderment'. Politically, this was a 'period of disillusionment'.[82] The subtitle of Bell's key work expresses this sentiment: *The End of Ideology : On the exhaustion of political ideas in the 1950s.*

On closer inspection the triumphalism of Fukuyama seems far from convincing. As in the case of a number of liberal thinkers, Fukuyama finds it far easier to gloat over the failures of his opponents than to elaborate a credible vision of what the end of history offers. To his credit, in his initial contribution Fukuyama did not attempt to present the realities of Western capitalism in a glorified form. Instead the future was presented as the continuation of the present. It was to be

a society characteristically banal and with little scope for the
expression of human creativity. A culture of profound boredom and
routine was the prize at the end of the road.

Not surprisingly, many took offence at this uninspiring picture of
the future Western capitalist society. Fukuyama responded in the
following terms:

> The idea that one should be anything other than unconditionally
> happy about the victory of liberalism, or that one could be bored in
> a society that offered perfect security and material well-being, is
> one that has caused a certain amount of indignation, particularly
> among the space-travel lobby. Some of the more literal-minded of
> my readers have not recognized that one can be a supporter of
> liberalism, believe passionately in the superiority of liberal
> democracy over any alternative system, and yet be aware of certain
> fundamental tensions and weaknesses in liberalism.[83]

This weakness relates to the absence of any consideration of the
meaning of life and the human potential. This life, by excluding
change, offers nothing but more of the same. In a round about way it
serves as confirmation of the exhaustion of ideas that preoccupied
Daniel Bell three decades earlier.

It is not merely the internal pessimism of Fukuyama's thesis that
convinces us that it should be situated within the end-of-the-West
literature. For Fukuyama the end of history represents the triumph of
the West. In his schema the ideas of capitalism and liberalism are
directly equated with the political culture of the West. In his first
published article on this subject Fukuyama wrote that the 'triumph
of the West, of the Western *idea*, is evident first of all in the total
exhaustion of viable systematic alternatives to Western liberalism.'[84]
Fukuyama differs in tone from the previous end-of-the-West
literature. At least in form, his is a celebrationist contribution. In this
sense Fukuyama's intervention is consistent with the more confident
right-wing intellectual offensive of the past ten to fifteen years.

It is interesting to note that the most distinctive feature of
Fukuyama's work is the aspect least commented on. Its
epistemological premise and theoretical orientation is in substance
part of the Western anti-historical literature. But unlike the previous
literature, he reverses the process and declares the West the winner.
Thus Fukuyama's conclusion is the direct antithesis of Spengler's.

Fukuyama also interprets his contribution as an alternative to the

Cold War end-of-ideology theories. As shown in previous chapters, these theories were integral to the postwar intellectual compromise. This 'third way' defensive posture indicated lack of confidence in the fight for absolute values. Fukuyama accepts that truth is historically relative, but feels the need to declare that history has come to an end, that henceforth it is 'impossible to state a philosophical proposition that was both true and new'. In other words Fukuyama is prepared to accept the relativity of truth for the past, but by closing off the possibility of further intellectual development, he endows the latest truths of the West with the character of an absolute. He justifies this closure in order to prevent 'historicism from degenerating into simple relativism'.[85]

The reassertion of absolute values, in Fukuyama's case, takes the form of making the present absolute. In this way Western liberalism is presented as the culmination of human development. Anxious to affirm the 'notion of progress', Fukuyama presents it in a teleological form, one where all previous historical stages are inexorably driving to towards realisation in the contemporary West. This positive defence of the West is far less compromising then the old Cold War versions. Fukuyama himself draws attention to this point:

> the century that began full of self-confidence in the ultimate triumph of Western liberal democracy seems at its close to be returning to where it started: not to an 'end of ideology' or a convergence between capitalism and socialism, as earlier predicted, but to unabashed victory of economic and political liberalism.[86]

Fukuyama's criticism of the intellectual heritage of the postwar compromise is unequivocal. Unlike the Raymond Arons, Daniel Bells and Edward Shils of the 1950s and 1960s, there is not even a hint of defensiveness in Fukuyama's defence of the West.

Nevertheless the very preoccupation with the West gives the game away. 'Endist' theorists have always expressed a semi-conscious fear regarding Western decline. In 1951, in what was probably the first substantial discussion of the end of ideology, Hughes accurately described the convergence of different political trends in Europe as a defensive Western response to the perception of threat posed by the Korean War. He observed that 'this time the West is at length united in a single bloc.' He pointed to what he perceived as an original development: the 'creeds of "progress" – liberalism, democracy, socialism – have made their peace with what remains of traditional conservatism.'[87] This convergeance or neutralisation of ideological emphasis Hughes described as the 'end of ideology'.

Four years later Edward Shils reported some good and some bad news from a CIA-funded conference in Milan. The good news was that the end of ideology had prevailed in the West. Cold War intellectuals could now relax; there was less need to be defensive then previously. There was a very widespread feeling that there was no longer any need to justify ourselves *vis-à- vis* the Communist critique of our society.'[88] The bad news was that the Third World delegates were less than enthusiastic about this end-of-ideology complacency. According to Shils, during the discussion on nationalism 'the distance between the African and Asian members on the one side and the Europeans and Americans on the other became tangible.' This session demonstrated to Shils the 'danger of Western complacency at having weathered the storm of ideologies'.[89]

A similar motif is evident in Bell's classic article, which is appropriately titled 'The End of Ideology in the West'. The geographical limits of the title underline one of its chief concerns. The West has not only failed to win the ideological battle in the Third World but was actually losing it. 'Russia and China have become models', warned Bell. During the 1960s and early 1970s the situation actually looked worse. The postwar economic boom had come to an end. The economic dislocation heightened the sense of decline in the West. Moreover this feeling of decline coincided with the rise, probably to its high point, of the Third World challenge to the West.

According to Bracher, there is a close relation between the defensiveness of the West in the aftermath of the 1960s and the rise of Third Worldism. He wrote that the 'crisis of growth after the mid-1970s was interpreted by an increasing number of contemporaries – either indignant or resigned – as a crisis of western civilization generally.'[90] The defensiveness of the Western posture was underscored by its sensitivity to the appeal of Third Worldism. Bracher himself personifies this reaction when he characterises Third Worldism as a new ideology. He argued:

That the decade of de-ideologization would not be the last word was reflected most clearly in the rise of the 'Third World', in the new nationalism and socialism of the developing countries.[91]

For Bracher the rise of the Third World led to a 'crisis of values upon which modern western policies were based'.

In reality, there was no such animal as a Third Worldist ideology. There was a collection of vague and unformed anti-imperialist sentiments among Western youth and liberal opinion. In this climate the traditional assumptions of Western superiority could not be publicly aired. The Western establishment no longer possessed the moral high ground.

Burdened by the presentiment of decline, the ideologues of the West panicked and feared the revenge of the Third World. Fukuyama disposes of these fears with a theory of history that seeks to provide the West with moral certitude.

Fukayama's thesis legitimates Western intervention and represents a coherent attempt morally to rearm imperialism. In line with Western intellectual prejudice, any assertion of Third World independence is dismissed as the act of unrepresentative tyrants. Fukuyama asserts that the 'end of the Cold War has allowed us to debunk the moral pretensions of Third World tyrants.'[92] This debunking means in practice criminalising and trivialising the actions of one's opponent. So Saddam Hussein's 'challenge to the international system' is dismissed as 'nothing more than the effort of a well-armed gangster to rob the world's largest bank'.[93] The force of Fukuyama's argument is directed towards the reconstruction of the old East-West couplet. It now acquires the form of the post-historical West and the still historical East. The duality which Shils and other Cold War theorists had already discussed is now recreated in a new triumphalist form. 'Post-history' is in fact the end of ideology with a smile.

Finally it is interesting to note that despite its internal consistency and robust defence of the West, Fukuyama's thesis has not gained much support. To an extent this is due to the fact that his celebratory tone jars too much in relation to sober reality. 'The triumphalist apotheosis celebrated in Fukuyama's essay "The End of History" was the briefest of interludes', wrote one British editor.[94] Nevertheless it is surprising that what probably constitutes the most coherent attack on historical thinking has not gained more influence amongst the right-wing intelligentsia. Probably the reason for this ambivalent reception is that its extremely open and explicit closure of history tends to deprive capitalist society of even semblance of a *promise* of the future. In effect, in this form, the eternalisation of history serves to systematise low expectations. Ultimately any representation of the sense of terminus must contradict its optimistic form. At the very least, as Fukuyama himself admits, it leaves unresolved all the basic questions about the meaning of life, culture and society.

Fukuyama's rehabilitation of nineteenth-century historicism seems to adopt a radically different perspective from that of Hayek. In Hayek's account, history is a story of accidents in the spontaneous evolution of society. There is no self-realisation of the Hegelian Idea here. Yet by different roads, both thinkers arrive at the same standpoint in relation to the role of the subjective factor in history. The expulsion of the subject from history becomes the hallmark of anti-historical thinking.

8

New historicism and the destruction of historical thinking

This chapter examines the other side of the conservative attack on the 1960s. It looks at the intellectual legacy of the 1960s and explores its subsequent development. To this day, the myth that everything started to go wrong in the 1960s retains its force. In recent years this posture has been supplemented by denunciations of the so-called inheritors of the 1960s: the cultural left and various radicals and liberals are accused of betraying the basic values of the West. In America numerous articles on 'political correctness' on campuses seek to convey the image of a university system firmly in the grip of academic terrorists.[1] Issues such as national identity, multi-culturalism and Western civilisation have become subjects of controversy either directly or indirectly in America and Western Europe.

Highly publicised debates about whether Beethoven was white or black tend to obscure the lack of substance of the discussion. It is ironical that so many words are exchanged in anger by two sides that share so many assumptions. The strident anti-historical stance of the right is more than matched by the left. On many subjects of debate, a depressing mirror-image prevails. To the so-called Eurocentrism of the right is counterposed not universalism but a self-conscious Afrocentrism. The methods of nineteenth-century historicism have been appropriated intact by radical thinkers, committed to constructing alternative identities by the invention of a competing past. The mystifications of Eurocentrism or ethnocentrism are seldom subjected to critical investigation.

Most of the controversies are about relatively trivial matters. Despite the vitriolic exchanges over specifics, the two sides share a common ground on essentials. The debate is about differences of form, with mutual acceptance of substance. Therefore it is not surprising that a section of the so-called cultural left has

225

enthusiastically adopted the term 'new historicism' to describe their stance. Despite its radical rhetoric, this stance is intensely conservative. In fact an old-fashioned nineteenth-century historicism seems to encompasses everyone on a spectrum from Gramscian Marxism to the tradition of American scepticism, including those who directly or indirectly situate themselves within the problematic of the post-modern. These contemporary historicists represent the most consistent opposition to historical thinking. The few traces of history left in the system of Hayek or Fukuyama are expunged in the scheme of the new historicist. Even those post-modern thinkers who formally criticise historicism adopt many of its basic premises.[2]

Until now the role of left and radical thought has not been explicitly considered. One of the arguments of this chapter is that on most issues to do with history it is difficult to detect a distinct left transformative approach to history. The differences between left and right are mainly formal, though of course there are important differences in subjective intent. An inspection of the past two decades suggests that radical currents have made a major contribution to the ascendancy of a conservative intellectual climate. They have done this by effecting a reconciliation between individual radicalism and anti-historical ideas. 1960s and post-1960s radicalism has emphasised the terrain of individual behaviour. This overdetermined sense of the individual helped shift intellectual concern from society to the realm of subjectivity. From the standpoint of the individual, strategies, no matter how radical, tend to devalue social engagement. This posits change at the level of the individual without necessarily questioning society. Hence militant individualism, which is highly sceptical of social change, leads to the deradicalisation of radical thought. The conservative reaction has been a direct beneficiary of this. As the left became more and more reluctant to discuss wider social issues, conservatives felt more comfortable promoting their own distinct world view.

Conservative thinkers hate new historicists because their radical individualism is often expressed in the form of extreme relativism. Those who express this relativism often come into conflict with prevailing conventions. For this reason they are denounced in rather extravagant terms as subversives or as Marxist agitators. In reality this charge is without foundation. In fact new historicists never tire of repeating that their standpoint represents as much a reaction to Marxism as to bourgeois convention.[3] At the same time new historicists do claim to stand in the tradition of the 1960s. One has argued that 'much new historicist work can be said to possess a remarkable continuity with certain cultural assumptions of the New Left.'[4] These assumptions are primarily to do with the centrality of the individual and the need to remove the old restraints on individual behaviour.

Given a common epistemological posture, it is increasingly difficult to establish definitively the meaning of what is *left* and what is *right*. Since the late eighteenth century, concepts such as reason, progress and universalism have been generally associated with the left. During the 1960s, the New Left began a fairly systematic demolition of these values by questioning the claims of reason, progress and universalism. This new philosophical posture was reflected in the political approach which acclaimed diversity and opposed universalistic claims. As the self-avowed new historicist Catherine Gallagher wrote: 'New Left activists notoriously invoked the principle of individual and group liberation in justifying rebellion instead of invoking their connection to the objective interests of a universal class.' A universalistic referent was no longer necessary to the New Left world view, she says: 'One no longer needed to justify her own cause by claiming that it ultimately substituted for the crucial cause, the cause of the universal class.' Instead of one 'crucial' cause, there were a 'number of local contests' without a 'privileged referent'.[5] Local communities and *differences* became the key sign points of the New Left.

The rejection of universalism and the adoption of particularism by the left has been widely commented on. However, the significance of this shift has not been assimilated by most of the commentators concerned. Thus Diane Ravitch, in her review of the particularist critique of American culture, argues that 'particularism has its intellectual roots in the ideology of ethnic separatism and in the black nationalist movement.'[6] In fact the intellectual roots of particularism are to be found in the conservative reaction to the Enlightenment; its most systematic expression is German historicism. The New Left was not in its origin motivated by a conservative impulse, but by rejecting universalism in general – because it confused the universalist form in which Western capitalism presented itself with the concept itself – it uncritically ended adopting a particularist epistemology. Unconsciously, the New Left reaction to postwar Western capitalism copied the methods and arguments of the conservative reaction to the Enlightenment.

Robert Nisbet, the prolific American conservative publicist, never tires of enjoying the spectacle of radical intellectuals embracing the community. He is one of the few observers who has noticed how conservative symbols appeal to the left. He writes that 'such conservative words as *family, kin, neighbourhood* and *community* have long held appeal to the political clerisy in the West.' Nisbet considers the 'clear hold' of conservatism upon these 'symbols and mystiques' to be a 'long-held advantage'.[7] The wholesale adoption of these symbols by the left seems to confirm Nisbet's argument.

During the 1960s, the left's adoption of historicism was hesitant and semi-conscious, but by the late 1970s, radical intellectuals and, more often, ex-radicals were speaking the language of Nietzsche. For once Bloom was right when he coined the term 'Nietzscheanization of the Left'. Repelled by modernism, the language of this process was moulded by its stress on 'heterogeneity and difference as liberation forces in the redefinition of cultural discourse'.[8] The concept of difference became part of a radical critique of the Western establishment which presented its particular interests in the form of universal truths. Heterogeneity and difference were used to focus on the reality of differential experience and to contest the universalistic claims of society. However, as the rebellion against the rhetoric of universalism turned into a celebration of difference, the process of intellectual deradicalisation became inescapable.

The original methodological orientation towards difference began as the defence of aristocratic and ruling-class privilege. Differences in moral and mental capacities were advanced to legitimise the social hierarchy. By the mid-nineteenth century, this perspective attached itself to racial differences and helped to legitimise the international hierarchy of people. As Greta Jones' valuable discussion of Social Darwinism points out, nineteenth-century sociology became 'obsessed with the question of mental and moral difference'.[9] The conceptualisation of 'backward' and 'advanced' races complemented the obsession on difference.

The radical left did not set out, as the Social Darwinists did, to provide intellectual sustenance to racial superiority. But, whatever the intentions, the conservative consequences of a particularist doctrine cannot be evaded. During the past decade the common ground of particularism has helped to erode the traditional distinction between left and right.

Take the example of the use that French right-wing racist discourse makes of the concept of difference. In France, right-wing intellectuals have acclaimed the 'right to be different' as a defence of their chauvinism, denouncing anti-racism as really racist for not respecting differences. Taguieff writes:

The latest New Right doctrine (since 1979–1980) places the utmost importance on *difference*. What Benoist terms anti-racism is a radical reinterpretation of 'the right to be different'. With racism defined by disrespect of differences, the New Right rejects the very idea of a 'differentialist racism'. Racism can only be an avatar of biblical universalism, an ideological heir of the monotheism that 'reduces' human diversity, the structure that eradicates differences.[10]

The right to be racist is the blur conclusion that the French New Right draws from the premise of the right to be different.

The appropriation by the right of the concept of difference has been a source of consternation for sections of the French left. Rather naively Alain Policar writes that 'given its left credentials, the praise of difference could hardly be claimed to be explicitly racist.'[11] Given the centrality of difference to Social Darwinism and to scientific racism in general, Policar's statement is truly astounding. Difference in the abstract is not racist as such. But by putting universalism to question, it undermines the commensurability of experience and therefore the possibility of common treatment. The logic of difference is the intellectual acceptability of differential treatment, which at least in principle raises the possibility of discrimination.

That the right to discriminate logically flows from the concept of difference was bought out with devastating consequences in America in the mid-1980s in the legal case of the Equal Employment Opportunity Commission v Sears, Roebuck and Company. This case, initiated by the Equal Employment Opportunity Commission, sought to prove that Sears discriminated against women by excluding them from equal access to the better-paid positions. According to Novick's excellent account of the case, Sears used material drawn from feminist history which highlighted the differences of women's values from those of men. Sears won the case by arguing that the less competitive values that women possessed suggested that they were less likely to apply for top jobs; it was not company discrimination but distinctive feminine qualities that accounted for the situation.[12] Whereas in the past it was the conservatives who speculated about natural differences in order to uphold the social hierarchy, today it is the left which theorises about the subject. In both cases the consequences are the same. *Difference* is inherently a conceptual device that has enormous potential for confirming the status quo.

What gave the Sears case its special poignancy was that the particularist methodology of feminist history was explicitly used by the company to rationalise its discrimination against women. As in the case of race in France, the idea of difference may well lead its practitioners towards a dramatically unexpected terrain.

This dilemma has been strikingly captured in relation to the historiography of the Third Reich. The emergence of studies of everyday life, of *Alltagsgeschichte*, was at least in part motivated by the desire to counter the view that reaction to the Nazi regime had been uniform. The new *locus* of this history was the everyday situation facing ordinary people. This history from below has tended to give pride of place to the particular and the different. One unfortunate unintended consequence of *Alltagsgeschichte* has been that in stressing the local and the different it tends to disaggregate the totality of the Nazi experience. The obsession with the local and the different distracts from the overriding realities of Nazi Germany. It can help render the events of the period everyday and banal. As Mary Nolan warns:

> In unravelling layer upon layer of subjective meaning, it is easy to forget that actions and attitudes operate in a world beyond the immediate environment of individuals and small groups, beyond the local and ostensibly unpolitical level on which *Alltagsgeschichte* focuses.[13]

Nolan has warned that 'while the intentions of *Alltagsgeschichte* are diametrically opposed to those of the right, the former may harbor strongly conservative implications and be readily used by conservatives.'[14] Just as the left has borrowed the method of the difference from the right, the right has used everyday history to normalise the experience of the Third Reich.

The lending and borrowing of ideas between the contemporary left and right is made possible by the common anti-Enlightenment assumptions which they share. As this chapter argues, the prevalence of this consensus threatens to destroy historical thinking altogether.

The annihilation of history

At least in the case of Fukuyama there was a history before it ended. In postmodernist theories the very idea of a history is questioned. To some extent this dismissal of history was originally motivated by a critical reaction to History, with a capital 'H'. But, as with the reaction to Western universalistic claims, historical thinking and not just History became abandoned.

'Life is too complex for simple answers', argued the nineteenth-century conservative reaction to the Enlightenment.[15] This banal insight, translated into the almost incomprehensible language of postmodernism, accounts for its rejection of 'meta-language, meta-theories, and meta-narratives of modernism'. According to Harvey this response is motivated by a 'concern for difference, for the difficulties of communication, for the complexity and nuances of interests, cultures, places'.[16] The complexity of life becomes the argument for a reorientation towards smaller places and aggregates.

It is suggested that since experience is so highly differential there can be no one history but instead a number of histories. A single History, encompassing a single knowledge, is said to violate the plurality of experience. A single History is usually labelled as a 'meta-narrative' and is denounced for attempting to monopolise the representation of reality. Lyotard, who defines postmodern as 'incredulity toward meta-narratives', offers his 'small narrative' as the sensible alternative.[17] This approach is very much in the tradition of German historicism in the nineteenth century. German society and culture was characteristically 'heterogeneous and provincial'. This encouraged particularist responses because German society was marked by 'strong local differences in religion and political organisation'.[18]

Nineteenth-century particularism, no less than Lyotard's 'small narratives' and local knowledges, leads to the destruction of historical thinking. Once history becomes 'histories' the fragmentation of human experience follows. There is no longer any point of reference or commensurability of human experience. Randomness and incoherence must follow once an overall point of view is rejected. This approach was eloquently outlined by Justus Moser, one of the best known of the eighteenth-century German particularist thinkers. In 1767, in his essay 'Concerning the Moral Perspective', Moser argued:

> everything has *its perspective* in which it *alone* is beautiful; as soon as you change it, as soon as you cut into the entrails with an anatomical knife, the previous beauty evaporates with the changed perspective.[19]

Moser's insistence on perspective restricts knowledge to partial insights and truth. Change itself, leading to a new perspective, shifts the terrain of meaning. From Moser to Lyotard, the perspectivist epistemology of extreme relativism leads to a sense of history that is necessarily arbitrary. Truth depends entirely on perspective.

Perspectivism can represent a rational response to the teleological claims of History. But by introducing the element of arbitrariness, chaos replaces meaning. Oxford academic Robert Young questions this point and asks why 'after all "history" at all?' He argues against conflating the 'concept of the differential with the notion of the random' and suggests that 'different histories may have different meanings'.[20] The consignment of meaning to little histories does not offer an alternative to the teleology of History. It represents a difference in scale but not in the content of this so-called meta-history. It means merely that there are little teleologies instead of big ones. But worse still, the recreation of meaning at the local level as partial and limited gives it a fragmented quality. Many meanings, involving many truths, in the end mean no truth at all.

The relativist perspective of postmodernism is directly focused against historical thinking. The many histories have their own different dynamic and the human subject is conspicuous by its absence. The human subject becomes fragmented into many different agents in different histories. The repulsion of the history-making human subject was theoretically justified by Foucault, who argued that the subject does not assume a unified form but is fragmented and scattered across various histories. Foucault boasts that his history does not have to 'make reference to a subject which is either transcendental in relation to the field of events or runs its empty sameness throughout the course of history.'[21]

The repudiation of the central role of the subject in the making of history leads to a shift from the social to the individual. The move from history to histories is paralleled by a comparable shift from society to societies and the recasting of the subject into subjects. For the new historicists, the focus of discussion is not social aggregates but the acts of individual agents. The cultural theorist Stephen Greenblatt, who claims to have invented the term 'new historicism', argues that 'methodological self-consciousness is one of the distinguishing marks of the new historicism in cultural studies.'[22] This methodological self-consciousness introduces an arbitrary subjectivity towards the question of method. This transforms method into a question of individual self-consciousness. In a roundabout way this turns out strikingly similar to the methodological individualism of the Austrian school of economics associated with thinkers such as

Popper and Hayek. The methodological individualism of the Austrian school explicitly asserts that all statements about groups are reducible to statements about the behaviour of individuals. Popper and Hayek reject the meaningfulness of social wholes and map out the interaction among individuals as the legitimate arena for analysis.[23] New historicists too feel comfortable mainly on the level of individual behaviour. The similarity between the individualistic orientation of the left and the right has been noted by the British radical historian Raphael Samuel. In an article on the ideas of former British Prime Minister Margaret Thatcher, he observed that 'her ideas, though aligned to right- wing politics, have disturbing affinities to the radical individualism recently in vogue on the left.'[24]

Using a number of metaphors such as 'currency' and 'negotiations', Greenblatt adopts the Austrian image of individuals maximising their interests in order to discuss the relation of art and society:

> In order to achieve the negotiation, artists need to create a currency that is valid for a meaningful, mutually profitable exchange ... I should add that the society's dominant currencies, money and prestige, are invariably involved, but I am here using the term 'currency' metaphorically to designate the systematic adjustments, symbolizations and lines of credit necessary to enable an exchange to take place.[25]

The close relation that Greenblatt establishes between individual action and calculation necessarily devalues the point of view of the social. As with little narratives, it loses sight of the overall point of view. For Greenblatt these metaphors are exclusively cultural terms, drained even of the analytic content they have for the Austrian school.

It is truly amazing just how far the methodology of Foucault, Greenblatt and Lyotard complements that of Hayek and the Austrian school. Both of these intellectual traditions share a fervent commitment to the individualising of the subject in history. Foucault's insistence that social agents are fragmented across numerous sites sits well with Hayek's desire to uphold the primacy of individual action.

Hayek has the merit of making explicit the implicit individualistic methodology of the post-modernist. In a chapter titled 'Our Poisoned Language', Hayek explains why he dislikes words like society and social. Without using the obscurantist language of Lyotard, Hayek professes an attachment to small groups rather than large ones. He cites with approval Bertrand de Jouvenel's romantic account of small communities: 'the milieu in which man is first found, which retains for him an infinite attraction: but any attempt to graft the same features on large society is utopian and leads to tyranny.'[26] Totalitarianism plays a role analogous to that of the totalising dangers of meta-narratives in the postmodernist schema.

Hayek despises the term 'society' because it seems to suggest patterns that are universal at the expense of the different awareness of individuals. He writes that society 'presupposes or implies a common pursuit of shared purposes that can be achieved only by conscious collaboration'.[27] Hayek wishes to contest this supposition on two grounds: first that the 'limits of individual awareness' call into question the conscious pursuit of common objectives, and second that the term 'society' tends to personify as one what are in fact numerous 'completely different formations'. He confesses to be disturbed by the view that 'society' ought to appear not 'as a plurality of persons' but as a 'single great person'.[28] In his own way Hayek celebrates *difference* with an enthusiasm that would put any contemporary new historicist to shame.

If Hayek dislikes the term 'society', he positively loathes what he calls the 'weasel word "social" '. His reaction to 'social' is motivated by a passion similar to the new historicist rejection of meta-narratives and meta-discourses. 'Social' implies values that transcend local knowledges and individual self-awareness. Hayek writes that 'it has increasingly been turned into an exhortation, a sort of guide-word for rationalist morals'.[29] It claims for itself truths – and Hayek believes that such a claim must be at the expense of individual knowledge.

Of course the main reason why Hayek dislikes the 'weasel word' is because 'social' implies phenomena that are the product of humans making history. What is social is neither natural nor permanent. It is by its very quality an arrangement subject to qualification and change. Hayek himself concedes that his reaction to the term 'social' is animated by the suggestion that history is made through the application of human consciousness. He writes that 'it tends pervertedly to insinuate ... that what has been brought about by the impersonal and spontaneous process of the extended order is actually the result of deliberate human creation.'[30] So the rejection of the social is an integral part of the repudiation of history as 'human creation'. In this reaction to the social, Hayek and Foucault are at one in rejecting the notion of a history that can be made.

With little histories and little communities, little changes

The reaction against meta-narratives and meta-history has driven postmodernists to find a home in little communities. The particularist methodology pushed to the fore everyday-life studies of communities. Novick has written that 'anthropologically influenced local holism was one of the major fragmenting influences at work within history in recent years.'[31] He is right to draw attention to the use made of anthropology by historians, but it is wrong to blame the influence of anthropology for the fragmentation of history. The tendency towards fragmentation came from within history itself – naturally this tendency would sooner or later make use of what is traditionally the most particularist of all the social sciences.

The new historicist tradition allowed historians to study local communities for their own sake, without context or any objective referent. Detailed descriptions of local communities, 'little histories' were now important in their own right. The anthropologist Clifford Geertz's method of 'thick description' was widely acclaimed by a spectrum from American community historians to the German *Alltagsgeschichte*. The emphasis on complexity and detail of thick description is necessarily at the expense of social context, structure and pattern.[32] There is also no sense of genesis, of process and change.

Local history is the appropriate form for the practice of particularism. Studies of small communities, especially over a short time scale, exaggerate peculiarities and differences. Without a wider social perspective many forms of human action appear as the consequence of specifically local factors. Developments are explained not as a result of wider social forces, but of accidental local details. This process of rendering history banal is clearly exposed by the British social historian Christopher Hill:

> if you concentrate narrowly on a short period of history, it is possible to suffer a loss of perspective. Events are most likely to seem determined by chance or by accidents of personality.[33]

New historicists actually like to view history as accident, since this invites a multiplicity of meanings; the interesting and the curious become objects to be discussed in their own terms. Veeser's new historicist manifesto is suspicious of 'any criticism predetermined by a Marxist or liberal grid, New Historicists eschew overarching hypothetical constructs in favour of surprising coincidences.'[34]

A reality (or should we say realities?) made up of surprising coincidences requires no explanation. Everything so expressed excludes the need for explanation. Accident instead of process destroys historical thinking altogether. In this anti-methodology, human beings have coincidences and accidents but they never make history.

The direction towards local and everyday studies risks giving every aspect of historical experience equal weight. There is the permanent danger of equating the banal with major developments. Moreover there is no way of distinguishing between an action that is part of wider social pattern and one that is the random reaction of the individual. By dissolving the connections that bind communities, the tendency is to interpret action individually rather then collectively. The elimination of wider social influences from the picture leads to a one-sided representation, where only the individual motive behind action seems to have meaning. Not surprisingly, individual motives play a large role in local histories.

The fragmented perspective of everyday history is clearly illustrated in the work of James Scott. His writings on peasant protest provide an illustration of how resistance can be reduced to an entirely individualised and technical act. Scott claims that the social and protest element of peasant life is not as important as their everyday struggle. He presents this struggle in a highly individualised and atomised form and warns against placing too much stress on organisation, common interest and collective identity. He projects a 'continuum of *resistance* ranging all the way from petty individual acts focused on the here-and-now to highly organized, durable movements of broad ideological purpose.'[35] Scott argues for a wide definition of resistance not only because he prefers to study the ordinary routine of life but because he believes that individual action is more rational than collective. He writes that 'if social movements, in the strict sense, are rarely found among peasants, this is in large part the result of a prudential, calculated and historically tested choice favouring other strategies.' This calculation is entirely sensible, suggests Scott, since 'everyday forms of resistance' can 'achieve many, if not all, of the results aimed at by social movements.'[36]

In this scenario, Scott not only equates everyday individual actions with those of the social movement but also offers the opinion that the former is more effective then the latter. Individual interests are more effectively defended through mundane routine events such as 'foot-dragging', 'dissimulation' or 'pilfering' than through collective organisation. Such routine reactions are held to be superior to collective organisation because they reduce the chance of retribution. To support his case, Scott endows 'everyday resistance' with an *a priori* conscious intent in order to justify its rationality. He writes that 'everyday resistance aims at an immediate and personal gain in a fashion that minimises the risk of open confrontation.' The inference of this statement is that whereas everyday resistance operates on the plane of rationality, open revolt is irrational. As with Hayek and others the shift from the individual to the collective implies a move away from the rational to the unknowable abstract.

By reducing the act of resistance to its subjective intent, Scott provides a history of atomised individuals. There is no mechanism through which the similar acts of individuals are transformed into collective action to become a social force. Scott insists that in any case the routine everyday action of peasants is more common than social protest. He exclaims that 'they command attention by their sheer empirical weight' and as he counts up the number of poachers concludes that the 'number of people involved over time in such resistance may also frequently dwarf the number drawn to a particular social movement.'[37] The sheer everyday routine of life certainly lasts longer than periods of social upheaval and change. But to discuss the two as comparable quantities is to reduce history to the biographical details of the individual. A false symmetry between the pursuit of individual survival and of social change allows for a static depiction of history.

The individualistic methodology of Scott simply cannot account for change. From the point of view of individual calculation the act of open defiance makes little sense. But in fact it is the close link that Scott tries to establish between individual calculation and a particular protest that is senseless. The relation between calculation and action is never unproblematic. Actions have unintended consequences that bear little resemblance to original intent. Sometimes even very ordinary acts at the level of a locality can converge to produce something very different at the level of society. What appears as a mere accident within the confines of the locality may turn into an understandable aspect of a society-wide pattern.

Local history, in line with the contemporary fashion for difference, shares with a number of intellectual trends – such as chaos theory in physics and postmodernism – a disposition for portraying history as a series of unconnected events that exist in an accidental relation to each other. This focus on difference and the deconstruction of historical experience into a series of parallel but unconnected relations is even influential among the advocates of the radical school of people's history. Raphael Samuel was to the point when he remarked on the 'regressive underside' which 'feeds on a nostalgia for visible social differences'.[38]

The heightened sense of difference has become a methodological bulldozer that drives over meaning, coherence and purposeful change. In a timely intervention, the historian Lawrence Stone has pointed to the new school of British empiricists who write 'detailed political narratives' on the English Revolution 'which implicitly deny that there is any deep-seated meaning to history except the accidental whim of fortune and personality.'[39] This intellectual fad influences a wide spectrum of opinion from postmodern to conservative.

The recent historiography of the English Revolution is not alone in displaying a predilection for deconstructing the meaning or pattern of its subject matter. In virtually every sphere of history where the question of social change, purposeful resistance, revolt or revolution is under consideration there is a discernible trend towards a narrative which queries the relevance of any universalistic themes. The criticisms are particularly strident against the linkage of action with conscious collective intent.

It is striking how European history has been deconstructed into a series of local events which are played out in isolation from one another. Lawrence Stone had drawn attention to the 'proliferation of local county or city studies' of the English Civil War which has led 'some to argue that there was no such thing as national politics in the early seventeenth century'. Influential writers argue that there was 'no clear social or economic division' between the two sides in the civil war and that the important source of conflict was local and cultural differences. Sixteenth-century English history thus becomes a series of isolated events inspired by parochial issues.[40] Nineteenth-century British social history is now also undergoing the localising treatment. During the 1980s a number of influential texts appeared which questioned the salience of class and other broad social influences. One representative of this trend has argued that it was the strength of local traditional communities that was the decisive factor in the emergence of radical resistance.[41]

The history of the French Revolution has also undergone a fragmentation in revision. Norman Hampson has remarked that the 'pragmatists have gone on marshalling the evidence that fragments the Revolution into a multitude of individual, local or sectional conflicts and aspirations.'[42] The recent revision of Irish nationalism by historians provides an example of the tendency towards the deconstruction of a coherent subject to its most caricatured form. This anti-nationalist literature not only denies the *national* status of the movement but succeeds in reducing the struggle against Britain to a series of morbidly parochial concerns. By casting doubt on the motives of the participants, the historian robs the Irish liberation struggle of even a hint of idealism or of political objective. Pointedly, Foster underlines that the 'idea of a "national" struggle can be exaggerated' as far as the Anglo–Irish War of 1919–21 is concerned. Foster prefers to highlight 'local feuds' as a key underlying dynamic of this event. Hoppen agrees and adds that 'many of the incidents commonly labelled IRA engagements were in reality no more than land seizures thinly disguised.' One could cite numerous examples of recent contributions where the Irish liberation struggle is treated as a 'morass of competing factional disputations' or as selfish land grabs and the settling of old scores. Local parochial concerns, it seems emerge time and again as the new transcendental force of history.[43]

Despite all the concern about difference, complexities and ambiguities, there is still the constant eternal theme of local concerns. The shift from a society-wide or universalistic perspective to the local and particularist merely reproduces the holism of the centre at the periphery. In this way local traditions and customs acquire an explanatory power simply by virtue of this shift in focus. All that has happened is that the field of operation for historicism has narrowed since the nineteenth century. Paradoxically, the more the world becomes internationalised, with every region brought into an intimate relationship with world market forces, the more the singularity of the experience of the parish-pump is insisted upon. Precisely when people's range of experiences are far wider than before, historians have decided to narrow the scale of their research. There must be a moral in this.

Local histories and small narratives call into question the making of history on a societal level. From this point of view the idea of change acquires a different quality. If every locality possesses its own dynamic then not only must change be uneven, it becomes chaotic and arbitrary. It is not merely a question of the speed or the breadth of change, *change itself* is driven by a different, local dynamic. There is no common element that would bestow upon change a social quality.

Since every locality follows its own instinct, it is at this level that human creativity can best be applied. Anything that happens beyond its confines is abstract. Moser argued that only local problems are susceptible to practical solutions. Writing over two centuries ago, Moser's caution is understandable. Not so with the new historicists of today. Meszaros' witty criticism of Lyotard's particularism indicates how the call of the latter to 'wage war on totality' actually represents a naive flight from reality.[44]

The localist approach also expresses a profound pessimism about the capacity of the human agent. According to a valuable account of Moser's work, his local/practical bias was motivated by his belief in the 'limited capacity of rationally oriented behaviour to alter life'.[45] The consequence of this understanding is that human beings are capable of tackling rationally the practical problems only of the locality! Beyond the confines of the local, there are only accidents or the unintended consequences of poorly informed action. This localisation of purposeful action resolves itself into a theory of little changes.

New historicists seldom work through the conservative bias of their argument. Indeed the form of their ideas continually affirms a critical stance. Their deconstruction of conventional prejudices often creates the impression of radical intent. Indeed many of them possess a radical subjectivity. However, since they adopt a historicist framework they cannot evade the conservative consequences of their arguments. In any case their ideas lend support to the conservative view of change. The language is different but the arguments bear an uncanny resemblance to each other. Local facts serve the role more generally assigned to tradition. They encompass the past, in a system of transcendental particularism. Periodically these local facts and traditions wreak their revenge as they expose the illusion of change. The eruption of communal and ethnic violence in post-Stalinist Eastern Europe has been seized upon as conclusive proof of the durability of local facts and traditions. There is almost an audible sigh of relief that ethnic violence has exploded in Eastern Europe, since this seems to confirm that little changes. Harold James, professor of history at Princeton, announced with ill-concealed triumph: 'socialist optimism thought that it could overcome age-old religious, national and racial animosities – and failed.'[46] Thank the Lord there are a few prejudices left.

The localisation of history provides the means through which an accommodation with society can be enforced. In the retreat to the local there is an implicit tendency to leave the fundamental structures of society as a whole uncontested. Traditionally, locally oriented histories have provided the medium for left-wing historians to reintroduce at a local level the values they have rejected for society as a whole. This point is well argued by Miles Taylor in his critique of British left-wing history:

> By 1941, therefore, many on the British left were unequivocal in their support for a patriotism which was rooted in popular, small-scale, often localized, struggles for democracy. In this qualified sense, patriotism was made acceptable.[47]

Taylor certainly cannot be accused of exaggeration. By the 1980s the lust of the British left for small-scale patriotism was positively indecent. Jeremy Seabrook and Trevor Blackwell declared:

> It is time for the Left to lay claim to another patriotism. A patriotism which concerns itself with the recreation of the local and the familiar – a patriotism which offers the possibility of belonging to a community of which one need not feel ashamed, a patriotism which encourages a love of place which poses no threat to all the other places that other people love – this would be a truer patriotism.[48]

Somehow the scale of the area makes everything right. This worship of parochialism actually reverses the traditional delineation between left and right. Not so long ago the parochial was a highly cherished conservative value while left-wing rhetoric was imbued with the rhetoric of internationalism. Today the adulation of the small is the key refrain in the radical tradition.

Judge not ... can't judge

The new historicism fully shares the fundamental premise of the old, that there is no objective standard of truth. It also follows nineteenth-century historicism in dismissing the central role that the Enlightenment accorded to reason. It is argued that there is no single road to understanding. The insistence on difference also pertains to methodology: there are truths that are arrived at by different methods.

The elaboration of the relativisation of methodology is one of the distinctive characteristics of the new historicism. It is based on the old romantic idea that the road to understanding is through subjectivity, specifically intuition. Postmodernists have elaborated this idea to suggest that since there are many truths, there are also many valid ways of getting there. It is also argued that those who live a particular experience are best capable of understanding it. Some would claim they are the *only* ones fit to comment on their particular experience.

The elaboration of methodological relativism is rarely made explicit. In general it assumes the polemical form of an accusation of cultural imperialism or ethnocentrism. For example, in the United States it has been strongly argued that only blacks had the right to write black history. Novick notes that at a 'minimum', black power meant that 'blacks rather than whites should have the power to define and interpret black history'.[49] This understandable reaction to racism was sometimes justified on the spurious ground that there is a special black or African epistemology.

The assertion of black – or in fact any – particularist epistemology represents the reformulation of the nineteenth-century cultural focus of historicism. Dwight W. Hoover puts the case for Black History in the following terms:

> In brief, the argument as presented by such writers as LeRoi Jones and Eldridge Cleaver is that the blacks in the world are forming a better community, one which has rejected the sterile rationalism of western white society in favour of emotion and creativity ... Out of this conviction came the word 'soul' which was a product of black experience, and an emphasis upon brotherhood and community among blacks.[50]

The affirmation of emotion and creativity represents not just the rejection of a particular form of rationalism, that is Western rationalism, but rationalism altogether. Following the methods of historicism it places experience within a cultural form, a form within which the unique and exclusive qualities of that experience dominate. The 'black soul' like the German soul, is beyond criticism; what it knows no one can possibly experience. And the French soul? Michel Falicon mobilises Renan's definition of the nation as its soul (*'Une nation est une âme, un principe spirituel'*) to justify his chauvinist defence of national identity.[51]

During the past two decades a number of groups have taken out a patent on their souls. Their unique way of knowing becomes the validation of their knowledge. Of all groups, academic feminism has the most elaborated particularist epistemology. In reaction to a male-centred world view, academic feminists often project a female-centred one. Moreover, 'for many feminists the ideology of "difference" extended to fundamental questions of cognitive style and epistemological values.'[52] Specific female qualities are abstracted by feminist historians to synthesise a women's perspective. Needless to say, from this exclusivist cultural point of view only women can know women. Novick reminds us that by the 'late 1970s the assertion that women's history could only be legitimately written from a feminist standpoint was no longer argued; it was a settled question, beyond argument.'[53]

The attack on 'Western rationality' or on 'male logic' assumes that theorising and knowing is reducible or to be equated with experiencing. At it worse this standpoint merely reproduces the object of its attack but in a different particularist form, such as 'women-centred' instead of 'men-centred' Thus it is not the centricity but the form of the centricity that is questioned.

More disturbing is the assumption of the new historicists that the development of knowledge is confined to subjective experience. Being black or white or male or female or German or Japanese does not confer a privileged access to the knowledge of the experience. As Mattick persuasively argues, being part of a culture does not give the individual greater understanding of that culture than those who study it from the outside. He writes:

> participants in a culture, even while they may (and indeed must) know the rules and criteria regulating social behaviour in that culture, may have only a very vague notion of how the parts of social life in which they participate fit together.[54]

To strengthen his point Mattick cites Fritz Machlup's illustration of an alien Martian anthropologist who observes the stock market and interviews its participants:

> Since probably 999 out of 1000 persons working on the stock market do not really know what it does and how it does it, the most diligent observer-plus-interviewer would remain largely ignorant. Alas, economics cannot be learned either by watching or by interviewing the people engaged in economic activities. It takes a good deal of

theorizing before one can grasp the complex interrelations in an economic system.[55]

Observation, like experience, is meaningless outside the framework of theory. The precondition for a sound account of how the stock exchange works is theory. Those who work at the stock exchange can write a sound account of how it operates, not because that is the locus of their activity, but because they possess a grasp of theory.

Particularist epistemology is inherently conservative. It makes no claims concerning anything except what is on its own terrain. In exchange for keeping to itself, it demands an absolute monopoly on its own culture. No matter how strident its rhetoric, implicit in its methodology is the demand for a non-aggression pact: 'I make no pretence to know about you; you must allow me the same privilege so that I can be the sole representative of my culture.' In the United States, for example, the particularist objects not to the dominant culture, but to that culture's claim to monopolise society. Elizabeth Fox-Genovese's observation of the historicist 'disinclination to engage general social theories of social cultural relations' is to the point. So is her conclusion that this 'leaves many of the new studies hostage to the models that they are attacking.'[56]

There is even an attempt to deny the reality of a dominant culture that influences society. Thus Barbara Herrnstein Smith places inverted commas around the term 'national culture' so as to question its existence in the United States. For Herrnstein Smith, the existence of an American 'national culture' is 'by no means self-evident'. Citizens belong to different communities and experience different cultures along with others in their localities. Following the old historicist mode, local communities are real and practical but societies are abstract and unreal. She writes:

> There is, however, no single, comprehensive macroculture in which all or even most of the citizens of this nation actually participate, no numerically preponderant majority culture in relation to which any or all of the others are 'minority' cultures, and no culture that, in Hirsch's term, 'transcends' any or all other cultures.[57]

Herrnstein Smith attempts to sustain her position by upholding the primacy of the particular. Using the inverted commas again, this time around 'national language', she argues that there is no such thing.

'There are only *particular* regional and other dialects.' Nothing hovers about the particular. It seems that everything else is an abstraction. There is no need to contest the dominant culture; it is sufficient to put inverted commas around it. The American military-industrial complex, its state institutions, the media, Hollywood ... these are just abstractions that do not intrude on the lives of people happily passing time in their particularist existence.

Instead of criticising the national culture, pointing out how it self-servingly projects a universalistic message but towards a sectional end, Herrnstein Smith declares that it is not a problem.

Those who take a more active critical stance often also fail to engage the dominant model. For example it had become fashionable to criticise Westernism or the concept of Western civilisation. The criticisms tend to concentrate on the West's claim to uphold objectivity and truth. Often the possibility of objectivity or of one truth is questioned. The canon or the grand narrative are attacked not for what they contain but because they exclude other narratives.

In reality the problem with the concept of Western civilisation is not that it contains canons but that it manipulatively uses the gains of history to create a particularist identity. The concept Western civilisation is as illogical as its opponents. Civilisation is not confined to a specific particularity, it is the sum total of the human experience. Just as an individual's knowledge is based on the experience of humanity as a whole, so there are no national, regional or religious boundaries to the development of civilisation. The powder used to make fireworks in China is subsequently used to fire guns in Europe. Whatever the rights and wrongs of these discoveries, they are part of the stock of human experience. To confine civilisation to a culture or a nation is to violate the experience of human development. From the point of view of historical thinking, the West has no more claim on the ideas of Aristotle than does the East on the insights of Mencius.

To criticise Western civilisation from a relativist point of view is to devalue the gains of human development. What ought to be criticised is the use made of human civilisation for nationalistic ends. Western civilisation seeks to appropriate the legacy of human development for its own particularistic end. Those who criticise the concept because it excludes this or that text or experience miss the point altogether. To quibble about its content or to want to have something included is to accept the particularist manipulation of the past. Those who project an alternative civilisation consisting of small narratives also fall into this trap. They are merely using a different form of the same particularist criteria that Western civilisation uses for itself. They too are perpetuating myths, just myths that run counter to the dominant ones.

Special-pleading history

The new historicism of the past two decades emulates not just the methodology but the concern of the old with the construction of identities. Nineteenth-century historicism was about identity-creation. History provided an idiom through which identity could be expressed. It could also provide a claim to territory and other resources. Often the histories that emerged in eastern and central Europe were a reaction to other histories. There was a veritable competition and no group felt it could afford to be left out.

Mihail Kogalniceanu, the founder of modern Romanian historical writing, illustrates the desire to convey nationalist claims through history. Like the new historicists who complain that a particular group has been excluded from history, he claimed recognition for Romania. His major work *Histoire de la Valachie, de la Moldavie, et des Valaques Transdanubiens*, published in 1837, seeks to counter prevailing views about Romania. In the preface he remarks on his project:

> Three years have already passed since I left Moldavia; since then I have traversed all of Germany and a part of France. Everywhere I have found that no one has the slightest true idea about Wallachia and Moldavia: their geographic position is hardly known; as for their history, their customs, their institutions, their misfortunes, even the most learned do not know them. The smallest countries of Africa and America are better known than these two principalities. In this century of enlightenment the Moldavians and Wallachians are still regarded as a savage people, brutalised, unworthy of liberty.[58]

The last point reveals Kogalniceanu's intent. Although ostensibly a history of Romania, the book's real aim is to demonstrate that its people are not savages and are therefore worthy of liberty. One of the paradoxes of particularist history is that despite its emphasis on special qualities of its culture it still appeals to a general standard.

So today, when it is suggested that a particular group or a number of groups are 'neglected' or 'excluded' from history, the implication is that they *ought to be included in something*. In other words, despite their excessively particularistic form, the new histories are not written simply for the people concerned. These histories provide the representatives of particular groups with *claims* that can be made on society as a whole. These claims are justified on the grounds that a particular group has been excluded from history and it is time their voices were heard. The claim for inclusion actually indicates the implicit acceptance of a common framework. Particularist history is oriented towards gaining a better deal from society as a whole.

Rosalind Miles justifies her special-pleading history of women on the following lines:

> It will also be objected that women should not be singled out for special pleading, since both sexes suffered alike. When both men and women groaned under back-breaking labour with the ever-present scourge of famine and sudden death, the women's afflictions, it is argued, were no worse than those of men. This is another widely held belief that will not stand up to any examination of the real differences between the lives of women and men. The male peasant, however poor and lowly, always had the right to beat his wife; the black male slave, though he laboured for the white master by day, did not have to service him by night as well.[59]

The arguments outlined by Miles contain all the essential elements of particularist history. They seek a remedy to past injustice through the mobilisation of the past and the emphasis is on the 'special' quality of the experience. Others would use the same method of argument to secure their special status: for example the same logic can be used to plead that blacks are worse off than women, since in Western societies most white women have a higher status than black men.

Since special pleading needs to stress the *special*, it is by its very nature exclusivist and potentially divisive. As the history of nineteenth-century eastern Europe shows, the construction of one special history unleashes a series of counter-responses. The same process has been evident during the recent decade. In Britain the assertion of Scottish and Welsh identity has led to the emergence of Cornish nationalism. In the United States there has been a mushrooming of special cases. What begins as women's history gradually fragments into black women's history, Jewish women's history, the history of lesbians. These examples do not exhaust the number of potential fragments. It appears that each cycle of particularism breeds a more intense form of parochialism.

The political direction of new historicism is towards the negotiation of a new pluralism. It is a plea for the recognition of new interests. As Fox-Genovese puts it: 'many of the new studies have, if anything, enthusiastically embraced fragmentation, variously described as diversity or pluralism.'[60] Special-pleading history is the political philosophy for the modernisation of traditional pork-barrel politics. Ultimately it represents an option for the reorganisation of society.

The angry exchanges between conservative politicians and the special pleaders can often obscure the issues at stake. The arguments of the particularist are often presented by the defenders of the establishment in all-or-nothing terms. Especially in the United States, the demands of special-pleading history are presented as a threat to the American way of life. The practitioners of new historicism are often denounced as radical subversives. Even a relatively restrained academic like Diane Ravitch tends to panic at the very mention of the word 'particularist'. She writes:

> But particularists have no interest in extending or revising American culture; indeed, they deny that a common culture exists. Particularists reject any accommodation among groups, any interactions that blur the distinct lines between them.[61]

Ravitch fails to grasp that the exclusivist logic of particularism is invariably tempered by a sense of political reality. The demand not to be 'neglected' or 'marginalised' from history is precisely a plea for accommodation, but one negotiated on a new basis.

Far from challenging society, the new historicism adopts the methodology of identity-creating history. In the first instance this involves inventing or finding the sense of worth or status in the past that evades a particular group in the present. That is what Rosalind Miles means when she observes that 'women's history' has 'only just begun to invent itself.'[62] This very preoccupation with the past indicates a conservative preference for the locus of intellectual labour. The implicit and sometimes explicit political objective of this history is to win recognition from society. Paradoxically, the particularistic rhetoric which romanticises marginalisation signifies the demand for inclusion.

Richard Rorty, probably the most popular living philosopher of the American cultural left milieu, captures the sense of accommodation contained within particularistic thinking well:

My hunch is that certain specific changes in the canon – those which will help students learn about what it has been like (and often still is like) to be female, or black, or gay – will be the chief accomplishment of the contemporary cultural left. This will be a very important accomplishment indeed. It will not amount to a transformation of society, but it will make life much less cruel for a lot of people, and will make America into a more decent place.[63]

Rorty's statement carefully delineates the objective of the cultural left. It is about changing the terms on which interaction takes place so that America will become a more decent place. The approach is similar to that adopted by successive groups of immigrants who also sought recognition as part of the American dream. Urban-machine politics and coalitions of interest groups such as the Democratic Party are the product of just such negotiations in the past.

The pluralistic orientation is by no means solely an American phenomenon. Left historians in Britain are also happy to co-exist with other histories. Anna Davin pleads for toleration:

A pluralist and international approach to national history could provide both large framework and 'patches' to explore in detail. It could situate Britain and its diverse population in relation to Europe and the world. It could teach that diversity means richness, that difference does not necessitate intolerance and sectarianism.[64]

Davin's plea for tolerance finds a resonance among a few individual conservatives, who recognise the need to reorganise the system of ideological support for society. In this vein, Jack Citrin has called for the revitalisation of the concept of the 'melting pot' in the United States. However tolerance, coexistence and accommodation are not usually the characteristics associated with the relation between competing histories.

Davin's plea for tolerance or Rorty's hope for a more decent America are perhaps good ideas that have arrived at the wrong time. In the context of the conservative intellectual offensive even the traditional forms of accommodation are being questioned. The contemporary revival of an explicit nationalist historiography restricts the scope for a pluralist revival. In this climate, particularist histories themselves must become increasingly more conservative too.

There is an irony in all of this. Earlier in this book, the growing activism of right-wing intellectuals and the attempt to restore History were discussed in detail. This activism was directly contrasted to the right's marginalisation in intellectual life as a result of the experience of the Second World War. There are many contributing influences that have shaped the revival of the right-wing intellectual project. One of those influences is suggested by the account contained in this chapter. It seems to us that the growing conservatism of the left, most clearly shown in its rejection of historical thinking, has provided an uncontested terrain for the advance of the right-wing intelligentsia.

This experience is evident throughout the advanced capitalist world. France, which has traditionally boasted a strong left-wing intelligentsia, exemplifies the trend. By the early 1980s it was the right-wing intellectuals, the *nouveaux philosophes*, who were taking the initiative. A symptom of this shift was the initiation of discussion on the 'Silence of the Intellectuals of the Left', by the French daily *Le Monde*. 'Has the Left abandoned its ideas', asked Max Gallo in an editorial that launched the discussion.[65] Clearly the answer was that the left could no longer offer a coherent intellectual alternative to the right. This reversal of fortune between the French right-wing intelligentsia, virtually annihilated in 1945, and the dominant left milieu reveals the full dimensions of the transformation that has taken place. It is immaterial that this transformation is primarily the result of a decline of the left rather than a renaissance of right-wing ideas. Whatever the cause, the balance of intellectual influence has changed.

It is precisely the adoption of anti-historical thinking by the left that has proved so decisive in the shaping of the new intellectual climate. There is no longer a debate between left and right about substantive issues to do with history. The discussion is over what kind of history, what kind of identity. To an astonishing extent the left has fully accepted the problematic of the right. It is difficult to find any contribution which actually questions the legitimacy of identity-creation. The critics of mainstream Western literature confine their objections to a particular identity. This mirror-image relationship between left and right is exemplified by the comments of the radical historian Raphael Samuel on the relationship between Margaret Thatcher and the British left:

> Mrs Thatcher was the only philosophically interesting prime minister of my adult lifetime. As much by accident as by design she stumbled on issue after issue of high principle, where there were genuinely incompatible moral choices to be made. Working less by reason than by the passions, she made the nationality question a

storm-centre of British politics and forced us to take up alternative definitions of what it means today to be British.[66]

Samuel's comments are symptomatic of the left-wing intellectual's reaction to the revival of History. It is a reaction that is above all about 'alternative definitions'. Instead of exposing nationalist historiography to a systematic critique, radical thinkers are content to quibble about definitions. Accepting that the celebration of Britishness is a legitimate enterprise, the left offers its alternative definition.

The uncritical posture of left historiography is based on its fatalistic appreciation of the past. It too, like conservative thinkers, believes that tradition and the past have the final say. Even the most incorrigible conservative romantic could not disagree with Robert Gray's justification for a left-wing British nationalism, published by *Marxism Today*:

> The Left cannot expect to undo three centuries or so of history quickly or easily. The very strong residues of empire and chauvinism in popular common sense will make our relationship to British nationhood an uneasy one for the foreseeable future.[67]

Gray is at least uneasy about his relationship to the past. Others lack no enthusiasm. Alternative identity-creation is a thriving business among Western academics, and the religion of multiculturalism has given scope for the invention of not a few new cultures.

With both sides accepting the authority of the past, historical thinking has been pushed to the margins of contemporary thought. The conversion of the left to conservative historicism is truly one of the most significant intellectual events of the postwar years. It represents a belated triumph for the conservative reaction against the Enlightenment. For those who consider that the achievements of the Enlightenment are well worth defending and developing, the project of restoring historical thinking needs to become the principal intellectual problem of the day.

9

A critique of history: Ideas for the restoration of historical thinking

The controversies about history discussed in Chapter two can now be seen as an attempt to contain the effects of the intellectual incoherence of contemporary capitalist society. The strident manner with which identities are contested can easily obscure the underlying uncertainties. It is difficult to detect any confidence behind the outward show of conviction. The narrow terms within which the debate is posed is symptomatic of a stagnation of the mind. As indicated in the previous chapter the debate between left and right is not about fundamentals but about the validity of specific types of identity.

In these contemporary debates, history is treated as a philosophical problem instead of a way of thinking. This leads to the objectification of history, whereby it is seen as a process untouched by the human agent and unyielding to the intervention of men and women. The only role for men and women is to speculate whether history has a meaning, a purpose, or whether it is chaotic and arbitrary.

As we have seen, the weakening of historical thinking is the product of profound disillusionment with the consequence of change. The intense scepticism regarding the desirability of change is strongly reflected in the general disenchantment with progress. There is no perceptible difference in political attitude towards the question of progress: the traditional model of left-wing enthusiasm and right-wing suspicion no longer has relevance. As we move into the new millennium it is difficult to find any systematic intellectual defence of the idea of progress. The very subject of this book, the politicisation of History, is itself an illustration of the all-pervasive reaction to change and the negative perceptions of progress.

If anything, in the recent period the reaction to progress is far more marked in the liberal-leftist milieu than anywhere else. The sensibility of catastrophe, particularly ecological, is widespread. The rejection of progress has been an evolving theme in left-wing literature since the

1930s. The resonance for the ideas of the Frankfurt School and critical theory was very much to do with their questioning of modernity. Max Horkheimer and Theodor Adorno's *Dialectic of Enlightenment*, published in 1944, is the representative work of this tendency. In this text, the Enlightenment impetus to dominate nature culminates in the barbarism of fascism. It was precisely this highly critical posture towards the Enlightenment and progress which later typified radical 1960s thought. This pessimistic and anti-modern perspective is personified by Herbert Marcuse, a central intellectual influence on the 1960s generation. His vision of progress was profoundly negative:

> intensified progress seems to be bound up with intensified unfreedom. Throughout the world of industrial civilization, the domination of man by man is growing in scope and efficiency. Nor does this trend appear as an incidental, transitory regression on the road to progress. Concentration camps, mass exterminations, world wars, and atom bombs are no 'relapse into barbarism', but the unrepressed implementation of the achievements of modern science, technology, and domination. And the most effective subjugation and destruction of man by man takes place at the height of civilization, when the material and intellectual attainments of mankind seem to allow the creation of a truly free world.[1]

This was no mere scepticism but an anguished condemnation of progress. That this view readily converged with that of 1960s radicalism is shown by the extensive reaction to science and technology, the explosion of interest in 'going back to the land' and the fashion for romanticising life in small, often rural communities.

The adoption of anti-progress sentiments by 1960s radicals led to a sort of role reversal. Those who attacked the 1960s were also forced to react against aspects of its anti-modernism. Consequently, at least outwardly, the right-wing critics of the 1960s sounded more positive about progress and modernity than the left.[2] This reversal of roles was more apparent then real, since the reaction of the right to the 1960s did not entail a revision of its antipathy to change. What was significant was that neither side in the political equation was prepared to defend progress – and neither could summon much enthusiasm for the achievements of science. The corollary of this reaction was the outburst of enthusiasm for the old: antiques, nostalgia and so on.

Marcuse's condemnation of progress reflects the general trend to objectify history. From an objectivist standpoint, history just happens and progress is reduced to the passing of time. The objectivist directly identifies anything that is new as aspects of progress. Whatever is new, positive or negative, is part of the drive of progress. Progress thus means simply changing reality. Consequently he can write about the 'growing destructiveness of present-day progress'. Marcuse accepts the reality of progress but characterises it in negative terms.

It is the equation of progress with reality that reveals an inherently anti-historical stance. Progress is what happens. In a fatalistic manner, the consequences of what happens are blamed on progress. Phenomena such as concentration camps are treated as the culmination of the drive to progress through the control of nature. The possibility that concentration camps exist precisely to prevent change and progress is not considered. Progress just happens, and whatever happens is progress – that sums up this simplistic formula.

Yet progress can be conceived of historically. Through historical thinking it is the *potential to progress* that becomes crucial. Progress conceived of naturalistically or in an objectified form ignores the fundamental point that the issue is *human* progress. Progress is not a blessing or a gift to humanity, it is the consequence of human history-making activity. Without human involvement, progress becomes an empty phrase or is mystified to mean the revelation of a god. It is the dramatic absence of humans from history-making that has led to the convergence of left and right-wing thought into a common reaction against progress.

The reaction against the idea of progress is one of the most tragic manifestations of the suspension of historical consciousness. It is an indirect attempt to freeze the present, to eternalise the existing social arrangements by renouncing the desirability of progress. The objectification of history provides intellectual support for this response. History without a subject rejects any responsibility for controlling our future. By encouraging passivity and fatalism it becomes an apologetic schema for confirming the status quo. History in this sense represents an evasion of responsibility for the future direction of society. For this reason alone it needs to be criticised.

Consciousness versus identities

The clearest indication of the decline of historical thinking is that the project of identity creation is virtually unquestioned. From left to right, intellectual energy is devoted to the plundering of the past. An unstated school of heroic history thrives. While the right celebrates the past of the establishment, the left romanticises the resistance of its people from below.

Critical thinking has been reoriented towards the past in a search for role models. This approach indicates a fatalistic acceptance of low expectations, for what is often celebrated is that a particular group survived. Particularist literature assures the contemporary reader of a heroic past by stretching the meaning of resistance. This theme is particularly striking in some of the discussion of the Jewish response to the experience of genocide. As Novick notes: 'resistance came to be equated with endurance and survival.'[3] The same tendency is to be found in the discussion of the experience of black slaves in the pre-civil war southern states of America. Everyday resistance is emphasised and it suggested that an independent culture emerged as a result. The transformation of routine into resistance is also evident in Scott's work on the peasantry, discussed in the previous chapter.

We have no wish to denigrate the experience of those who survived intense forms of oppression in the past. Our objection is to the romanticisation of oppression, a tendency which is marked in left-wing historiography. In reality the romanticisation of the ordinary lives of ordinary people reflects the patronising sensibility of the writer. It assumes that the role of history should be to pacify ordinary people. This view of history is based in turn on the ahistorical assumption that people have an inherent need for an identity. The role of the radical historian is to provide one. This conclusion is inspired by the conservative assumption that people are moved by the tradition of the past rather then a vision of the future. Harvey Kaye, a left-wing academic expert on Marxist historiography, cites with approval the statement by the German Marxist Walter Benjamin to the effect that working-class political struggle is 'nourished more by the image of enslaved ancestors than liberated grandchildren'.[4] This self-awareness, which redirects energy away from the future towards the past, represents the sensibility of low expectations. It is the radical equivalent of the conservative view which counts on the force of tradition to outweigh every attempt at social transformation.

Even writers who profess to be Marxists accept the transcendental need of the individual for an identity. G. A. Cohen's work on historical materialism has been widely greeted as a significant contribution to the subject. In his attempt to systematise historical materialism he criticises Marx for underestimating the need of the individual for an identity. He writes:

I claim, then, that there is a human need to which Marxist
observation is commonly blind ... It is the need to be able to say not
what I can do but who I am, satisfaction of which has historically
been found in identification with others in a shared culture based
on nationality, or race, or some slice or amalgam thereof.[5]

Cohen's observation that the need for self-identity is an eternal
human need assumes not only a history that is objectified but also a
static view of humanity. Yet the need for self-identity is itself a
product of history rather than a pre-given characteristic of humanity.
For example the problem of individual identity emerged only in
particular circumstances. It did not exist, for example, in feudal
communities, where one's position in a clearly defined social
hierarchy was determined at birth. By eternalising the question of
identity, Cohen projects backwards the anxieties of our own time and
legitimises a History with a capital 'H'.[6]

Cohen explicitly links the need for self-identity to an attack on
Enlightenment universalism. To what he calls the 'abstractness of
Enlightenment universalism' he counterposes an abstracted
particularism: 'Marx is guilty of the idea that people can, should, and
will relate to each other just as people, an idea that ignores the
particularization needed for human formation and human
relationship.'[7] This mechanistic counterposition of the universal to
the particular abstracts the relationship from real history. The
universal and the particular exist in a relation with each other, a
relation that is subject to change through human action. Conversely
it is through the exclusion of human action from history that a static
eternalised need for the particular can be retained.

By transforming the need for identity into a human constant,
particularist history is reintroduced through the back door. The need
for identity is never substantiated empirically, but treated as self-
evident. Many Marxist thinkers emulate their conservative counterparts and simply assert that there is a demand for identity creating
history. So while in one breath Kaye warns of the danger of the 'abuse
of history', in the next he urges that 'we must acknowledge – nay,
subscribe to – *the necessity of history*'. To demonstrate that history is
necessary, all Kaye needs to do is to state that it is in wide demand:

we must recognise that however much the demand for the past may
seem to be caught up in nostalgia, the demand itself arises out of
the real and legitimate needs and aspirations of working people

themselves. If our goal truly is the making of *democratic* socialist movements and, ultimately, *socialist democracies*, then it remains fundamental to articulate these needs and aspirations in a dialectical and democratic fashion.[8]

The aspiration of working people for the past seems to be an unsubstantiated proposition. In fact there seems to be a confusion of the historian's desire to provide a past with a popular demand for it.

Is there a popular demand for the past or is History used to pacify the masses? Is the romanticisation of the past by Marxists any different from the heroic history of the right? Kaye is obviously of the view that there is a difference. He writes that one of the important contributions of British Marxist historians has been 'the recovery and assemblage of a "radical democratic tradition" in which have been asserted what might be called "counter-hegemonic" conceptions of liberty, equality and community.' It appears there is tradition and tradition. Kaye seems to imply that they have theirs and we have ours. Ours is 'counter-hegemonic', theirs is 'hegemonic'. There is a mirror-image relationship between the two traditions; for example, 'alongside the Magna Carta we are offered the English Rising of 1381'.[9]

The adoption of a conservative historiographical methodology by Marxists is a source of bemusement to mainstream historians. Oxford historian Michael Howard hits the nail on the head when he observes the reversal of orientation from the future to the past in Marxist studies. He writes:

> The study of the past 'for its own sake' is normally a characteristic of conservative rather than of radical historians. Traditional Marxist history and morality were impregnated with the sense of the historical process: those elements which 'objectively' forwarded that process were applauded ... those who stood in its way or did not contribute to it were condemned. But today the criteria are reversed. Distinguished Marxist historians like E. P. Thompson and Christopher Hill reserve their sympathy for the losers, the little men whose values and livelihood were swept away by the power structures of the historical process but on older and more enduring concepts of equity and social justice with which most of us would have considerably more sympathy.[10]

An element of exaggeration and sarcasm notwithstanding, Howard is justified in drawing a parallel between the romanticisation of the underdog by Marxist historians and traditional conservative concerns.

The counterposition to establishment History of a history from below still depends for authority on the sanction of the past. There is of course nothing wrong with the critical representation of the history of ordinary people. But when history becomes used for identity-creation it strengthens the passive side of men and women. Identity is the passive by-product of history. It is conferred on the individual without effort. As it were, one is simply born into it, history supplies the rest. People's consciousness, on the other hand, is the product of human history-making. It develops the active side of men and women. Unlike identity, consciousness is not pre-given; it develops through interaction and experience. To put matters bluntly, the attempt to achieve status by finding one's 'roots' or through one's history is an evasion of the possibility of making history in the here and now. By accepting the sanction of the past, human beings give up their own power to make history. It does not matter whether this past is radical or conservative. In both cases it is the past that is *active* and men and women, the grateful recipients of identities, are *passive*.

The denigration of the human potential

The conservative historical methodology of many Marxist intellectuals is closely linked to the low estimation they have of the human potential. In this respect their view of the masses is not qualitatively different from that of the elitist anti-mass thinkers who were considered in Chapter 7.

Antonio Gramsci, the Italian Marxist known for his interest in popular thought and the role of ideology, was also concerned with the limited culture of the masses. One of the main dilemmas for Gramsci was that the political culture of the masses was far lower than that of the elite. He noted that for 'didactic' reasons Marxism 'was combined into a form of culture which was a little higher than the popular average (which was very low) but was absolutely inadequate to combat the ideologies of the educated classes.'[11] He suggests that in adapting Marxism to the level of the popular masses, it had become 'prejudice' and 'superstition'. As the example of the British Marxist tradition-oriented historians shows, Gramsci's conclusion is probably accurate.

The main problem with Gramsci's analysis is that he offers a static

view of popular consciousness. In his schema there is no solution to
the low level of culture of the masses. Gramsci seeks to resolve this
dilemma by envisaging the emergence of a group of intellectuals who,
because they are close to the people, are able to articulate their
aspirations.[12] Thus Gramsci adopted a semi-conscious elitist
perspective. In this scenario the intellectual intervenes to educate the
passive, inert masses. His advice is 'never tire of repeating' the
argument, since 'repetition is the best didactic means for working on
the popular mentality.'[13]

Gramsci draws a false relationship between the level of culture and
the ability to learn. The human potential is only constrained, not
negated, by a low level of culture. Experience shows that consciousness is susceptible to great fluctuations and becomes transformed as
reality changes. Just as Gramsci underestimates the human potential
so too he overestimates the capacity of the intellectual to educate.
Gramsci's call for 'repetition' is as likely to be as ineffective as Kaye's
call to construct an alternative tradition.

Both Gramsci and Kaye express a disenchantment with the capacity
of the masses. Miles Taylor's article 'Patriotism, history and the left
in twentieth-century Britain' indicates that this was part of a wider
tendency. Taylor writes that there was a widely held view on the left
that mass opinion was guided by instincts rather then intelligence:

> Doubts about the capacity of the working class, in particular, to
> overcome their apathy or their elementary emotions fuelled the
> inter-war debate over what constituted the best form of leadership
> within the modern political party. By the 1930s some communists
> and socialists were advocating the establishment of a priestly party
> elite or even the consolidation of power in a single figure of
> personal authority.[14]

The experience of fascism seemed to confirm these elitist sentiments.
Leading representatives of the Frankfurt School wrote about the
'eclipse of rationality' and were deeply pessimistic about the capacity
to reason.

The pessimism which Gramsci expressed in relation to the low level
of culture of the masses becomes unrestrained in the literature of the
Frankfurt School. Herbert Marcuse, a product of this tradition,
explicitly rejects the history-making potential of human beings. He
argues that democratic societies assimilate the capacity to revolt. The
'effectiveness of the democratic introjection' has 'suppressed the

historical subject, the agent of revolution', writes Marcuse.[15]

The suppression of the historical subject implies the total objectific-ation of history. Men and women stand entirely outside history, waiting to discover their destiny. Their only hope is the enlightened intellectual who can help them find their identity through history.

With the suppression of the historical subject there can be no historical thinking. The consciousness of history is stimulated and reinforced by the experience of human beings making history. But in its absence, the sense of change does not give way to a sense of permanence. The world has become too fast to return to a sense of stability. In the absence of historical thinking change is reflected only *passively*. As a result change is experienced as further fragmentation and atomisation. Awareness of only the fragmenting consequence of change breeds a conservative reaction. Containing the effects of fragmentation leads to a search for wholeness, which in an atomised society is resolved through the wholeness of the particular. So the suppression of the historical subject, which leads to its exclusion from history, enhances the sensibility of atomisation. The particularist history of the left is a clear expression of this sensibility.

One by-product of the particularist response is objectified history. It means the left no less then the right can conceptualise history only as an objectified process. There may be debates on its meaning or whether it has any meaning at all but there is no argument that history is somewhere out there carrying on without the historical subject.

From this discussion it follows that the revival of History cannot achieve results which are entirely satisfactory to its practitioners. The consolidation of the past and the suspension of historical thinking are obviously helpful in fostering a conservative mood in society. But as indicated previously, the changing world overwhelms tradition and exposes a society that is highly atomised and ill at ease with itself. As a result the decline of historical thinking does not automatically mean the triumph of History. Its most characteristic manifestation is a sense of intellectual malaise that afflicts all sections of society.

The transformation of historical materialism into History

Even Marxism has not been able to avoid the consequences of the decline of historical thinking. Since most Marxists themselves accepted the project of recovering the past, albeit a more radical past than others, they have become complicit in turning historical materialism away from the future. More specifically, historical materialism has been turned into a philosophy of history. Except for a handful of thinkers, it is widely accepted that historical materialism provides a general theory of history.[16] Consequently it is not surprising that Marx's opponents routinely accuse him of deterministically believing in history and of reducing history to an inevitable process. Although there is an element of polemical excess in the attacks on Marx, the regularity with which he is accused of an attitude towards history which he explicitly renounced indicates that the accusers actually believe their own case.

The most common charge levelled at Marx is that, because of his deterministic and mechanical view of history, he claimed to be able to predict its outcome in the future. So for example Hayek observes that 'those philosophers like Marx and August Comte who have contended that our studies can lead to laws of evolution enabling the prediction of inevitable future developments are mistaken.'[17] Nisbet reiterates the accusation of inevitability and refines the point to suggest that Marx's view of history was entirely a fatalistic one. He notes that Marx assumed that 'what we are developing (trans.) *would* develop (intrans.) if we just left it alone and allowed indefinite time.'[18] Since history was characterised as an automatic process, it seems, according to Nisbet, that Marx thought he had all the answers; Marx 'was convinced that *he* had discovered the law of motion or development that would thenceforth render obsolete prior opinions on fixity and change in society.'[19] Certainly from this portrait, it is difficult to avoid the conclusion that Marx must have been a singularly stupid man.

The view that Marx was a simpleton is upheld by virtually all the mainstream writers considered in this book. J. H. Plumb accuses Marx of an explicitly tendentious use of the past. He writes:

> Yet it was a past that was being used, and not always history. The dialectic was simple, clear, rigid and uniform: all societies had to pass through the same stages of development, and the history of China had to be forced into the same strait-jacket as the history of Europe.[20]

Everything then is 'simple, clear, rigid and uniform'; all societies go through the same stages. Hall repeats this by now not so original criticism: 'Marxism as a universal and unilinear theory suggested that each society had to go through every stage specified.'[21] Hans Kohn chips in and adds that Marx 'claimed a mechanical course for history'. It was for Marx 'an inevitable teleological reality'.[22]

By now Marx's mechanical views predicting some inevitable teleological process sound dangerously like a religion in expectation of the Second Coming. This is the conclusion that Alan Bloom draws when he announces that 'Marx denied the existence of God but turned over all His functions to history, which is inevitably directed to a goal fulfilling of man and which takes the place of Providence.'[23] Marxism, then, is a secular religion, and it only remains for von Mises to point out that, given Marx's complete determinism, his interest in revolution is nothing less then bizarre. 'If Marx had been consistent, he would not have embarked upon any political activity.'[24]

There are a number of curious aspects to these criticisms of Marx. First, it is well worth asking why so many highly gifted thinkers feel the compulsion to expand their energies attacking what are manifestly ludicrous ideas. The second, and in many ways even more curious, feature of their criticism is that Marx does not hold even *one* of the ideas attributed to him by the writers above. It is always possible to quibble about nuances, but in this case Marx and his colleague Engels explicitly argue against precisely the attitudes attributed to them.

First the point that Marx knew in advance the course of history and that he possessed a unilinear and general theory. In numerous places he argued precisely against the legitimacy of a general philosophy of history. This argument is a constant theme throughout his work. In *The German Ideology*, written with Engels in 1845, criticism is levelled at general historicism. The book's argument is that history is specific: 'empirical observation must in each separate instance bring out empirically and without any mystification and speculation, the connection of the social and political structure with production.'[25] This insistence on empirical observation was motivated by the conviction that there were no ready-made models through which history could be understood. It is a point to which Marx returned time and again. For example 18 years later he challenged the quest of Proudhon and other utopian socialists for a ready-made model which needed only to be applied to reality. He accused them of 'hunting for a so-called "science" by means of which they want to devise *a priori* a formula for the "solution of the social question", instead of deriving their science from a critical knowledge of the historical movement.'[26]

There is nothing inevitable or predictable in Marx's theory of history. He explicitly criticised those who depicted history as going through necessary stages. He wrote of his critic Mikhailovsky:

> He insists on transforming my historical sketch of the genesis of capitalism in Western Europe into an historico-philosophic theory of the general path of development prescribed by fate to all nations, whatever the historical circumstances in which they find themselves.

But, he remarks:

> Events strikingly analogous but taking place in different historical surroundings led to totally different results. By studying each of these forms of evolution separately and then comparing them one can easily find the clue to this phenomenon, but one will never arrive there by using as one's master key a general historico-philosophical theory, the supreme virtue of which consists in being supra-historical.[27]

The orientation of Marx's analysis was very much against prediction and general theories. Nothing could be assumed as unproblematic or as self-evident.

Take a couple of illustrations of the demand for *historical specificity*. Engels objected to those who attempted to use Marxist concepts as a rigid analytic framework. He insisted that 'all history must be studied afresh.' He also insisted that historical materialism was a guide to social investigation rather than a system of concepts that could be mechanically imposed on history. He warned that 'the materialist method turns into its opposite if it is not taken as one's guiding principle in historical investigation but as a ready-made pattern according to which one shapes the facts of history to suit oneself.'[28]

The charge that Marx possesses a teleological view of history is patently absurd. Marx in fact wrote at great length against such a conception of history. He was for example critical of the 'intellectual laziness' of Social Darwinists and contemptuously dismissed their view that 'all history may be subsumed in one single great natural law'.[29] He explicitly attacked the teleological view of history for the distortion whereby 'later history is made the goal of earlier history'. This objection is sustained on the ground that teleological views exclude human beings from history, that is the objectification of history excludes the subject; thus 'life appears as non-historical, while the historical appears as something separated from ordinary life, something extra-superterrestrial.'[30]

Finally, from the above it is clear that Marx could not have held the view of a unilinear sense of history and of progress. His statements on this subject allow no scope for any ambiguity. He wrote:

> In spite of the pretensions of *'Progress'*, continual *retrogressions* and *circular movements* occur ... the category *'Progress'* is completely empty and abstract.[31]

Elsewhere, the unevenness and complexity of historical development is discussed by Marx in detail.

The distortions of Marx are not casual nor rare. They have a systematic quality which itself ought to be of interest to the historian of ideas. For example words such as 'inevitable', 'unilinear', 'rigid' or 'uniform', which are consistently coupled with Marx's theory of history by his opponents, are conspicuously absent from his own discussions of the subject. It is always possible that Marx unconsciously subscribed to these views and his critics have discovered a hidden agenda – but in that case one would expect it would be a matter of intellectual integrity to point out that at least *outwardly* Marx rejected the views attached to him. From the sheer consistency of their criticism of Marx, it seems likely that the authors actually believe their own arguments. Their criticism is part of an already established consensus for which Marx's unilinear view of history is an article of faith. Such critics can be accused of intellectual shoddiness or of not bothering to read the targets of their attack but not of self-conscious dishonesty. At most, carried away by polemical excess, they stand accused of a cavalier attitude towards facts.

The transformation of Marx's view of history into a History, with a very big capital 'H', is itself a product of an intellectual climate where historical thinking is inconsistently applied. Above all this interpretation is made possible by the dualism between history and the subject, a dualism which seems to predominate in left and right-wing literature alike. Once the role of human history-making is suppressed it is possible to treat the subject mechanistically. There is no sense of interaction. Indeed history stands external to society; it imposes its dictates on the passive individual.

In the previous section it was argued that many Marxists have adopted an objectified view of history. If Marxists possess such a view of history then it is not surprising that mainstream critics attribute such views to Marx. Once the historical subject is suppressed and taken out of the picture then many of the criticisms made of Marx actually become plausible.

Take the question of change. Outside the context of humans bringing about change through the making of history, change can have no purpose. That is why some of the liberal theories which regard change as accidental are logically consistent. If change is not the product of human action, then this leaves only two other possibilities. It is the product either of accidents or of some supra-historical divine force. That is why the philosophy of history always contains some pre-given meaning or purpose. Interpreted from this perspective, that is one where there is no historical subject, Marx's view of history can be readily transformed into a religion.

With the exclusion of men and women from history, the process of change becomes truly incomprehensible and mystifying. Once the connection between human action and its consequences is lost sight of, then the cause of those consequences can be ascribed to something extra-human. The outcome of human interaction is then generally explained as either accidental, that is *arbitrary*, or the product of some transcendental purpose. The couplet of history as either *accidental* or *purposeful* is reproduced in the debate on relative and absolute values that were considered in earlier chapters.

The controversy over the essential character of history treats as unproblematic the subject of the debate. But before the question regarding its character can be considered, it is necessary to ask what this history is. The very attempt to discuss history and to inspect its essence implies that it exists in some objectified form. But what are the objective qualities of history? Chronology, time and the passing of time can be objectively measured and discussed. But the passing of time is not necessarily the same as history. The passing of time is certainly not the same as change. In many societies, seasons can come and go without there being a conception of past, present and future. The passing of time, or time itself, is not synonymous with history.

History clearly cannot have a fixed character or essence. History is about the consciousness that people have about time, the passing of time, the past, the changing present and the future. So any discussion of history is really a shorthand for the consideration of different consciousnesses towards the subject. And these perceptions of history are shaped by contemporary experience. So when the question 'what is history?' is considered, this is a roundabout way of asking what shapes society and what are the forces that govern our social arrangements.

As long as human beings seem unable to control their lives in the present, it seems to us highly unlikely that they could do so in the past. As a result it is easy to acquire the perception that the past is separate from human activity. This way the past is endowed with autonomy, it becomes an independent force that moves in accord with its own logic. In reality it is the human being who endows history with autonomy. His or her limited understanding creates the mystery of history. The real mystery, however, is the lack of control that men and women have over their own lives. Once this is understood then the connections that bind human beings into one society become clear. And once the connections are clarified, then it becomes evident that even forces that are most out of our control – the stock exchange, currency fluctuations, supply and demand – are the product of human construction. History too is a human construction. There is only a history of humans acting and interacting. An understanding of these interactions is what provides insight into history.

Historical thinking developed through the conviction that human beings can shape their circumstances and make history. This form of thinking emphasises subjectivity, the act of change through transformation. But it isn't simply subjective, for it comprehends that there are real constraints to human action. These constraints are themselves historical. For example the constraint of physical strength, which was crucial in one epoch, is entirely insignificant today. Even within specific constraints, historical thinking does not imply that human action can directly realise its objectives. The accumulated experience of the past, formalised through tradition, can slow down, even neutralise, social experimentation. It is rare for men and women to simply 'break with the past'. A humanist view of history does not argue that men and women can simply make history; it argues that men and women have *the potential* to make history. The realisation of this potential depends not on an act of will but on the cumulative effects of historical constraints, tradition and prevailing consciousness in society.

From the above it follows that there are no general truths waiting to be revealed. There are truths but they are truths only for the specific historical relation that they seek to explain. The relative character of truth, however, does not mean a relativistic epistemology. It does not renounce objectivity; rather it specifies objectivity in relation to its problem. The absolute–relative value debate exists at the level of historical speculation. This tension is resolved in practice in the tackling of real problems, where there are *absolute truths that are historically relative*.

The importance of a human-centred practical epistemology is shown by the fate of Marxism as an intellectual discipline. Once the subject is expunged from its theory it can be readily turned into a History. The formal transformation of Marxism into a philosophy of history by both the left and the right is itself the product of the decline of historical consciousness. It is to the implications of this problem for the future that we now turn.

For a critique of history

The worldwide debates on history should be seen as attempts to recast or modernise the past in order to make it into a usable source of authority. The systematic character of this revival of identity-creating history indicates that, in today's intellectual climate, the balance has swung very much against the sense of historical temporality. The sense of terminus at once indicates not only the absence of a sense of change but also an outlook which fears change. This closure of the historical mind is the flip-side of the crusade for the revival of the past.

The controversies that have exploded over identities and cultures underline the difficulty of recasting the past. This difficulty has nothing to do with historiographic issues. It mirrors the unresolved tensions that prevail in most industrial capitalist societies. The very process of inventing identities creates claims and counter-claims for others. It is of course illusory to imagine that the substitution of one history textbook for another is likely to make much difference. Nevertheless, by elevating the past into an unquestioned source of authority the scope for human action becomes restrained.

This is the nub of the problem. Regardless of the actual content of the debates on history, making the past the main point of reference is to lose sight of the possibility of influencing the future. From this perspective radical and left-wing alternatives to conservative or mainstream histories are not particularly helpful. The recovery of the radical past tends to confirm that the enterprise of recasting the past is a legitimate one. The counterposition of one sort of History to another in the end validates History as the point of reference. Any difference is secondary to a commonly held methodology. Radical history, labour history, women's history or black history fully share the problematic of conservative historiography. The debate is about means to a commonly shared end.

The alternative of a different History is undesirable because whatever its content it can do no more than flatter people about their past. There is nothing necessarily wrong with flattery, except that this process tends to orient the interest of men and women to who they were, and away from considering what they could be. Even when the past is used to inspire, it retains the initiative; it is the active element. That is why the more people become preoccupied with the past, the less they are likely to consider their future. It would be naive mechanically to counterpose the past to the future. Through a critical stance towards the present, men and women necessarily interrogate both the past and the future. The problem emerges only when the past is endowed with authority and the power to confer identity. When that happens, human action becomes subject to the constraint of the past.

The formalised past is not some benevolent, neutral source of authority. It directly influences the conduct of society and prescribes the values that conserve society. The past is charged with legitimising what exists, it is an instrument of the status quo. That is why the project of developing alternative pasts is irrational. Such pasts may help provide identities, but do so within the context of existing reality.

Instead of alternative history or radical pasts, we require a critique of history. More specifically, we require a critique of the consciousness which gives the past the privilege of defining human values and identities. A critique of history is essential to the restoration of the human subject to the centre of history. It is through such a critique of history that society can be consciously understood as the product of human action rather than as the mysterious outcome of the past.

A critique of history is essential for the restoration of the consciousness of *reason*, the *human potential*, and the possibility of *change*.

Reason

The elevation of tradition which takes place with the closure of the historical mind directly puts to question the claims of reason. One of the most destructive consequences of the suspension of historical thinking is the flourishing of non-rational or irrational thought. Parallel with the revival of History during the past 15 years or so has been a consistent tendency to disparage understanding. This tendency takes on different forms but they all work towards the same end: restricting the applicability of human reason.

For example the recent period has seen the revival of theories of socio-biology. Numerous writers have publicly admitted their conversion from social explanations to naturalistic ones. This conversion is usually justified on the ground that some scientific discovery shows that this or that human characteristic in fact has not a social but a biological foundation.[32] In physics and elsewhere chaos theory has become respectable. Among environmentalists there is a manifestly mystical trend which enjoys widespread respectability. In all these cases, and others, the field for the application of human reason has been narrowed. It is suggested, in other words, that causes to do with mysterious natural or biological forces or accidents are not susceptible to human reasoning. The narrowing of the field of reasoning highlights the insignificance of the human race.

If the use of reason is so significantly circumscribed, there is little that human beings can do to develop their understanding. As E. H. Carr once remarked in relation to his criticism of the accidental view of history, 'randomness is an enthronement of ignorance.'[33] It is this ignorance that traditionalists presuppose when they demand that society respect the past. For them the wisdom of the past can help guide the ignorant.

The tendency to mystify problems by assigning causation to nature, biology or God – or by denying the possibility of determining causality altogether – needs to be confronted. The human consciousness can grasp problems. Indeed new problems extend the field of human consciousness. The restriction placed on knowledge by the restraining of reason helps create a climate where superstition and prejudice can thrive. Tackling those who seek to limit the relevance of human knowledge is the first priority for those committed to the restoration of historical thinking.

Human potential

History, in its contemporary objectified form, requires the exclusion of men and women. According to most views human beings are extraneous to the whole business. Either history is the property of a divine force, a force that determines its direction, or history is too complicated and too random for the application of human understanding. Either way humans have no business for making history.

The anti-humanist posture of the historicist standpoint is sceptical about the potential that men and women possess for influencing their destiny. This belittling of the human potential is not unconnected from the sentiment that the attempt by humans to control their destiny is not only unrealistic but also very dangerous. Attempts at any form of social experimentation are often condemned as unnatural. It is suggested that it is far better to leave things to work themselves out than to intervene and upset things. The rejection of the human potential is coupled with the fear that this potential may be exercised in the project of change.

The celebration of tradition and the disparaging of reason are reinforced by the rejection of social experimentation. Thus it is not surprising that the conservative reaction directs its fire not merely at the restoration of History but also against social experiments. Tradition demands *conformity*, not experimentation. During the past decade the call to conform has been justified by pointing to the failures of experiments. For example the collapse of Stalinism is used to prove the futility of the project of social transformation. At a more domestic level, the disease AIDS was deployed to discredit sexual experimentation; some suggested that it was God's way of punishing the sinner. Whatever the specifics of the argument, the underlying theme is that of human limitations and the danger that through experimentation the situation will become worse.

The restoration of historical thinking demands the rescuing of the awareness of the human potential. The significance of this potential lies precisely in the fact that through doing things, acting on things and transforming things, men and women learn, change themselves and develop their potential. Every advance in the development of men and women has been based upon experimentation of one sort or another. Humanity learned by doing things and by sometimes trying out something new. One needs to get on to the saddle before one can master the art of riding a bicycle. Like all experiments, things can go wrong. Millions of bruised knees attest to that fact. But without bruised knees there would be no bicycle riders. And humanity would have been that much more impoverished.

An awareness of the human potential developing through experimentation is key to the recovery of the consciousness of history. Human beings change their circumstances. That is real history.

Change

The sense of change has as its precondition a confident view of the scope of reason and of the human potential. Once knowledge and science are seen from this perspective then the conclusion that human beings can solve the problems thrown up by history makes sense. Human consciousness now grasps that at least to a limited extent the world is of its own making. Or, more to the point, it can alter the circumstances within which it lives. A consciousness of change, a sense of the transience of social arrangements, implies a human-centred view of the world. That means people start thinking that what they do may count for something, that individual or collective action can make a difference.

It is this sensibility towards change which represents the negation of History. The consciousness that nothing is beyond change strengthens the faculty of criticism. This attitude does not recognise that anything is self-evident. It is no respecter of tradition. Indeed it insists that tradition and custom account for themselves and justify their existence.

This is a consciousness that seeks to liberate men and women from an arrogant not-to-be-questioned tradition. By questioning tradition and criticising history, people set themselves up as the sole authorities for their action. Finally, the rejection of History must imply the rejection of all forms of History. Instead of changing identities our conclusion is that it is better to change the realities that make identities necessary.

Notes and references

Chapter 1: History under siege

1. Cited in *Guardian*, 13 July 1991.
2. R. Holton, 'Problems of crisis and normalcy in the contemporary world', in Alexander and Sztompka (1990), p.39.
3. See J. K. Galbraith, 'The price of world peace', in *Guardian*, 8 September 1990, and *Financial Times*, 7 January 1991. There is now a substantial body of literature in international relations which argues that the ending of the Cold War is potentially a major threat to world peace. See for example the main contributions to *Foreign Affairs*, vol.69 (4), Fall 1990.
4. *Wall Street Journal*, 18 January 1991.
5. Cited in *New York Times*, 15 April 1990.
6. See *Far East Economic Review*, 26 April 1990, and *Economist*, 21 April 1990. For an interesting background to these developments see C. Gluck, 'The Idea of Showa', in *Daedalus*, 1990.
7. Bennett and Bauer cited in D. B. Fleming, 'Foreign Policy Issues in Social Studies Textbooks in the USA', in Berghahn and Schissler (1987) p.117.
8. Elton (1984) pp.11 and 16.
9. Scruton (1990) p.283.
10. *Frankfurter Rundschau*, 14 January 1987.
11. *Sunday Times*, 10 March 1991.
12. J. J. Mearsheimer, 'Why we will soon miss the Cold War', in *Atlantic Monthly*, August 1990, p.50.
13. Pfaff (1990) p.3.
14. *Financial Times*, 4 September 1990.
15. Bloom (1988) p.56.
16. A. Meyerson, 'The Vision Thing Continued', in *Policy Review*, Summer 1990, p.2.
17. Himmelfarb (1982) p.170.
18. *Frankfurter Allgemeine Zeitung*, 25 April 1986.
19. *The Times*, 25 June 1990.
20. *Guardian*, 14 February 1991.

21. See the discussion in *Guardian*, 8 May 1991.
22. Clark (1990) p.4.
23. Cited in *Independent*, 21 September 1989.
24. J. C. Alexander, 'Between progress and apocalypse: social theory and the dream of reason in the twentieth century', in Alexander and Sztompka (1990).
25. C. N. Degler, 'In Pursuit of an American History', in *American Historical Review*, vol.92 (1), February 1987, p.1.
26. The contemporary politicisation of history is not yet a subject of serious comparative discussion. There are some useful studies of past attempts to politicise history. See for example the very interesting collection of essays edited by Laquer and Mosse (1974). Richard Evans' article on the German history debate also shows a sensitivity to the international trends. See his 'The New Nationalism and the Old History: Perspectives on the West German *Historikerstreit*', in *Journal of Modern History*, vol 59 (4) December 1987, pp.793–4.
27. See Gardiner (1990).
28. Carr (1987) p.42.
29. Independent, 28 April 1990.
30. Scruton (1990) p.11.
31. Cited in G.Eley, 'Nazism, Politics and the Image of the Past: Thoughts on the West German *Historikerstreit* 1986–1987', in *Past and Present*, no.121, November 1988, p.193.
32. Elton (1984) pp.14–15.
33. Cited in *Independent*, 7 September 1990.
34. *Sunday Telegraph*, 17 March 1991.
35. Cited in N. Birnbaum, 'History and the Holocaust', in *Nation*, 22 May 1989.

Chapter 2: History in demand

1. J. Lukacs, 'American History? American History', in *Salmagundi*, no.50–1, Fall 1980–Winter 1981, pp.172–3.
2. R. Mayne, 'Superpower Emeritus: The British Example', in *Encounter*, December 1989, p.53.
3. Novick (1988) p.574.
4. B. Bailyn, 'The Challenge of Modern Historiography', in *American History Review*, vol.87, February 1982, p.3.
5. J. Turner, 'Recovering the Uses of History', in *Yale Review*, vol.70, no.2, January 1981. See also the discussion in Hamerow (1987).
6. K. Robbins, 'National Identity and History: Past, Present and Future', in *History*, vol.75, no.245, October 1990, p.383.
7. Plumb (1978) p.40.
8. Cited in Grainger (1986) p.32.

9. French history education is 'probably responsible for the remarkable morale of the French soldiers during the Great War'. See Scott (1926) p.24.
10. For a discussion of Seeley's preoccupation with the national stock see Grainger (1986) p.46.
11. Cited in P. Burroughs, 'John Seeley and British Imperial History', in *Journal of Imperial and Commonwealth History*, vol.1, no.2, p.194.
12. Earl of Meath, 'The Cultivation of Patriotism', in Dawson (1917) p.11.
13. Cited by C. Lasch, 'The Politics of Nostalgia', in *Harper's*, November 1984, pp.66–7.
14. Gluck, 'The Idea of Showa', p.23.
15. Robbins, 'National Identity', p.369.
16. Plumb (1978) p.44.
17. S. Hoffman, 'Fragments Floating in the Here and Now', in *Daedalus*, no.108 (1), Winter 1979, p.9.
18. Hoffmann, 'Fragments', p.26.
19. Thomas (1990) p.70.
20. Elton (1984) pp.8–9.
21. Nisbet (1980) p.324.
22. Nisbet (1980) p.332.
23. Bennett (1985) p.43.
24. Bennett (1985) p.44.
25. Bloom (1988) p.34.
26. W. H. McNeill, 'Mythistory, or Truth, Myth, History, and Historians', in *American Historical Review*, vol.91 (1), February 1986, p.6.
27. Thatcher (1977) p.29.
28. Cited in J. Z. Muller, 'German Historians at War', in *Commentary*, vol.87 (5), May 1989, p.37.
29. Cited in Thomas (1990) p.15.
30. Elton (1984) p.28.
31. Turner, 'Recovering', pp.226–7.
33. See *Frankfurter Allgemeine Zeitung*, 25 April 1986.
33. See Sir K. Joseph, 'Why Teach History in School?', in *Historian*, no.2, Spring 1984, p.11, and Beattie (1987) p.9.
34. Bennett (1985) p.45.
35. McNeill, 'Mythistory', p.6.
36. *Far Eastern Economic Review*, 23 March 1989.
37. Joseph, 'Why Teach', p.12.
38. *Far Eastern Economic Review*, 23 March 1989.
39. J. Torpey, 'Introduction: Habermas and the Holocaust', in *New German Critique*, no.44, Spring/Summer 1988, p.23.
40. Cited in *Guardian*, 30 October 1990.
41. R. Skidelsky, 'Going to war with Germany', in *Encounter*, November 1972, p.16.

42. *Auf Wiedersehen Pet* was a popular television situation comedy portraying a group of British migrant workers living in Germany. See M Steyn, 'The Fawlty school of international affairs', in *Independent*, 15 October 1990.
43. Interview reprinted in *Daily Telegraph*, 13 July 1990.
44. The extravagant vision of the stab-in-the-back perspective is well illustrated by Butt in his article 'Remaking History', in *The Times*, 25 June 1990.
45. N. Stone, 'At the crossroads of history', in *Sunday Times*, 8 April 1990.
46. A. D. Harvey, 'The Future of British History', in *Salisbury Review*, December 1987, p.44.
47. M. Thatcher, 'Introduction' to Thomas (1985) p.5.
48. See Yoshihisa Komori, 'The re-writing of war history: A Japanese view', in *Independent*, 23 February 1989.
49. See L. Botstein, 'Haunted by History', in *New Republic*, 3 April 1989, p.142.
50. O. Handlin, 'The Vulnerability of the American University', in *Encounter*, no.35, July 1970, pp.25 and 28.
51. Bloom (1988) p.29.
52. Strictly speaking this point could be refuted by the argument that conservatives are 'revisers' of the so-called new history that emerged in the 1960s. However it is more profitable to understand conservative historiography as actually conserving that past which was challenged by the new history.
53. F. Fitzgerald, 'Changing the Paradigm', in Berghahn and Schissler (1987) p.20.
54. See *Newsweek*, 14 January 1991.
55. Cited in B. Shapiro, in *Nation*, 21 May 1990, p.707.
56. D. W. Hoover, 'Black History', in Ballard (1970) p.39.
57. Hoffmann, 'Fragments', p.12.
58. McNeill, 'Mythistory', p.9.
59. D. Ravitch, 'Multiculturalism', in *American Scholar*, vol.59, no.3, Summer 1990, p354.
60. See report in *The Times*, 22 October 1990.
61. See Moses (1975) p.7.
62. Cited in A. Rabinbach, 'The Jewish Question in the German Question', in *New German Critique*, no.44, Spring/Summer 1988, pp.184–5.
63. *Frankfurter Allgemeine Zeitung*, 29 August 1986.
64. Thomas (1990) p.49.
65. See Hayek (1976) pp. 4 and 125. Similar arguments are also be found in Hayek, 'The Counter-revolution of Science', in *Economica*, n.s.8, 1941.
66. Popper (1952) p.255.
67. M. Nolan, 'The *Historikerstreit* and Social History', in *New German Critique*, no.44, Spring/Summer 1988.

68. Eley, 'Nazism, Politics', p.193.
69. Evans, 'The New Nationalism', p.787.
70. Eley, 'Nazism, Politics', p.176.
71. For a good overview of this debate, see Maier (1988) and Thomas (1990). *New German Critique*, no 44, Spring/Summer 1988, is a 'Special Issue on the *Historikerstreit*'.
72. Rabinbach,'The Jewish Question', p.179
73. Cited in Eley, 'Nazism, Politics', p.196.
74. Nolan, 'The *Historikerstreit*', p. 65. Hans-Ulrich Wehler and Martin Broszat are both on the left/liberal side of the debate.
75. Cited in Holstein (1990) pp.156–7.
76. Cited in Holstein (1990) p.157.
77. I. Buruma, 'Why Japan Hides Its Guilt', in *Spectator*, 7 January 1989, pp.9–10.
78. Ishihara (1991) pp.27, 28 and 29.
79. Shimizu Ikutaro, 'The Nuclear Option: Japan, be a State!', in *Japan Echo*, vol.7, no.3, 1980, p.35.
80. See Y. Masato, 'History Textbooks That Provoke an Asian Outcry', in *Japan Quarterly*, January–March 1987, p.53.
81. Masato,'History Textbooks', p.53.
82. Cited in *Independent*, 13 January 1989.
83. Thomas (1990) p.70.
84. H. Schulze, 'The *Historikerstreit* in Perspective', in *German History*, vol.6, no.1, 1988, p.67.
85. Masato, 'History Textbooks', p.55.
86. A. Davin, 'Introduction: Special Feature: History, the Nation and the Schools', in *History Workshop*, no.29, Spring 1990.
87. This point is well documented in Taylor (1990).
88. Hill (1990) p.252.
89. See F. Furedi, 'Not-so Great Britain', in *Living Marxism*, February 1991, p.27.
90. Robbins, 'National Identity', p.383.
91. For a useful survey of historians' views on this debate, see Gardiner (1990).
92. M. Prowse, 'Leaving it to the History Man', in *Financial Times*, 11 April 1990.
93. *Sunday Times*, 29 July 1990.
94. D. Cameron Watt, 'Battle of the History Men', in *Evening Standard*, 22 March 1990.
95. R. Honeyford, 'The Gilmore Syndrome', in *Salisbury Review*, April 1986, p.11.
96. See *Sunday Telegraph*, 18 February 1989.
97. J. Casey, 'The other side of racialism', in *Evening Standard*, 24 May 1990.
98. *Sun*, 7 February 1991.

99. R. Porter, 'Healthy History', in *History Today*, November 1990, p11.
100. R. Samuel, 'Forum', in *History Today*, vol.34, May 1984, p.9.
101. R. Samuels, 'History, the Nation and the Schools', in *History Workshop*, no.29, Spring 1990, p.127

Chapter 3: History and society

1. Aron (1978), p.5.
2. Novack (1972), p.15.
3. E. Hobsbawm, 'The Social Function of the Past: Some Questions', in *Past and Present*, no.55, May 1972, p.3.
4. Hobsbawm, 'The Social Function'. p.5.
5. Hobsbawm, 'The Social Function'. p.6.
6. Hobsbawm, 'The Social Function'. p.6.
7. P. Abrams 'The Sense of the Past and the Origins of Sociology', in *Past and Present*, no.55, May 1972, p.23.
8. Hobsbawm, 'The Social Function', p.10.
9. R. W. Davies, 'From E. H. Carr's Files: Notes Towards a Second Edition of *What is History*', in Carr (1987) p.173.
10. Marwick (1990), p.14.
11. Joll (1985) p.20.
12. Cited in Joll (1985) pp.6–7.
13. Marwick (1990) p.41.
14. Benda (1959) p.42.
15. Soffer (1987) pp.77–104.
16. Soffer (1987) p.80.
17. Joll (1985) p.5.
18. Macaulay (1979) p.52.
19. F. Ringer, 'Review Essay of C. Simon: *Staat und Geschichtswissenschaft in Deutschland und Frankreich 1871–1914*', in *History and Theory*, vol.30, no.1, 1991, p.103.
20. Cited in Ringer, 'Review Essay', p.96.
21. Stokes (1986) p.451.
22. Woodward (1988) p.2.
23. Soffer (1987) p.103.
24. Benda (1959) p.14.
25. Carr's response to the question 'what is history?' provides a useful point of departure: 'it is a continuous process of interaction between the historian and his facts, an unending dialogue between the present and the past'. See Carr (1987) p.30.
26. Plumb (1978) p.11.
27. Plumb (1978) p.18.
28. Plumb (1978) pp.12–13.
29. The relationship of objectivity to history is discussed in chapter 9.

30. Plumb (1978) p.111.
31. Plumb (1978) pp.140–2.
32. Plumb (1978) p.17.
33. Chesneaux (1978) p.12.
34. 'Another strengthening of national passions comes from the determination of the peoples to be conscious of *their past*, more precisely to be conscious of their ambitions as going back to their ancestors and to vibrate with "centuries-old" aspirations, with attachements to "historical" rights'. See Benda (1959) p.16.
35. Samuel and Thompson (1990) p.19.
36. Vico (1961) pp.52–3.
37. Cited in Grainger (1986) p.9.
38. Rieff (1975) pp.15 and 39.
39. Marx (1979) p.106.
40. Marx and Engels (1975) p.93.
41. Gamble (1987) p.255.
42. Cited in Grossman (1943) p.383. This essay provides a most stimulating account of the new sense of historical temporality that developed within the Enlightenment.
43. Iggers (1968) p.41.
44. Zeitlin (1968) p.36.
45. Elton (1968) p.7.
46. Namier (1962) pp.25–6.
47. G. Steiner, 'Aspects of Counter-revolution', in Best (1988) p.151.
48. Nietzsche (1977) pp.6–7.
49. Berlin (1976) p.215.
50. C. C. O'Brien, 'Paradise Lost', in *New York Review of Books*, 25 April 1991, p.58.
51. Barnes (1963) p.187.
52. See Knudsen (1986) p.161.
53. Kohn (1953) p.18.
54. Barnes writes that 'there developed, especially in England and the United States, that notorious and specious myth representing the Anglo-Saxon peoples as the perfect examples of political quietism and, hence, of inherent political capacity. An equally erroneous doctrine pictured the French as the typical instance of a revolutionary and unstable nation, utterly devoid of all political capacity.' See Barnes (1963) p.179.
55. Fryer (1989) p.73.
56. Langer (1965) p.85.
57. Nietzsche (1977) p.42.
58. Moses (1975) p.5.
59. Kohn (1953) p.20.
60. P. M. Kennedy, 'The Decline of Nationalistic History in the West 1900–1970', in *Journal of Contemporary History*, vol.8, no.1 1973, p.77.

61. Barraclough (1979) p.8.

62. Kennedy, 'Decline of', p.96.

63. See 'Introduction' to Berghahn and Schissler (1987) p.11, and A. Hearnden, 'The Education Branch of the Military Government of Germany and the Schools', in Pronay and Wilson (1985).

64. Kennedy argues: 'the anti-nationalistic trend in historical writing has not been so noticeable in Britain, perhaps because it has had no National Socialist past or is fighting no Vietnam war over which liberal/radical circles can become angry and critical; perhaps also because its historians have long been busy attacking previous government policies.' See Kennedy, 'Decline of', p.87. Another element in explaining the lack of critical anti-nationalist historiography may well be the explicit patriotic commitments of left-wing and radical historians.

65. Public Record Office (PRO), Kew Gardens: INF12/303, 'COI: Far East Publicity Committee – Minutes', 13 March 1950.

66. Barraclough (1979) p.51 and Moses (1975) p.131.

67. Berghahn and Schissler (1987) p.3.

68. For example historians sought to find alternative traditions to that used by German right-wing nationalists. Hofer wrote in 1947 that instead of a Prussian there was a healthy German tradition, one that was liberal and humanistic. He argued that 'Germans must now turn their own neglected traditions to the forces upon which to rebuild their life and state. They must learn again to see that alongside and within the Prussian-German historical stream, there was also a German historical stream.' See W. Hofer, 'Toward a Revision of the German Concept of History', in Kohn (1953) p.205.

69. Iggers (1968) p.286.

70. D. B. Fleming, 'Foreign Policy Issues in Social Textbooks in the USA', in Berghahn and Schissler (1987) p.120.

71. See H. C. Schroder, 'England's "Special Constitutional Development" in the Seventeenth and Eighteenth Centuries', and K. Rohe, 'The Constitutional Development of Germany and Great Britain in the Nineteenth and Twentieth Centuries in German and English History Textbooks', in Berghahn and Schissler (1987).

72. Novick (1988) p.316.

73. Cited in Novick (1988) p.318.

74. Fischer (1970) p.156.

75. Berghahn and Schissler (1987) p.10.

76. Cited in Fryer (1989) p.77.

77. Elton (1968) pp.20–2.

78. Elton (1968) p.17.

79. Berghahn and Schissler (1987) p.14.

80. See Carr (1987) pp.173–4.

81. Hirsch (1987) p.18.

82. See I. Buruma's 'England, whose England?', in *Spectator*, 9 September 1989.

Chapter 4: The moral impasse

1. Even the immediate past is not immune from this tendency. The retrospective idealisation of the Cold War era is a case in point. The introduction to a recently published collection of essays, *The Lessons of History*, concludes: 'yet at risk of appearing complacent, we can say that we have not ¹one too badly over the past forty years'. See Howard (1991) p.5. This only shows that the past has the privilege of being the last terrain where optimism is possible.

2. McNeill, 'Winds of Change', in *Foreign Affairs*, Fall 1990, p.161. He added: 'this time, unless some new foreign danger raises its head, American politicians and the public will have to think about what ought to happen at home.'

3. Howard (1991) p.4.

4. Howard (1991) p.4.

5. Shklar (1957) p.vii.

6. Lasch (1979) p.30.

7. Pfaff (1990) p.185.

8. Giner (1976) p.201.

9. C. Mongardini, 'The decadence of modernity: the delusions of progress and the search for historical consciousness', in Alexander and Sztompka (1990) p.54.

10. Cited in Zeitlin (1968) p.39.

11. Zeitlin (1968) pp.52–8.

12. Cited in Zeitlin (1968) p.67.

13. Giner (1976) p.39.

14. Jones (1980) p.121.

15. Giner (1976) p.39.

16. Giner (1976) p.40.

17. Durkheim (1968) p.427.

18. Durkheim (1968) p.427.

19. Durkheim (1968) p.427.

20. Durkheim (1968) p.419.

21. Bell (1979) p.155.

22. Hughes (1988) p.33.

23. Garbett (1956) p.67.

24. Jones (1980) p.vii.

25. Cited in Darby (1987) p.37.

26. See PRO:CO 875/19/12, 'Report of Committee on Long Range Publicity', May 1943. For the discussion of this report see CO 875/19/10, 'Minutes of meeting on Long Range Propaganda'.

27. Giner (1976) p.3.
28. Smith (1989) p.179.
29. *Time*, 1 April 1991, and *Sunday Times*, 5 May 1991.
30. Kimball (1990) and Scruton (1985) p.7.
31. Cited in B. Shapiro, 'Red-Baiting comes to Brookline', in *Nation*, 21 May 1990.
32. See *Evening Standard*, 22 March 1990.
33. See M. Nagai and T. Nishijima, 'Postwar Japanese Education and the United States', in Iriye (1975).
34. Bloom (1988) p.26.
35. Cited in Hewison (1981) p.42.
36. Bloom (1988) p.34.
37. Arendt (1961) p.173.
38. Arendt (1961) p.193.
39. Arendt (1961) p.193.
40. Arendt is far clearer than most about the necessity for a morally oriented system of education. The American commentator Christopher Lasch underestimates its importance when he argues: 'Even patriotism, the inculcation of which once constituted one of the school's most important tasks, has become superfluous in the defense of the status quo. The deterioration of training in history, government and philosophy reflects their increasingly marginal status as part of the apparatus of social control.' See Lasch (1979) p.225.
41. Shor (1987).
42. Rieff (1975) p.12.
43. See Appleyard (1989) p.28. T. S. Eliot wrote in this vein: 'Go, go, go, said the bird: human kind / Cannot bear very much reality.' (The Four Quartets).
44. Cited in D. Edgar, 'The Free or the Good', in Levitas (1986) p.61.
45. Bloom (1988) p.247.
46. Bell (1979) p.29
47. Koestler (1951) pp.173–4.
48. Gassett (1963) pp.142 and 144.
49. Niebuhr (1949) p.41.
50. Niebuhr (1949) p.8
51. Johnson (1980) p.147.
52. Scruton (1990) p.11.
53. *The Times*, 5 December 1984.
54. P. Anderson, 'Nation-States and National Identity', in *London Review of Books*, 9 May 1991.
55. T. Nipperdey, 'In Search of Identity: Romantic Nationalism, its Intellectual, Political and Social Background', in Eade (1983) p.8
56. Cited in G. Seidel, 'Culture, Nation and "Race" in the British and French New Right', in Levitas (1986) p.128.

57. J. Casey, 'The other side of racialism', in *Evening Standard*, 24 May 1990.
58. Bloom (1988) p.39.
59. Cited in *Guardian*, 23 April 1991.
60. *Sunday Times*, 28 April 1991.
61. *Sunday Times*, 2 December 1990.
62. Cited in Seidel, 'Culture, Nation', pp.109–10.
63. Bell (1980) p.206.
64. Bell (1980) p.195.
65. Edgar, 'The Free or the Good', in Levitas (1986) p.71.
66. J. Citrin, 'Language politics and American identity', in *The Public Interest*, no.99, Spring 1990, p.96.
67. Benda (1959) p.16.
68. PRO: FO.370/721, MOI 'Special Issues Committee', *The Projection of Britain Paper*, no.28a, 23 June 1943.
69. PRO: FO.370/721.
70. Bennett (1988).
71. Novick (1988) pp.313–14.
72. Cited in Novick (1988) p.312.
73. Chirol (1924) pp.ix and 4.
74. Bell (1980) pp.150 and 206.
75. See Clough (1960).
76. 'Only in the Western nations, i.e. those influenced by Greek philosophy, is there some willingness to doubt the identification of the good with one's own way.' (Bloom (1988) p.36).
77. Thomas (1981) pp.xv and xvi.
78. Johnson (1980) p.206.
79. Scruton (1990) p.vii.
80. See *The Times Higher Education Supplement*, 31 May 1991.
81. See Kohn (1953).
82. Kohn (1966) p.267.
83. Kohn (1966) p.267.
84. Von Mises (1958) pp.332–3.
85. Aron (1978) p.233.
86. *Sunday Telegraph*, 3 February 1991.
87. Bloom (1988) pp.27 and 56.
88. Cited in *Guardian*, 9 October 1990.
89. See for example Bennett (1985).
90. Gellner (1974) p.176.
91. Scruton (1990) p.11.
92. Cited in Giner (1976) p.40.
93. Iggers (1968) pp.35 and 8.
94. Iggers (1968) p.13.
95. Iggers (1968) p.14
96. Hughes (1964) p.13.

97. See Lukacs (1980) p.322 and Nietzsche (1967) p.3.
98. See for example C. Becker 'What Is Historiography?', in *American Historical Review* vol.44, October 1938.
99. Gerth and Mills (1977) p.146.
100. Meszaros (1989) p.148.
101. Hughes (1964) p.14.
102. See Novick (1988) p.157.
103. Dance (1969) p.9.
104. These points are elaborated in Chapter 7.
105. Hughes (1988) p.42.
106. Shklar (1957) pp.272–3.
107. Berlin (1969) p.12.
108. Berlin (1969) p.114.
109. Berlin (1969) p.115.
110. Cited in C. Cruise O'Brien, 'Paradise Lost', in *New York Review of Books*, 25 April 1991, p.55.

Chapter 5: Attempts to recover absolutes

1. Bell (1980) p.149.
2. Thomas (1990) p.46.
3. *Guardian*, 10 May 1991.
4. Burnham, in his extensive treatment of the problem, resolves the issue by marshalling the power of assertion. He suggests that *'prima facie* evidence is sufficent to refute the opinion that Nazi Germany is a type of capitalism and to show that it is on the contrary an early stage of a new type of society.' See Burnham (1942) p.222.
5. H. Mommsen, 'Totalitarian Dictatorship versus Comparative Theory of Fascism', in Menze (1981) pp.148–9.
6. Mommsen, 'Totalitarian Dictatorship', p.153.
7. Rich (1986) p.117.
8. PRO:INF/560, 'Plan of Propaganda to the British West Indies', 12 January 1943.
9. See Thorne (1978) pp.142–3.
10. PRO: CO.847/35/47234/1(47), 'Governor Mitchell to Secretary of State for the Colonies', 30 May 1947.
11. Cited in Thomas (1990) p.17.
12. Barnett (1986) p.19.
13. Cited in Hewison (1981) p.4.
14. Cited in Brick (1986) p.190.
15. Mannheim (1943) p.7.
16. Schlesinger (1949) pp.254 and 256.
17. Honeyford, 'The Gilmore Syndrome', p.11.
18. Aron (1977) p.136.

19. Aron (1977) p.227.
20. Eley, 'Nazism, Politics', p.174.
21. Cited in Novick (1988) p.618.
22. Novick (1988) p.620.
23. See for example J. P. Stern's review 'Germans and the German Past', in *London Review of Books*, 21 December 1989.
24. Cited in P. Mattick, 'Competition and Monopoly', in *New Essays*, vol.6, no.3, p.26.
25. Burnham (1942) p.216.
26. Popper (1952) p.255.
27. Hayek (1941) p.316.
28. Hayek (1979) p.4. This text, published in 1943, clearly foreshadows many of the arguments of the conservative ideological offensive of the late 1970s.
29. Hayek (1979) p.3.
30. Hayek (1979) pp.7 and 125.
31. Von Mises (1958) p.197.
32. Hughes (1951) p.148.
33. Hughes (1951) p.148.
34. Hughes (1951) p.151.
35. Hughes (1975) p.120.
36. Schlesinger (1949) p.63.
37. Koch (1985) p.9.
38. Koch (1985) p.373.
39. Emphasis added. See E. Nolte, 'Between Myth and Revisionism', in Koch (1985) p.36.
40. D. Horowitz, 'Socialism: Guilty as Charged', in *Commentary*, vol.90, no.6, December 1990, p.24.
41. F.Furet, 'From 1789 to 1917–1989', in *Encounter*, September 1990, p.5.
42. For example the German historian Eberhard Jackel has argued that the 'theory of totalitarianism amounted to a partial justification of the Nazis.' This comment, made at a symposium on German history, provoked a strong response from the proceedings. See Thomas (1990) p.84.
43. See for example a discussion of militant Islam in *Guardian*, 8 June 1991. The author notes that in Algeria 'it is not Islam that wants to take power, but individuals tempted by totalitarianism and authoritarianism', and adds: 'in Europe, 60 years ago, that gave rise to fascism.' Here totalitarianism is treated as an autonomous urge or force, which exists independently to the movements to which it attaches itself.
44. Taylor (1990) p.974. The Jameson Raid was an incident in the Boer War.
45. *Daily Express*, 21 October 1949.
46. Fitzgerald (1979) p.55.
47. The issues raised in this section are elaborated at length in my forthcoming work *The Silent Race War*.

48. *Economist*, 2 December 1939.
49. *The Times*, 1 April 1940.
50. *The Times*, 4 April 1940.
51. *The Times*, 18 April 1940.
52. *The Times*, 22 April 1940.
53. The *Economist* warned that in the United States 'there is a certain readiness to accept the war as just another "selfish clash of rival imperialisms".' See *Economist*, 24 February 1940.
54. See PRO: FO.953/136, 'A. A. Dudley to K. W. Blackburne', 28 June 1948.
55. Burns (1957) p.73.
56. S. Pearce, 'Swann and the Spirit of the Age', in Palmer(1986) p.142.
57. See Johnson (1980) p.206 and R. Honeyford, 'Anti-Racist Rhetoric', in Palmer (1986) p.55.
58. Dance (1969) p.33.
59. Indeed some of the most eloquent apologies for the British empire are authored by Americans. In one of the most widely read books on the subject, Emerson writes: 'A plausible case can, however, be made from the proposition that the future will look back upon overseas imperialism of recent centuries, less in terms of its sins of exploitation, and discrimination, than as the instrument by which the spiritual, scientific, and material revolution which began in Western Europe with the Renaissance was spread to the rest of the world.' See Emerson (1960) p.6.
60. Kohn (1966) p.126.
61. Arendt (1967) p.133.
62. Aron (1959) pp.4–7.
63. Aron (1978) p.221.
64. Bell (1980) p.191.
65. See Aron (1978) p.19, Arendt (1967) p.xxix, and Kohn (1966) p.274.
66. B. W. Jackson, 'Britain's Imperial Legacy', in *Foreign Affairs*, vol.35, no.3, April 1957, p.147.
67. D. Fromkin, 'The Strategy of Terrorism', in *Foreign Affairs*, vol.53, no.4, July 1975, p.683.
68. For an illustration of vitriolic anti-Third Worldism by a French author see Bruckner (1983).
69. See P. A. Taguieff, 'The New Cultural Racism in France', in *Telos*, no.83, Spring 1990, p.111.
70. Taguieff, 'The New Cultural Racism', p.111.
71. See for example E. Mortimer, 'White man eyes his burden', in *Financial Times*, 15 May 1991.
72. *Wall Street Journal*, 22–3 February 1991.
73. Cited in *Guardian*, 25 February 1991.
74. 'A wave of self-criticism swept over the West in connection with the Vietnam war, and with the rapid social transformations brought about by material progress', writes Bracher (1984) p.203.

75. Horowitz and Lipset (1978) p.146.
76. K. L. Kusmer, 'An American Tradition: Governmental Action to Promote Equality in American History', in *Amerikastudien*, vol.34, no.3, 1989, p.263.
77. R. Nisbet, 'The Conservative Renaissance in Perspective', in *The Public Interest*, no.81, Fall 1985, pp.134–5.
78. J. Z. Muller, 'German Historians at War', in *Commentary*, vol.87, May 1989, p.35.
79. *Die Welt*, 31 December, 1990.
80. Davies (1975) p.202.
81. Plumb (1978) p.66.
82. See Podhoretz (1980).
83. See Kimball (1990).
84. *Sunday Times*, 22 July 1990.
85. *Guardian*, 23 January 1991.
86. Cited in *Nation*, 22 May 1989.
87. Johnson (1980) p.161.
88. Bracher (1984) p.x.
89. S. Hook, 'The academic ethic in abeyance: Recollections of *Walpurgisnacht* at New York University', in *Minerva*, vol.22, nos.3–4, Autumn–Winter 1984, pp.297 and 299.
90. Bloom (1988) p.313.
91. Bloom (1988) p.314.
92. Gellner (1974) p.72.
93. Bell (1979) p.128.
94. Shor (1987) p.25.
95 Hayek (1954) p.v.
96. Hayek (1954) p.4.
97. Sandel (1987) p.1.
98. See Hayek (1989) p.157.
99. J. Gray, 'Conservatism, Individualism and the Political Thought of the New Right', in Clark (1990) p.99.
100. Hayek (1989) p.137. Emphasis in the original.
101. Thomas (1981) p.738.
102. R. Gruner 'The Old Virtues', in *Salisbury Review*, vol.8 no.3, March 1990, p.19.
103. A. Meyerson, 'The Vision Thing, Continued', in *Policy Review*, Summer 1990, p.2.

Chapter 6: The other 1960s and the fatal compromise

1. Cited in Sontag (1971) p.209.
2. Valery (1927) pp.1 and 54.
3. Cited in Kohn (1966) p.259.

4. Sontag (1971) p.172.
5. Orwell (1950) p.6.
6. Fussell (1975) p.21.
7. W. McNeill, 'World History in the Schools', in Ballard (1970) p.20.
8. McNeill, 'World History', p.20.
9. The intellectual reaction and indeed *fear* of progress will be examined at greater length in the next chapter.
10. According to Bracher: 'even an expert on the human psyche like Sigmund Freud, unlike some of his progressivist disciples who saw themselves as successful engineers of the soul or as revolutionaries, now proclaimed the rather pessimistic realization that civilization was possible only at the cost of a psychological restriction or inhibition, indeed the neurosis of the individual through the sublimation of his aggression.' See Bracher (1984) p.140.
11. See Green (1977) pp.65 and 69.
12. It is interesting to note how even at this point optimism was linked to America. It was already assumed that Europe was beyond optimism. It will take another three decades for America to catch up. Lord Eustace is cited in P. Rich, 'Imperial decline and the resurgence of British national identity 1918-1979', in Kushner and Lunn (1989).
13. Hughes (1969) p.15.
14. Carr (1944) p.xxi.
15. Carr (1944) p.xv.
16. Cited in Kohn (1966) p.259.
17. Niebuhr (1949) pp.10–11.
18. This point is developed further in the next chapter.
19. Hall (1986) p.4.
20. Popper (1952) p.5.
21. Aron (1978) p.10.
22. Aron (1978) p.18.
23. Aron (1977) p.xv.
24. Hughes (1969) p.6.
25. Cited in Hughes (1969) p.136.
26. See Berlin's article on 'Historical Inevitability' in Berlin (1969). This critique of 'historical determinism' seeks to avoid relativist consequences by reintroducing the 'basic notions of our morality'. Since these notions are basic, Berlin does not feel compelled to argue their consistency with the rest of his critique.
27 Shklar (1957) p.273.
28. Carr (1944) pp.102 and 106.
29. Carr (1944) p.106.
30. Koestler (1983) p.170.
31. Hayek (1976) p.29.
32. J. Friedman 'The New Consensus: The Fukuyama Thesis', in *Critical*

Review, vol.3, nos.3 and 4, 1989–90, p.383. 'Of all the intellectual triumphs of the communist regime – and they are vast – it seems to me the greatest is to have made these eminent and influential writers so completely lose their heads', wrote Michael Polanyi in 1957. See Friedman 'The New Consensus', p.383.

33. Mannheim (1943) p.1.
34. Mannheim (1943) p.8.
35. Mannheim (1943) pp.7 and 25.
36. Niebuhr (1949) p.241.
37. Schlesinger (1949) pp.10 and 254.
38. Schlesinger (1949) pp.10 and 201.
39. Schlesinger (1949) p.viii.
40. Schlesinger (1949) p.256.
41. Schlesinger (1949) p.174.
42. Barnett (1986).
43. Bell (1979) p.42.
44. Bell (1980) p.302.
45. Mannheim (1943) p.12.
46. Mannheim (1943) p.25.
47. Mannheim (1943) p.7.
48. Mannheim (1943) p.7.
49. See Orwell (1941) pp. 46–8. Orwell's inspiration and influence is evident in the American neo-conservative thinker Norman Podhoretz's *The Present Danger*. See Podhoretz (1980).
50. Orwell (1941) p.55.
51. See Giner (1976).
52. Hayek (1954) pp.8–9.
53. Benda (1959) p.30.
54. Benda (1959) p.30.
55. Benda (1959) p.86.
56. Benda (1959) p.39.
57. Benda (1959) p.21.
58. For a classical illustration of this literature, see Hook (1984).
59. Koestler (1983) p.84.
60. Schumpeter (1951) p.153 also see pp.145–55.
61. Schumpeter (1951) p.154.
62. B. de Jouvenel 'Treatment of Capitalism by Intellectuals', in Hayek (1954) pp.105–6.
63. de Jouvenel 'Treatment of Capitalism', p.123.
64. de Jouvenel 'Treatment of Capitalism', p.122.
65. J. Carroll 'With the Death of God is Everything Permitted?', in *Salisbury Review*, December 1990, pp.23–4.
66. Johnson (1980) p.160.
67. See Horowitz and Lipset (1978) pp.24–5.

68. Bell (1964) p.373.
69. Brick (1986) p.22.
70. Wilson (1940) pp.431–2.
71. Bracher (1984) p.149.
72. See report in *Encounter*, November 1955.
73. For an example of this view, see Galbraith (1967).
74. Aron (1978) p.228.
75. Bell (1964) p.373.
76. Bell (1964) p.373.
77. Bell (1964) p.375.
78. Pells (1985) p.201.

Chapter 7: Dreading change

1. Comte (1910) p.21.
2. Comte (1910) p.133
3. Hobsbawm (1972) p.11.
4. Namier (1962) p.203.
5. He writes: 'that better educated people should be more reluctant to submit to some unintelligible direction – such as the market ... thus has the result ... that they tend to resist just what ... would increase their usefulness to their fellows.' See Hayek (1989) p.82.
6. This point is eloquently argued by Lukacs in his critique of Schopenhauer: 'So pessimism means primarily a philosophical rationale of the absurdity of all political activity. In order to reach this conclusion the chief necessity is to devalue society and history philosophically.' See Lukacs (1980) p.203.
7. Cited in Nisbet (1986) p.29.
8. Cited in Kumar (1986) p.166.
9. Nietzsche (1967) p.3.
10. Cited in Lukacs (1980) pp.326 and 336.
11. Cited in Jones (1980) p.37.
12. Cited in Jones (1980)
13 Cited in Giner (1976) p.47.
14. Cited in Giner (1976) pp.45–6.
15. Cited in Giner (1976) p.47.
16. Jones (1980) p.42.
17. Jones (1980) p.122.
18. Shklar (1957) p.viii.
19. Green (1987) p.32.
20. Green (1987) p.136.
21. Hayek (1978) p.19.
22. See P. Jenkins, 'New dreams of liberty', in *Independent*, 14 May 1991.
23. Cited in *The Times*, 28 December 1988.

24. Cited in *Independent*, 31 May 1991.
25. Cited in Nisbet (1986) p.89.
26. Cited in Nisbet (1986) p.93.
27. Hayek (1989) p.7.
28. Hayek (1989) p.21.
29. Hayek (1989) p.10.
30. Hayek (1989) p.137.
31. Hayek (1989) p.136.
32. Hayek (1989) p.137. Emphasis in the original.
33. Hobson (1901) p.18.
34. For a useful discussion of Le Bon, see Giner (1976) pp.57–60.
35. Schumpeter (1951) p.144.
36. Schumpeter (1951) p.144.
37. Schumpeter (1951) p.264.
38. Schumpeter (1951) p.264.
39. In this respect we take issue with aspects of Lukacs' otherwise excellent study of irrationalism. In line with the Popular Front tradition on this subject, the relation he draws between irrationalist trends in Germany and the subsequent emergence of fascism is too unmediated. See Lukacs (1980).
40. Cited in Jones (1980) p.129.
41. M. Weber, 'Science as Vocation', in Gerth and Mills (1977) p.138.
43. Wittgenstein (1989) p.73. My understanding of analytical philosophy derives from the discussions I have had with my friend James Heartfield on the subject. From this perspective any meaning of history must perish. 'We cannot infer the events of the future from those of the present.'
43. Wittgenstein (1989) p.7.
44. Alexander, 'Between progress', p.26.
45. Shklar (1957) p.17.
46. Bloom (1988) p.245.
47. Bloom (1988) pp.56–9 and 229–33.
48. Hayek (1989) p.23.
49. Hayek (1978) p.31.
50. B. Thomas, 'The New Historicism and other Old-fashioned Topics', in Veeser (1989) p.188.
51. Thomas, 'New Historicism', p.188.
52. Hayek (1978) p.31.
53. Hayek (1978) p.30.
54. Hayek (1989) p.27.
55. Popper (1952) p.195.
56. Bell (1964) p.371.
57. Cited in Moses (1975) p.10.
58. Elton, in Gardiner (1990) p.10.
59. Bell (1964) p.373.

60. Nisbet (1986) p.187.
61. Mommsen, 'Totalitarian Dictatorship', pp.151–2.
62. See 'Editorial', in *Salisbury Review*, September 1990, p.2.
63. Bloom (1988) p.247.
64. In Britain television programmes hosted by David Attenborough have emphasised this point.
65. L. Wirth, 'Preface' to Mannheim (1960) p.xiii.
66. Wirth, 'Preface' to Mannheim (1960) p.xxvii.
67. Spengler (1926) pp.38–9.
68. Spengler (1926) p.358.
69. Eliot (1948) pp.123–4.
70. Carr (1944) p.275.
71. Koestler (1983) pp.103–4.
72. Niebuhr (1949) p.267.
73. Kumar (1987) p.193.
74. Thomas, 'The New Historicism', p.200.
75. See F. Fukuyama, 'Forget Iraq – history is dead', in *Guardian*, 7 September 1990.
76. E. Shils, 'The End of Ideology?', in *Encounter*, November 1955, p.57.
77. F. Fukuyama, 'A Reply to My Critics', in *The National Interest*, Winter 1989/90, p.22.
78. With Fukuyama this is presented in an idealist form of 'human consciousness thinking about itself and finally becoming self conscious'. See Fukuyama, 'A Reply', p.22. While we would agree with the stress on the self-knowledge of reality, this can be achieved not through consciousness thinking about itself but through conscious action.
79. Fukuyama, 'A Reply', p.22.
80. Spengler (1926) p.454.
81. Bell (1964) p.370.
82. Bell (1979) p.41.
83. Fukuyama, 'A Reply', p.28.
84. F. Fukuyama 'The End of History?', in *The National Interest*, no.16, Summer 1989, p.3.
85. Fukuyama, 'A Reply', p.23.
86. Fukuyama, 'The End', p.3.
87. Hughes (1951) p.158
88. Shils (1955) p.54.
89. Shils (1955) pp.55–6.
90. Bracher (1984) p.x.
91. Bracher (1984) p.202.
92. Cited in *Independent*, 7 September 1990.
93. Cited in *Independent*, 7 September 1990.
94. See *The Times Higher Educational Supplement*, 31 May 1991.

Chapter 8: New historicism

1. See for example 'Upside Down in the Groves of Academe', *Time*, 1 April 1991.
2. See for example Young (1990).
3. See 'Introduction' to Veeser (1989) p.xi
4. C. Gallagher, 'Marxism and the New Historicism', in Veeser (1989) p.43.
5. Gallagher, 'Marxism and the New Historicism', pp.40–1.
6. D. Ravitch, 'Multiculturalism', p.342.
7. Nisbet (1986) p.107.
8. Harvey (1989) p.9.
9. Jones (1980) p.151.
10. P. A. Taguieff, 'The New Cultural Racism in France', in *Telos*, no.83, Spring 1990, p.118.
11. A. Policar, 'Racism and Its Mirror Images', in *Telos*, no.83, Spring 1990, p.99.
12. See Novick (1988) pp.503–6.
13. Nolan, 'The *Historikerstreit*', p.67.
14. Nolan, 'The *Historikerstreit*', p.65.
15. See Knudsen (1986) p.21.
16. Harvey (1979) p.113.
17. Lyotard (1984).
18. Knudsen (1986) p.x.
19. Cited in Knudsen (1986) p.162.
20. Young (1990) p.22.
21. Foucault, 'Truth and Power', in Gordon (1980) p.117.
22. S. Greenblatt, 'Towards a Poetics of Culture', in Veeser (1989) p.12.
23. For a useful explanation of methodological individualism from an 'Austrian' point of view see Shand (1984) pp.4–6.
24. See *The Times*, 4 July 1991.
25. Greenblatt, 'Towards a Poetics', p.12.
26. Hayek (1989) p.113.
27. Hayek (1989) p.112.
28. Hayek (1989) p.113.
29. Hayek (1989) p.114.
30. Hayek (1989) p.116.
31. Novick (1988) p.587.
32. See Geertz (1973).
33. Hill (1990) p.2.
34. 'Introduction' to Veeser (1989) p.xii.
35. J. C. Scott, 'Resistance without Protest and without Organization: Peasant Opposition to the Islamic Zakat and the Christian Tithe', in *Comparative Studies in Society and History*, vol.29, 1987, p.419.
36. Scott, 'Resistance without Protest', p.422.

37. Scott, 'Resistance without Protest', p.421.
38. R. Samuel, 'Introduction: Exciting to be English', in Samuel (1989) p.xlix.
39. Stone (1987) p.93.
40. See Stone (1987) p.168, Russell (1979) and Underdown (1985).
41. See Calhoun (1982).
42. N. Hampson, 'The French Revolution and its Historians', in Best (1988) p.232.
43. See Foster (1988) pp.500–1, Hoppen (1989) p.107, and P. Bew, 'Sinn Fein, Agrarian Radicalism and the War of Independence, 1919–21', in Boyce (1988).
44. See Meszaros (1989) pp.42–6.
45. Knudsen (1986) p.26.
46. Cited in *Sunday Telegraph*, 22 April 1990.
47. Taylor (1990) pp.982–5.
48. See *New Statesman*, 24 September 1982.
49. Novick (1988) p.476.
50. D. W. Hoover, 'Black History', in Ballard (1970) p.47.
51. Michel Falicon, *'L'indifferenciation contre l'identité nationale'*, in Michel (1985) p.23.
52. Novick (1988) p.494.
53. Novick (1980) p.496.
54. Mattick (1986) p.32.
55. Cited in Mattick (1986) p.32.
56. Fox-Genovese (1990).
57. B. Herrnstein Smith (1990) p.71.
58. Cited in B. Jelavich, 'Mihail Kogalniceanu: Historian as Foreign Minister, 1867–8', in Deletant and Hanak (1988) p.89.
59. Miles (1990) pp.15–16.
60. Fox-Genovese (1990) p.23.
61. Ravitch, 'Multiculturalism', p.341.
62. Miles (1990) p.12.
63. Rorty (1990) p233.
64. Davin (1990) p.94.
65. See *Le Monde*, 26 July 1983.
66. See *The Times*, 4 July 1991.
67. Cited in A. Barnett, 'After Nationalism', in Samuel (1989).

Chapter 9: A critique of history

1. Marcuse (1972) p.23.
2. For a conservative attempt at the defence of progress, see Nisbet (1980).
3. Novick (1988) p.486.
4. H. J. Kaye, 'E. P. Thompson, the British Marxist Historical Tradition and the Contemporary Crisis', in Kaye and McClelland (1990) p.254.

5. Cohen (1988) p.140.
6. For a development of these ideas, see Furedi, 'Introduction' to Jakubowski (1990).
7. Cohen (1988) p.146.
8. H. J. Kaye, 'The Use and Abuse of the Past', in Miliband and others (1987) p.358.
9. Kaye, 'E. P. Thompson', p.255.
10. Howard (1991) p.194.
11. Gramsci (1982) pp.392–3.
12. Gramsci (1982) pp.396–7.
13. Gramsci (1982) p.340.
14. Taylor (1990) p.978.
15. Marcuse (1972) p.13.
16. Mattick is one those few who rejects the 'possibility of general theories of society'. See Mattick (1986) p.105.
17. Hayek (1989) p.26.
18. Nisbet (1986) p.34. Interjections and emphasis in the original.
19. Nisbet (1986) p.41.
20. Plumb (1978) p.99.
21. Hall (1986) p.11.
22. Kohn (1966) p.53.
23. Bloom (1988) p.196.
24. Von Mises (1958) p.81.
25. Marx and Engels (1976) p.35.
26. 'Marx to Schweitzer', 24 January 1863 in, Marx and Engels (1975a) p.148.
27. 'Marx to the Editorial Board of the *Otechestvenniye Zapiski*', November 1977, in Marx and Engels (1975a) pp.293–4.
28. 'Engels to Schmidt', 4 August 1890, and 'Engels to Ernst', 5 June 1890, in Marx and Engels (1975a) pp.393 and 390–1.
29. 'Marx to Kugelman', 27 June 1870, in Marx and Engels (1988) p.527.
30. Marx and Engels (1976) pp.50 and 55.
31. Marx and Engels (1975) p.83. Emphasis in the original.
32. These arguments have thrived in relation to explanations of difference of sex. See Moir and Jessel (1989) and Wilson (1989).
33. Carr (1987) p.173.

Bibliography

Abrams, P. (1972) 'The sense of the past and the origins of sociology', *Past and Present*, no.55.

Alexander, J. C. and Sztompka, P. (1990) *Rethinking Progress* (Boston: Unwin Hyman).

Anderson, P. (1991) 'Nation-states and national identity', *London Review of Books*, 9 May 1991.

Appleyard, B. (1989) *The Pleasures of Peace: Art and Imagination in Post-War Britain* (London: Faber & Faber).

Arendt, H. (1961) *Between Past and Future* (London: Faber & Faber).

— (1967) *The origins of Totalitarianism* (London: George Allen and Unwin).

Aron, R. (1959) *Imperialism and Colonialism: The Seventeenth Montague Burton lecture* (Leeds: University of Leeds)

——(1961) *Introduction to the Philosophy of History* (London: Allen & Unwin).

——(1977) *The Opium of the Intellectuals* (Westport: Greenwood Press).

——(1978) *Politics and History* (New York: The Free Press).

Ballard, M. (editor) (1970) *New Movements in the Study and Teaching of History* (London: Temple Smith).

Barnes, H. E. (1963) *The History of Historical Writing* (New York: Dover Publishers).

Barnett, C. (1986) *The Audit of War* (London: Macmillan).

Barraclough, G. (1979) *Main Trends in History* (New York: Holmes and Meier).

Bailyn, B. (1982) 'The Challenge of Modern Historiography', *American History Review*, vol.87, no.1.

Beattie, A. (1987) *History in Peril* (London: Centre for Policy Studies)

Bell, D. (1964) *The End of Ideology; On the exhaustion of political ideas in the Fifties* (New York: The Free Press).

——(1979) *The Cultural Contradictions of Capitalism* (London: Heinemann).

——(1980) *Sociological Journeys: Essays 1960–1980* (London: Heinemann).

Bennett, W. (1985) 'Lost Generation', *Policy Review*, no.33, Summer 1985.

——(1988) 'Why the West?', *National Review*, May.

Benda, J. (1959) *The Betrayal of the Intellectuals* (Boston: The Beacon Press).

Berghahn, R. and Schissler, H. (editors) (1987) *Perceptions of History: International Textbook Research on Britain, Germany and the United States* (Oxford: Berg Publishers).

Berlin, I. (1969) *Four Essays on Liberty* (London: Oxford University Press).
——](1976) *Vico and Herder: Two Studies in the History of Ideas* (London: The Hogarth Press).
Best, G. (editor) (1988) *The Permanent Revolution: The French Revolution and its Legacy 1789–1989* (London: Fontana).
Billington R. A. and others (1966) *The Historian's Contribution to Anglo-American Misunderstanding* (London: Routledge and Kegan Paul).
Bloom, A. (1988) *The Closing of the American Mind: How higher education has failed democracy and impoverished the souls of today's students* (London: Penguin).
Blumenthal, S. (1986) *The Rise of the Counter-Establishment: From conservative ideology to political power* (New York: Times Books).
Boyce, D. G. (editor) (1988) *The Revolution in Ireland 1879–1923* (London: Macmillan).
Bracher, K. D. (1984) *The Age of Ideologies* (London: Weidenfeld and Nicolson).
Brick, H. (1986) *Daniel Bell and the Decline of Intellectual Radicalism* (Madison: The University of Wisconsin Press).
Bruckner, P. (1983) *Le Sanglot de l'Homme Blanc* (Paris: Du Seuil).
Burke, P. (1990) *The French Historical Revolution: The Annales School 1929–1989* (Oxford: Polity Press).
Burnham, J. (1942) *The Managerial Revolution* (London: Putnam).
Burns, A. (1948) *Colour Prejudice* (London: George Allen and Unwin).
——(1957) *In Defence of Colonies* (London: Macmillan).
Burroughs, P. (1973) 'John Seeley and British Imperial History', *Journal of Imperial and Commonwealth History*, vol.1, no.2.
Butterfield, H. (1951) *The Whig Interpretation of History* (London: Bell and Sons).
Calhoun, C. (1982) *The Question of Class Struggle: Social foundations of popular radicalism during the industrial revolution* (Oxford: Basil Blackwell).
Cannadine, D. (1987) 'British history: past, present – and future?', *Past and Present*, no.116, August 1987.
Carr, E.H. (1944) *Conditions of Peace* (London: Macmillan).
——(1987) *What is History?* (London: Penguin).
Carroll, J. (1990) 'With the death of god is everything permitted?', *Salisbury Review*, December.
Chesneaux, J. (1978) *Past and Futures or What is History For?* (London: Thames and Hudson).
Chirol, V. (1924) *The Occident and the Orient* (Chicago: University of Chicago Press).
Clark, J. C. D. (editor) (1990) *Ideas and Politics in Modern Britain* (London: Macmillan).
Citrin, J. (1990) 'Language politics and American identity', *The Public Interest*, no.99, Spring.
Clough, S. B. (1960) *Basic Values of Western Civilization* (New York: Columbia University Press)

Cohen, G.A. (1988) *History, Labour and Freedom* (Oxford: Oxford University Press).

Comte, A. (1910) *Republic of the West, Order and Progress: A general view of Positivism* (London: Harrison).

Crowley, B. L. (1987) *The Self, the Individual and the Community* (Oxford: Clarendon Press).

Dance, E. H. (1969) *History the Betrayer: A study in bias* (London: Hutchinson).

Darby, P. (1987) *Three Faces of Imperialism* (New Haven: Yale University Press).

Davies, C. (1975) *Permissive Britain* (London: Pitman Publishing).

Davin, A. (1990) 'Introduction: Special feature: History, the nation and the schools', *History Workshop*, no.29.

Dawson, W. H. (editor) (1917) *After-War problems* (London: George Allen and Unwin).

Degler, C. N. (1987) 'In Pursuit of an American history', *American Historical Review*, vol.92, no.1.

Deletant, D. and Hanak, H. (editors) (1988) *Historians as Nation-builders (London: Macmillan)*.

Durkheim, E. (1968) *The Elementary Forms of the Religious Life* (London: George Allen and Unwin).

Eade, J. C. (editor) (1983) *Romantic Nationalism in Europe* (Canberra: Australian National University: Humanities Research Centre Monograph no.2).

Eley, G. (1988) 'Nazism, politics and the image of the past: thoughts on the West German *Historikerstreit* 1986–1987', *Past and Present*, no.121.

Eliot, T. S. (1948) *Notes Towards the Definition of Culture* (London: Faber & Faber).

Elton, G. R. (1968) *The Future of the Past* (Cambridge: Cambridge University Press).

——(1984) *The History of England* (Cambridge: Cambridge University Press).

——(1989) *The Practice of History* (London: Fontana).

Emerson, R. (1960) *From Empire to Nation* (Cambridge, Massachusetts: Harvard University Press).

Evans, R. (1987) 'The New Nationalism and the Old History: Perspectives on the West German *Historikerstreit*', *Journal of Modern History*, vol.59, no.4.

Fischer, D. (1970) *Historians' Fallacies* (New York: Harper and Row).

Fitzgerald, F. (1979) *America Revised* (Boston: Little Brown).

Foster, R. M. (1985) Modern Ireland 1600–1972 (London: Allen Lane).

Fox-Genoveses, E. (1990) 'Between individualism and fragmentation: American culture and the new literary studies of race and gender', *American Quarterly*, vol.42, no.1.

Friedman, J. (1989) 'The New Consensus: The Fukuyama Thesis', *Critical Review*, vol.3, nos.3 and 4.

Fromkin, D. (1975) 'The strategy of terrorism', *Foreign Affairs*, vol.53, no.3.

Fryer, P. (1989) *Black People in the British Empire* (London: Pluto Press).

Fukuyama, F. (1989) 'The End of History', *The National Interest*, no.16.

——(1989-90) 'A reply to my Critics', *The National Interest*, no,18.

Füredi, F. (1991) 'Not-so great Britain', *Living Marxism*, February.

Furet, F. (1990) 'From 1789 to 1917–1989', *Encounter*, September.

Fussell, P. (1975) *The Great War and Modern Memory* (London: Oxford University Press).

Galbraith, J. K. (1967) *The New Industrial State* (London: Hamish Hamilton).

Gamble, A. (1987) *An Introduction to Modern Social and Political Thought* (London: Macmillan).

Garbett, C. (1956) *In an Age of Revolution* (Harmondsworth: Penguin).

Gardiner, J. (editor) (1990) *The History Debate* (London: Collins and Brown).

Gassett, Y. O. (1963) *The Revolt of the Masses* (London: Unwin Books).

Geertz, C. (1973) *The Interpretation of Cultures* (New York: Basic Books).

Gellner, E. (1974) *Contemporary Thought and Politics* (London: Routledge and Kegan Paul).

Gerth, H. H. and Mills, C. W. (editors) (1977) *From Max Weber: Essays in Sociology* (London: Routledge and Kegan Paul).

Giner, S. (1976) *Mass Society* (London: Martin Robertson).

Glazer, N. and Kristol, I. (1971) *The American Commonwealth* (New York: Basic Books).

Gluck, C. (1990) 'The Idea of Showa', *Daedalus*, Spring.

Gordon, C. (1980) *Power-Knowledge* (New York: Pantheon).

Grainger, J. H. (1986) *Patriotism, Britain 1900–1939* (London: Routledge and Kegan Paul).

Gramsci, A. (1982) *Selections from Prison Notebooks* (London: Lawrence and Wishart).

Green, D. G. (1987) *The New Right* (Brighton: Wheatsheaf Books).

——(1977) *Children of the Sun* (London: Macmillan).

Grossman, H. (1943) 'The evolutionist revolt against classical economics', *Journal of Political Economy*, vol.21, no.2.

Gruner, R. (1990) 'The Old Virtues', *Salisbury Review*, vol.8, no.3.

Hall, J. A. (1986) *Powers and Liberties: The Causes and Consequences of the Rise of the West* (Harmondsworth: Penguin).

Hamerow, S. (1987) *Reflections on History and Historians* (Madison: University of Wisconsin Press).

Hampson, N. (1982) *The Enlightenment* (London: Penguin).

Handlin, O. (1970) 'The vulnerability of the American university', *Encounter*, no.35.

Harvey, D. (1989) *The Condition of Postmodernity* (Oxford: Basil Blackwell).

Hay, D. (1968) *Europe: The Emergence of an Idea* (Edinburgh: Edinburgh University Press).

Hayek, F. A. (1941) 'The Counter-Revolution of Science', *Economica*, NS vol 8.

——(editor) (1954) *Capitalism and the Historians* (London: Routledge and Kegan Paul).

——(1976) *The Road To Serfdom* (London: Routledge and Kegan Paul).

——(1978) *The Three Sources of Human Values* (London School of Economics).

——(1989) *The Fatal Conceit: The Errors of Socialism* (London: Routledge).

Herrnstein Smith, B. (1990) 'Cult-Lit: Hirsch, literacy, and the "National Culture",' *South Atlantic Quarterly*, vol.89, no.1.

Hewison, R. (1981) *In Anger: British Culture in the Cold War* (New York: Oxford University Press).

Hill, C. (1990) *The Nation of Change and Novelty* (London: Routledge).

Himmelfarb, G. (1982) *The New History and the Old* (Cambridge Massachusetts: Harvard University Press).

Hirsch Jr., E. D. (1987) *Cultural Literacy: What Every American Needs to Know* (Boston: Houghton Mifflin).

Hobson, J. A. (1901) *The Psychology of Jingoism* (London: Grant Richards).

Hobsbawm, E. (1972) 'The social function of the past: some questions', *Past and Present*, no.55.

Hoffmann, S. (1979) 'Fragments floating in the here and now', *Daedalus*, 108.

Holstein, W. (1990) *The Japanese Power Game* (London: Macmillan).

Honeyford, R. (1986) 'The Gilmore Syndrome', *Salisbury Review*, April.

Hook, S. (1984) 'The academic ethic in abeyance: Recollections of *Walpurgisnacht* at New York University', *Minerva*, vol.22, nos.3–4.

Hoppen, K. T. (1989) *Ireland Since 1800: Conflict and Conformity* (London: Longman).

Horowitz, D. (1990) 'Socialism: Guilty as Charged', *Commentary*, vol.90, no.6.

Horowitz, I. L. and Lipset, S. M. (1978) *Dialogues on American Politics* (New York: Oxford University Press).

Howard, M. (1991) *The Lessons of History* (Oxford: Clarendon Press).

Hughes, H. S. (1951) 'The End of Political Ideology', *Measure*, no.2.

——(1964) *History as Art and as Science* (New York: Harper Torchbooks).

——(1969) *The Obstructed Path: French Social Thought in the Years of Desperation* (New York: Harper and Row).

——(1975) *The Sea Change: The Migration of Social Thought, 1930–65* (New York: Harper and Row).

——(1988) *Consciousness and Society* (Brighton: Harvester Press).

Iggers, G. C. (1968) *The German Conception of History* (Middletown: Wesleyan University Press).

Ishihara, S. (1991) *The Japan that can say No* (London: Simon and Schuster).

Iriye, A. (editor) (1975) *Mutual Images: Essays in American-Japanese Relations* (London: Harvard University Press).

Jakubowski, F. (1990) *Ideology and Superstructure in Historical Materialism* (London: Pluto Press).

Johnson, P. (1980) *The Recovery of Freedom* (Oxford: Basil Blackwell).

Joll, J. (1985) *National Histories and National Historians: Some German and English Views of the Past* (London: German Historical Institute).

Jones, G. (1980) *Social Darwinism and English Thought: The interaction between biological and social theory* (Brighton: Harvester Press).

Joseph, K. (1984) 'Why Teach History in School?', *The Historian*, no.2 Spring.

Kaye, H. J. and McClelland, K. (editors) (1990) *E. P. Thompson: Critical Perspectives* (Cambridge: Polity Press).

Kennedy, P. M. 'The decline of nationalistic history in the West, 1900-1970', *Journal of Contemporary History*, vol.8, no.1.

Kimball, R. (1990) *Tenured Radicals* (New York: Harper and Row).

Knudsen, J. B. (1986) *Justus Moser and the German Enlightenment* (Cambridge: Cambridge University Press).

Koch, H. W. (editor) (1985) *Aspects of the Third Reich* (London: Macmillan).

Koestler, A. (1951) *The Age of Longing* (London: Collins).

——(1983) *The Yogi and the Commissar and Other Essays* (London: Hutchison).

Kohn, H. (editor) (1953) *German History: Some New German Views* (London: George Allen and Unwin).

——(1966) *Political Ideologies of the Twentieth Century* (New York: Harper and Row).

Kumar, K. (1986) *Prophecy and Progress* (Harmondsworth: Penguin).

Kushner, T. and Lunn, K. (editors) (1989) *Traditions of Intolerance* (Manchester: Manchester University Press).

Kusmer, K. L. (1989) 'An American tradition: Governmental action to promote equality in American history', *Amerikastudien*, vol.34, no.3.

Langer, W. H. (1965) *The Diplomacy of Imperialism* (New York: Alfred Knopf).

Laquer, W. and Mosse, G. L. (editors) (1974) *Historians in Politics* (London: Sage).

Lasch, C. (1979) *The Culture of Narcissism: American Life in an Age of Diminishing Expectations* (New York: Warner Books).

Levitas, R. (1986) *The Ideology of the New Right* (Cambridge: Polity Press).

Lukacs, G. (1980) *The Destruction of Reason* (London: Merlin Press).

Lukacs, J. (1980–1) 'American History? American History', *Salmagundi*, no.50–51.

Lyotard, J. F. (1984) *The Postmodern Condition: A Report on Knowledge* (Manchester: Manchester University Press).

Macaulay, T. B. (1979) *The History of England* (Harmondsworth: Penguin).

McNeill, W. H. (1986) 'Mythistory, or truth: Myth, History, and Historians', *The American Historical Review*, vol.91, no.1.

——(1990) 'Winds of Change', *Foreign Affairs*, Fall.

Maier, C. S. (1988) *The Unmasterable Past: History, Holocaust, and German National Identity* (Cambridge Massachusetts: Harvard University Press).

Mannheim, K. (1943) *Diagnosis of our Time* (London: Kegan Paul).

——(1960) *Ideology and Utopia (London: Routledge and Kegan Paul)*

Marcuse, H. (1972) *Eros and Civilisation* (London: Abacus).

Marwick, A. (1989) *The Nature of History* (London: Macmilan).

Marx, K. and Engels, F. (1975) *Collected Works* vol.4 (London: Lawrence and Wishart).

——(1975a) *Selected Correspondence* (Moscow: Progress Publishers).

——(1976) *Collected Works* vol.5 (London: Lawrence and Wishart).

——(1979) *Collected Works* vol.11 (London: Lawrence and Wishart).

——(1988) *Collected Works* vol.43 (London: Lawrence & Wishart).

Masato, Y. (1987) 'History textbooks that provoke an asian outcry', *Japan Quarterly*, January–March.

Mattick, P. (1939) 'Competition and Monopoly', *New Essays*, vol.6, no.3.

Mattick Jr., P. (1986) *Social Knowledge: An Essay on the Nature and Limits of Social Science* (London: Hutchison).

Mayer, A. (1989) *Why did the Heavens not Darken?* (London: Verso).

Mayne, R. (1989) 'Superpower Emeritus: The British Example', *Encounter*, December.

Mearsheimer, J. J. (1990) 'Why we will soon miss the Cold War', *The Atlantic Monthly*, August.

Menze, E. A. (1981) *Totalitarianism Reconsidered* (Port Washington, N.Y.: Kennikat Press).

Meszaros, I. (1989) *The Power of Ideology* (New York: Harvester Wheatsheaf).

Meyerson, A. (1990) 'The Vision Thing Continued', *Policy Review*, Summer 1990.

Michel, A. (1985) *L'Indentité de la France* (Paris: Le Club de l'Horloge).

Miles, R. (1990) *The Women's History of the World* (London: Grafton Books).

Milliband, R. and others (editors) (1987) *The Socialist Register 1987* (London: Merlin Press).

Moir, D. and Jessel, D. (1989) *Brainsex: The real difference between men and women* (London: Michael Joseph).

Moses, J. A. (1975) *The Politics of Illusion: The Fischer Controversy in German Historiography* (London: George Prior Publishers).

Muller, J. Z. (1989) 'German Historians at War', *Commentary*, vol.87, no.5.

Namier, L. (1962) *Vanished Supremacies* (Harmondsworth: Penguin).

Niebuhr, R. (1949) *Faith and History* (London: Nisbet).

Nietzsche, F. (1967) *The Will to Power* (New York: Random House).

——(1977) *The Use And Abuse of History* (Indianapolis: Bobbs-Merill).

Nisbet, R. (1980) *History of the Idea of Progress* (London: Heinemann).

——(1985) 'The Conservative Renaissance in Perspective', *The Public Interest*, no.81

——(1986) *Conservatism* (Milton Keynes: Open University Press).

Nolan, M. (1988) 'The *Historikerstreit* and Social History', *New German Critique*, no.44.

Novack, G. (1972) *Understanding History* (New York: Pathfinder).

Novick, P. (1988) *That Noble Dream: The 'Objectivity Question' and the American Historical Profession* (Cambridge: Cambridge University Press).

Orwell, G. (1941) *The Lion and the Unicorn* (London: Secker and Warburg)

——(1950) *Shooting an Elephant and Other Essays* (London: Secker and Warburg).

Palmer, F. (editor) (1986) *Anti Racism – An assault on education and value* (London: The Sherwood Press).

Pells, R. H. (1985) *The Liberal Mind in a Conservative Age: American Intellectuals in the 1940s and 1950s* (New York: Harper and Row).

Pfaff, W. (1990) *Barbarian Sentiments: How the American Century Ends* (New York: The Noonday Press).

Plumb, J. H. (1986) *The Death of the Past* (London: Macmillan).

Podhoretz, N. (1980) *The Present Danger* (New York: Simon and Schuster).

Policar, A. (1990) 'Racism and its Mirror Images', *Telos*, no.83.

Pollard, S. (1968) *The Idea of Progress: History and Society* (Harmondsworth: Penguin),

Pompa, L. (1975) *Vico: A Study of the 'New Science'* (Cambridge: Cambridge University Press),

Popper, K. (1952) *The Open Society and Its Enemies* (London: Routledge and Kegan Paul).

——(1986) *The Poverty of Historicism* (London: Ark Paperback).

Porter, R. (1990) 'Healthy History', *History Today*, November.

Pronay, N. and Wilson, K. (editors) (1985) *The Political Re-education of Germany and her Allies after World War II* (London: Croom Helm).

Rabinbach, A. (1988) 'The Jewish Question in the German Question', *New German Critique*, no.44.

Ravitch, D. (1990) 'Multiculturalism', *The American Scholar*, vol.59, no.3.

Rich, P. (1986) *Race and Empire in British Politics* (Cambridge: Cambridge University Press).

Rieff, P. (1975) *Fellow Teachers* (New York: Dell Publishers).

Ringer, F. (1991) 'Review of *Staat und Geschichte wissenschaft in Deutschland und Frankreich*', *History and Theory*, vol.30, no.1.

Robbins, K. (1990) 'National Identity and History: Past, Present and Future', *History*, vol.75, no.245.

Rorty, R. (1990) 'Two Cheers for the Cultural Left', *The South Atlantic Quarterly*, vol.89, no.1.

Russell, C. (1979) *Parliaments and English Politics 1621–1629* (Oxford: Clarendon Press)

Samuel, R. (1984) 'Forum', *History Today*, vol.34, May.

——(editor) (1989) *Patriotism: The Making and Unmaking of British National Identity* (London: Routledge).

——(1990) 'History, the Nation and the Schools', *History Workshop*, no.29.

Samuel, R. and Thompson, P. (editors) (1990) *The Myths We Live By* (London: Routledge).

Sandel, M. I. (editor) (1984) *Liberalism and its Critics* (Oxford: Basil Blackwell).

Schlesinger, A. M. (1949 *The Vital Center* (Boston: Houghton Mifflin).

Schulze, H. (1988) 'The *Historikerstreit* in Perspective', *German History*, vol.6, no.1.

Schumpeter, J. (1951) *Capitalism, Socialism and Democracy* (London: Allen and Unwin).

Scott, J. C. (1987) 'Resistance without Protest and without organization: Peasant Opposition to the Islamic Zakat and the Christian Tithe', *Comparative Studies in Society and History*, vol.29.

Scott, J. F. (1926) *The Menace of Nationalism in Education* (London: George Allen and Unwin)

Scruton, R. (1985) *Thinkers of The New Left* (London: Longman).

——(1990) *The Philosopher on Dover Beach* (Manchester: Carcanet Press).

Shand, A. H. (1984) *The Capitalist Alternative: An introduction to Neo-Austrian Economics* (Brighton: Wheatsheaf).

Shils, E. (1955) 'The End of Ideology?', *Encounter*, November.

Shklar, J. (1957) *After Utopia: The Decline of Political Faith* (Princeton: Princeton University Press).

Shor, I. (1987) *Culture Wars: School and Society in the Conservative Restoration 1969–1984* (London: Routledge and Kegan Paul).

Smith, A. D. (1989) *The Ethnic Origins of Nations* (Oxford Basil Blackwell).

Smith, F. L. (1990) *When Choice becomes God* (Eugene,Oregon: Harvat House).

Soffer, R. (1987) 'Nation, Duty, Character and Confidence: History at Oxford, 1850–1914', *Historical Journal*, vol.30, no.1.

Sontag, R. J. (1971) *A Broken World: 1919–39* (New York: Harper and Row).

Spengler, O. (1926) *Decline of West* (London: George Allen and Unwin).

Stern, F. (1974) *The Politics of Cultural Despair* (Berkely: University of California Press).

Stokes, M. (1986) 'American Liberalism and the Neo-Consensus School', *Journal of American Studies*, vol.20, no.3.

Stone, L. (1987) *The Past and the Present Revisited* (London: Routledge and Kegan Paul).

Taguieff, P. A. 'The New Cultural Racism in France', *Telos*, no.83.

Taylor, M. (1990) 'Patriotism, History and the Left in Twentieth-Century Britain', *Historical Journal*, vol.33, no.4.

Thatcher, M. (1977) *Let Our Children Grow: Selected speeches 1975–77* (London: Centre for Policy Studies).

Thomas, G. (1990) *The Unresolved Past: A Debate in German History* (London: Weidenfeld and Nicolson).

Thomas, H. (1981) *The Unfinished History of the World* (London: Pan Books).

——(1985) *History, Capitalism and Freedom* (London: Centre for Policy Studies).

Thorne, C. (1978) *Allies of a Kind* (London: Hamish Hamilton).

Torpey, J. (1988) 'Introduction: Habermas and the Holocaust', *New German Critique*, no.44.

Turner, J. (1981) 'Recovering the Uses of History', *The Yale Review*, vol.70, no.2.

Underdown, D. *Revel, Riot and Rebellion: Popular Politics and Culture in England* (Oxford: Basil Blackwell).

Valery, P. (1927) *Variety* (New York: Harcourt Brace).

Veeser, H. A. (1989) *The New Historicism* (London: Routledge).

Vico, G. (1961) *The New Science* (New York: Anchor Paperback).

Von Mises, L. (1958) *Theory and History* (London: Jonathan Cape).

Weisz, G. (1983) *The Emergence of Modern Universities in France, 1883–1914* (Princeton: Princeton University Press).

Wilson, E. (1940) *To the Finland Station: A Study in the Writing and Acting of History* (Garden City: Doubleday).

Wilson, G. (1989) *The Great Sex Divide: A Study of Male–Female Difference* (London: Peter Owen).

Wittgenstein, L. (1989) *Tractatus logico-philosophicus* (London: Routledge).

Woodward, W. (1988) 'America as a Culture: Some emerging Lines of Analysis', *Journal of American Culture*, vol.11 no.1.

Yeo, S. (1986) 'Whose story? An argument from within current historical practive in Britain', *Journal of Contemporary History*, vol.21.

Young, R. (1990) *White Mythologies: Writing History and the West* (London: Routledge).

Zeitlin, I. M. (1968) *Ideology and the Development of Sociological Theory* (Englewood Cliffs, New Jersey: Prentice-Hall).

Index

305